Lost Honour, Betrayed Loyalty

Lost Honour, Betrayed Loyalty

The Memoir of a Waffen-SS Soldier on the Eastern Front

Herbert Maeger

Translated by Geoffrey Brooks
Foreword by Charles Messenger

Frontline Books, London

Original German language edition title *Verlorene Ehre, Verratene Treue.*
First published by Rosenheimer Verlagshaus in 2002.

This English edition first published in 2015
and reprinted in 2016 and 2018 by
Frontline Books
An imprint of Pen & Sword Books Limited
Yorkshire - Philadelphia

ISBN 978 1 84832 748 1

A CIP catalogue record for this book is
available from the British Library

Printed and bound in England by TJ International Ltd, Padstow, Cornwall.

Pen & Sword Books Limited incorporates the imprints of Atlas, Archaeology, Aviation,
Discovery, Family History, Fiction, History, Maritime, Military, Military Classics,
Politics, Select, Transport, True Crime, Air World, Frontline Publishing, Leo Cooper,
Remember When, Seaforth Publishing, The Praetorian Press, Wharncliffe Local History,
Wharncliffe Transport, Wharncliffe True Crime and White Owl.

For a complete list of Pen & Sword titles please contact:
PEN & SWORD BOOKS LIMITED
47 Church Street, Barnsley, South Yorkshire, S70 2AS, England
E-mail: enquiries@pen-and-sword.co.uk
Website: www.pen-and-sword.co.uk
Or
PEN AND SWORD BOOKS
1950 Lawrence Rd, Havertown, PA 19083, USA
E-mail: Uspen-and-sword@casematepublishers.com
Website: www.penandswordbooks.com

DEDICATION

'For Sigrid, who persisted in encouraging me to write this book'.

'My Honour is Loyalty' was the motto embossed
on a Waffen-SS soldier's belt-clasp.

'One must keep repeating the true facts, because the false facts
are continuously stated all around us, and not just
by the odd individual, but by the masses.
In newspapers and encyclopaedias,
in schools and universities, false facts are everywhere,
for it is a comfortable feeling to have the majority on your side.'
Goethe to Eckermann, 16 December 1828.

Contents

Plates

Berlin-Lichterfelde: No. 4 Company Reserve Battalion Leibstandarte SS Adolf Hitler paraded for roll-call.

Berlin, the training group from Room 14, the author at the extreme left.

No. 4 Company Reserve Battalion LSSAH on the march during training.

Berlin-Lichterfelde: the author in front of the barracks swimming baths.

March 1942: the author in captured Soviet uniform at an MG post on the main frontline.

In the bunker, SS-Quartermaster-Sergeant 'Marinus' and SS-Lance Corporal 'Laban'.

Yegorovka June 1942: off duty with Ukrainian women.

Yegorovka: a small concert with two violins and a bass mandolin.

The author during home leave, August 1943.

LAH parade on the Champs-Elysées, Paris, July 1942.

The author as an MG gunner before the Canadian landings at Dieppe, September 1942.

Excursion to Paris, September 1942.

In front of the Boissy 'manor house'.

A heavy MG group at the beginning of an attack.

Olshany, May 1943: the company collecting rations.

The Battle of Kharkov, March 1943; conference in front of A KFZ 69.

KFZ 15/Horch V8; the Wehrmacht's best cross-country vehicle.

Battle of Kursk-Belgorod: troops of an SS panzer division recovering a seriously wounded Red Army soldier. (J. K. Piekalkiewicz Photo Archive)

Kursk-Belgorod, July 1943.

Kursk-Belgorod: captured Soviet soldiers.

Battle of Kursk-Belgorod: MG group of the '9th' in expectation of a Soviet attack.

SS-Lieutenant General Sepp Dietrich, commander of 1st SS Panzer Division.

On the transport to Italy, July 1943, at the left the author.

Italy: 'Farmhouse Holidays'.

Commander's tent with Horch V8.

Proud in Italian summer uniforms.

Bernd Kloska, a recruit in Berlin together with the author.

Others from the company in short trousers.

Croatia, October 1943.

Istria, September 1943.

Maeger's release document No 299; release document from Trebbin PoW Camp; and Displaced Person's Index Card issued by the 'Belgian Military Mission'.

Foreword

This is an unusual story. Herbert Maeger was a Belgian who served in the Waffen-SS during the Second World War. For much of the time it was not in the so-called Foreign Legions of the Waffen-SS, but at its very heart as a member of the Leibstandarte SS Adolf Hitler, the Führer's own bodyguard. The origins as to why this should have been lie in the fact that Maeger was born in easternmost Belgium, Eupen-Malmedy, the scene of much of the heaviest fighting during the December 1944 Ardennes offensive. The region had been part of Germany, but Belgium annexed it under the Treaty of Versailles. Even though the majority of those who lived there considered themselves German – Maeger's father had served with distinction in the German Army during 1914–18 – a rigged plebiscite ensured that it remained part of Belgium. This lasted until 1940 when it once more became part of Germany and Maeger, now aged 18, found himself liable for conscription into the Wehrmacht.

The author was destined for the German Artillery, but, according to him, a remark insulting to Hitler made by his mother in September 1939 was reported to the German authorities. This enabled them to blackmail Maeger into volunteering for the Leibstandarte, joining its reserve battalion at Lichterfelde in Berlin in August 1941. Maeger makes the point that already by this stage in the war the Leibstandarte had lost its pre-war purity and its ranks were being filled by conscripts, as well as Luftwaffe transfers. The recruit training was tough, but Maeger survived and joined the Leibstandarte west of Rostov-on-Don as a machine gunner at the end of the year.

The author's descriptions of the period of static warfare following the Russian counter-offensive of December 1941 are grim. The German Army was totally ill-equipped to face the Russian winter and Maeger and his comrades only survived through stripping

Russian dead of their winter clothing. He was sick during the spring 1942 fighting around Kharkov, but rejoined in time for the Leibstandarte's move to France, where it was expanded into a full Panzer division. Here Maeger's French proved handy. He also became a company truck driver and eventually his company commander's driver. Much of this was due to his quick wittedness and eagerness to learn. Back in Russia in time for the Kharkov battles of spring 1943 and Operation 'Citadel' at Kursk that July, Maeger again survived to enjoy the Leibstandarte's sudden deployment to Italy in the face of Mussolini's overthrow.

It was now that Maeger left the Leibstandarte. While he considered that it had many faults, he had high praise for its basic tenet of never leaving a comrade in the lurch. A minor wound which he received during 'Citadel' turned badly septic and he was hospitalised. Thereafter he trained as a medic, which was what he originally wanted, but this was interrupted by posting to an SS officer training school. Maeger, had little liking for National Socialism and soon fell foul of the authorities. Posting to a punishment unit seemed inevitable, but somehow Maeger managed to delay this until early 1945, when he joined the notorious 36th SS Grenadier Dirlewanger Division on the Eastern Front, serving as a medical orderly in the equivalent of a casualty clearing station. He eventually joined over 100,000 other German servicemen and women trapped in the notorious Halbe pocket east of Berlin. Eventually caught by the Russians, only his quick-wittedness and good luck saved him from being sent to Siberia. Released on medical grounds, his final hurdle was getting from the Russian to the British zone of occupation. He could not, however, return to his native Belgium until the mid-1970s, since he had been found guilty of treachery and sentenced to life imprisonment *in absentia*.

If true, this is a remarkable tale of survival against the odds. It also provides revealing insights into the mindset of the Waffen-SS and its *modus operandi*. If there is one theme that runs throughout the book it is hunger. Herbert Maeger is always hungry and seldom enjoys a full stomach, whether it is the monotony of Army rations or in wartime Germany as a whole. Even his skills as a scrounger seldom leave him contented.

CHARLES MESSENGER

Translator's Note: SS Ranks

SS	Wehrmacht equivalent	British equivalent
SS-Mann		Private
SS-Sturmmann/ Oberschütze	Gefreiter	Private (trained soldier status)
SS-Rottenführer	Obergefreiter	L/Corporal
SS-Unterscharführer	Unteroffizier	Corporal
SS-Scharführer	Unterfeldwebel	Sergeant
SS-Oberscharführer	Feldwebel	Staff Sergeant
SS-Hauptscharführer	Oberfeldwebel	Quartermaster Sergeant
SS-Stabsscharführer	Hauptfeldwebel	Warrant Officer II
SS-Sturmscharführer	Stabsfeldwebel	Warrant Officer I
SS-Untersturmführer	Lieutnant	2nd Lieutenant
SS-Obersturmführer	Oberleutnant	1st Lieutenant
SS-Hauptsturmführer	Hauptmann	Captain
SS-Sturmbannführer	Major	Major

Author's Foreword

I decided decades ago not to write this book. The experiences and entanglements of that fearsome war made a dispassionate portrayal seem impossible. As a result of this attitude many of my peers took their experiences to the grave, thus allowing free rein to interpretations by other interested parties.

History is a very exhausting discipline based on interpretations made centuries after the event, only unassailable as to calendar dates. This is much more the case for Modern History, its factual basis having imponderable – often purely material – motives, which with regard to the subject matter under consideration are necessarily of a subjective nature. Good and evil are terms which no longer retain a stable meaning in principle, but are assigned such interpretation as the occasion demands. This change in values is heightened amongst the Germans by their inherent propensity for opportunism and conformity.

For objective research painstaking historians bewail the lack of reports of pure experience from the Second World War. The attempt to close this gap is an extremely difficult undertaking, for it requires that one pay no heed to the unscrupulous political and military leadership of the Third Reich and instead evaluate it according to the criteria, which were the valid standards at the time of the events reported. These include the imperishable military principles of loyalty to one's oath, bravery and readiness to sacrifice oneself, which were often mis-used by an irresponsible regime and were to a large extent weakened as social maxims.

I am aware that despite my effort for the greatest possible honesty, and strictly confining myself to facts, I do expose myself to criticism. I must accept this risk; I ask only for fairness in that those who judge me do not do so from under that banner of 'political correctness', which prevails in the current epoch.

In the portrayal of one's own experiences 'as the whole truth and nothing but the truth' one can only speak relatively and then on the basis 'Everything that I experienced personally, and nothing which I did not experience myself.' So much happened in those nearly four years that the choice is limited to a selection of experiences: I have given prominence in the text to especially impressive examples of facts and emotions.

All reported speech as I remember it is recorded verbatim. I have changed personal names where it seemed right to do so to avoid incorrect associations. I have aimed for balance in the choice of quotations from foreign authors to elucidate the framework of events.

I hope, therefore, that my modest contribution will go in some measure towards satisfying the need to reduce the deficit of information and at the same time do justice to my many comrades-in-arms who cannot speak for, or justify, themselves: and also for those in the hecatomb of a fearsome war, obliged by fate to die in the bloom of their youth and which, in the judgement of the contemporary period, was a death without purpose, or even somehow deserved.

Herbert Maeger, Krefeld, October 2000.

Introduction: Between Two Fatherlands

My first inner conflict arose when I was six and attended Belgian elementary school, where I was taught to read. On the first page of our German-language reader was quoted Ernst Moritz Arndt's question: 'What is a person's Fatherland?' and also his answer: ' . . . there, where God's sun first shone upon him, and the stars first glittered . . . '. This made me think. Was my Fatherland, where the sun first shone upon me, Belgium, the country which according to Caesar and the reading book was settled by 'the bravest of all the Gauls'? Or was my Fatherland the country in which my parents had been born and who, like nearly everybody else in the Belgian 'Eastern Cantons', spoke German as their mother tongue, with the exception of French-speaking Malmedy and a few surrounding villages? Was my father—proud to have served with the 4th Prussian Guard Regiment in Berlin and who in 1915, as a young reservist at Arras in Northern France, was so seriously wounded that he barely survived—a German? And how could he now be a Belgian and no longer German?

I began to ask questions, and received only the most sparing replies from my parents from which to form my world-political picture: Germany was the great Fatherland from which we had been cut off, Belgium the small Fatherland in which we were forced to live because some people lacking in education or conscience in a place called Versailles had decided that it should be so. Actually, the treaty signed in 1919 said that there should be a referendum in Eupen-Malmedy so that the inhabitants could choose to which of the two Fatherlands the province should belong.

A referendum on what might be called democratic principles was never held. Some time in February 1920, posters announced that

1

whoever wanted to opt for Eupen/Malmedy to be German had to report to the office of the relevant mayor and sign his or her name on a list. Before this there had been a massive campaign of intimidation. Only a few reported, the great majority were simply afraid – and in Germany there was famine and despair. Families were led to understand that whoever opted for Eupen/Malmedy to be German would be taken to the German border in handcuffs and pushed over it, all his property and possessions in Belgium being forfeit to the state. The official Belgian history denies all this, but the fact is that only 271 out of a population of approximately 60,000 in Eupen/Malmedy dared to vote for the province to be German.[1]

My father loved his home village of Hergenrath, where he had inherited his house and land from his German forefathers. Like almost all other Eupen-Malmedyers he wanted to keep the property, and so the result of the 'referendum', which in reality never happened, was clear: the population of Eupen/Malmedy was 'definitively' Belgian and so were their children. At the end of the 1920s there was an unofficial ballot held by the pro-German 'Heimattreue Front', which claimed that over 90 per cent of the population wanted it to be German. In 1920 itself, however, a few had voted with their feet, left their Eupen/Malmedy homeland for Germany and made for themselves a new existence 'over there'.

In practice it was really not such a bad thing to be a Belgian in the new circumstances. My father, no longer able to carry on his trade as a baker in the family business as a result of his war wounds, and who on his medical discharge had become an employee of the German state railway in 1917, was accepted into the Belgian State Railway and appointed stationmaster at the village of Astenet after a crash course in French. He wore a red cap, which made him look like a French general, and became well respected: he was still relatively young when he was elected to the village council in Walhorn where we lived.

The Belgians did everything they could to get their new citizens to forget the dubious referendum and gave them – retrospectively – all their rights. My father received a war pension, as if he had shed his blood on the battlefield for Belgium, and even a Belgian

2

decoration for fighting at the front: this amused him, but nevertheless he kept it with great care in the same box containing his German Iron Cross and Wound Badge.

My province was a Catholic stronghold: the highest honour was to have a priest in the family. As my father had inherited the parental bakery as the eldest of three sons, the honour fell on his brother Lambert. He was still a theology student when he fell at Arras in 1916. His grave is in a beautifully cared-for military cemetery at Bapaume, a small village in the valley of the Somme. In the seminary he was a fellow student of my maternal uncle, Josef, then also the pride of his family as an incipient theologian. He is still spoken of: my parents met each other through this religious relationship.

Apart from the festive celebration of a young priest's first mass in his home community, the annual children's first communion was the most important event in the life of a village, and celebrated by the families accordingly. After high mass in the parish church a feast would be thrown for all those attending and this would turn into an extended coffee afternoon with marvellous rice and fruit pancakes – round, flat fancy pastries just like one sees in Breughel's paintings – followed in the evening by frankfurter sausages and potato salad. It was best of all when there were five children present at the house of my Hergenrath uncle, Martin, and his lovable wife, Malchen, for the festivities were arranged with the children in mind.

As I grew older a significant change in the Church Rule involved me. Previously it had been the custom to link the first communion to confirmation at the age of fourteen. I was amongst the first who were now allowed to take part in the church ritual at the age of nine. It was more trying for me than uplifting: a crowd of relations arrived, to whom I was presented in a blue naval cadet's uniform with long trousers; dessert was delicious ice cream, of which I never got my share because the main course had taken so long that I had to leave without delay for the festive afternoon vespers at the parish church.

On this occasion my grandmother gave me the present of a gold-plated pocket watch with lid, totally inappropriate for a child. She was a pious and cheerful woman, although widowed at the age of forty and had had to bring up five children on a modest pension. She had a phenomenal memory and at age seventy could quote for a half hour without pause from her husband's love letters. Even today I still weave a couple of her sayings into my text when I make a speech. Her favourite rule for life she liked to express in the Aachen dialect: *'Wä gett, wat hä hatt, es wäet, datt hä leeft, en mot ästimeert wäede!'* (Whoever gives what he has is worthy of his life and must be respected!) I like to use it when addressing my observations to politicians or economists.

My church obligations took up a considerable part of my early youth. My father had been an altar boy and had taken it upon himself to teach me the Latin of the mass before I could read and write. The most difficult was the sacrificial prayer 'Suscipiat', which I was obliged to recite at the age of five without understanding a word of it. This stirred my mother's pride and she entered my name as a novice to serve at mass in the Ursuline convent at Astenet. This was an excellent boarding school for young ladies, with nuns as teachers, but apart from one housemaster and the boys of the convent dairy, there were no males. A pensioned-off priest who lived in the old people's home inside the convent took the church services. The inhabitants of Astenet, a small hamlet outside Walhorn, had made a considerable contribution towards the building of the chapel and, thus, had the right to attend all services there. This saved them the two-kilometre walk to the parish church at Walhorn, whose pastor did not look upon this division of his flock with much favour.

As a result of my mother's initiative, as a pre-schooler I was an altar boy alongside two or three others older than myself. At first I only had to attend punctually a couple of times each week, but as time went on my duties became more onerous. Especially when I started school – aged not yet quite six – it took a lot of my time. For chapel mass I had to walk almost a kilometre. The mass lasted half an hour, beginning at half past six and finishing at seven. I attended school from eight until midday, and from two to four. In the morning and afternoon I had to walk to and from school, almost two kilometres each way, thus eight kilometres daily, and all this in the coldest months of the year.

Worst of all for me were the holidays, increasingly unpleasant when clergymen arrived at the convent for rest and recuperation. They held their masses daily and the altar boys were indispensable. If only two such guests were present, that meant three masses daily, and on Sundays three early ones and the regular mass for the villagers at nine. The other altar boys gradually threw in the towel, and thus I was called upon all the more frequently: even in the holidays I had a full, restful sleep only once or twice per week.

The excessive physical and mental demands on me at such a tender age led eventually to the first rebellion of my life. After being the only altar boy three times a day for a whole week I went on strike. My mother was more bewildered than annoyed, but accepted my refusal, probably because my change of school to Eupen meant a daily round-trip of twenty kilometres.

I know that I owe much to the religion of my childhood years, and I feel very closely bound to it today. My ethic arising from my life's experiences is simple: We are part of a creative purpose impossible for us to understand. God has created us as individuals capable of respecting his creative will: each of our fellow humans is an elementary part of this Creation. Whoever causes one of them to suffer, wounds the Creator and commits a serious sin. In comparison I see any offence against the dictates of the Church as a mere trifle. I believe that every prayer, no matter what the religion or language, reaches the Godhead, as do the three Hail Marys, which I have recited every evening since my early childhood. In fear and suffering – especially in the war years – I drew much help from this, for which I am grateful.

The official Church is something we cannot do without, it is the framework for the maxims of human dealings. Because of my personal experiences I distanced myself from the Church for many years. These experiences included – beyond relatively harmless attempts at pederastic contact by priests to whom I was exposed as a child – the brutal and totally unjustified accusations made with threats of corporal punishment by a clerical teacher in the senior class of primary school. I was accused of having made an obscene drawing in a book. I had no idea what it was supposed to represent.

The primitive female torso, which I thought looked like an owl, had been drawn in a French reader I had obtained from an older pupil. The affair was investigated and decided in my favour; but the dirty-minded fantasies of the teacher set up a barrier that was very difficult to surmount.

So as not to give anybody the wrong idea of what I am saying, I must emphasise that the majority of clergymen whom I met in my childhood and youth, and especially at school and in my later life, were personalities of the highest quality whom I remember with reverence and respect.

Much later another experience shocked me greatly. I had begun the study of medicine in 1944. After I was released from Soviet captivity I went to Rheydt where, through her contacts, my aunt Ottilie had obtained for me a place as a pre-clinical practitioner in the city hospital. My uncle Otto, rector of the school at Frechen and like everyone in our family very close to the Church, also wanted to weigh in with help and drove me to Bonn, to the Catholic Students' priest, in order to solicit his assistance in getting me a place there. Despite the dreadful shortage of food in those times, I noticed how well fed the churchman was. He asked me some questions, heard me out and then declared tersely and in conclusion: 'We have no places here for criminals!'

My uncle protested: 'But he was in a penal battalion!' I had no desire to argue the point, stood up and took my leave with the words: 'I saw similar examples of such cynicism in the Waffen-SS!' Then I left and slammed the door behind me.

That happened many years later, of course. In our 1930s 'New Belgium' we lived in the long shadow of those events which would soon unfold over Europe to become the catastrophe of the century. The so-called 'New Belgians' actually had it good materially, far better than the 'Reichsdeutsche', whose Fatherland was much larger in size but had worse butter, not much chocolate and not much else either, particularly in the years of hyperinflation, the payment of reparations and the occupation of the Rhineland. Our relations on the other side of the border were always highly delighted to be invited to come over for a good meal. Certain foodstuffs, 'Calba' chocolate, eggs with a strong golden yolk from poultry fed on maize and above all the prized Walhorn butter were especially praised. Margarine was never served at table, not even when Göring declared that the phrase 'Guns before butter' was binding upon the entire German nation.

We found much in the new Germany to be remarkable. In particular I remember a visit to my uncle Joseph and aunt Laura, one of my father's sisters, and their five children. Uncle Joseph, a headmaster at Zweifall/Stolberg, was born at Hergenrath like my father and had been a highly decorated senior lieutenant in the 1st Guards Regiment. He had not needed much reflection to opt for Germany. As a very devout Catholic, keen churchgoer and organist he had not had it easy with the new political masters, but his community had supported him energetically in every respect.

One day we were invited to Zweifall for lunch, a simple bourgeois meal. Just after the pudding was served there was a knock at the door and two brown-uniformed men entered the dining room rattling a collecting tin, into which aunt Laura dropped a few coins. One of the visitors looked down at the meal with a frown to which my uncle Joseph assured him quickly: 'We have relatives visiting from Belgium and did not want to give them the impression that we are short of food.' This seemed to satisfy them, and once they had gone my uncle explained the situation: It was the first Sunday in the month, a day when all German citizens aware of their duty were urged to prepare only a stew and donate the money saved to the winter relief organisation. Pudding was an infringement, if only a minor one, against the principle of community spirit. 'Nobody should go cold and hungry' also implied in the total National Socialist sense: 'And nobody should eat better than his neighbour either!'

My 'Reichsdeutsch' cousins left it in no doubt, however, that in the development of the human race the Belgians came pretty low down the ladder. What else could one expect of a country squeezed in somehow between Holland and France, no wider than the Eifel mountains to the English Channel, and which was a by-product of the Congress of Vienna? It bore no comparison to a Reich which, as the second verse of the German national anthem announced, stretched potentially from the Meuse to Memel, from the Adige in Tyrol to the waters of the Kattegat. Even the Belgian high school cap that I wore, which resembled a Basque beret with a peak, could not measure up to its German equivalent whose shape looked like a 'pre-destined' officer's cap.

In my home village of Walhorn-Astenet, whoever was conscious of reputation sent his son to the Kaiser Karl high school at Aachen, barely eight kilometres away. After I had completed four years' elementary schooling, my parents sent me to the Collège Patronné at Eupen to save on the school fees. Later I realised that the Collège, which came under the aegis of the Bishop of Liège, was an excellent school, especially in the teaching of logical thinking and creativity. The upper classes were taught in the French language and the teachers were Jesuits, to whom I owe much: when I attended the German upper school between the invasion of 1940 up to my school-leaving certificate in 1941, it soon became clear that this successor from the Reich did not match up to the Collège. The classes at the Collège up to the end of my secondary education used German textbooks for Greek, History and Geography.

My favourite subject was History: the four volumes of *Welters Weltgeschichte*, published by the University bookshop Franz Coppenrath of Münster, I knew more or less by heart. It was primarily a book with a German bias and this brought me into conflict with my teachers, who in my opinion were not neutral politically, which looked at objectively was quite natural. I was feeling myself increasingly German and an 'enforced Belgian' and was discovering ever more contradictions between what was happening every day in my home province, and political and historical justice as I understood it. That discrepancies of this kind occur quite normally in all political connections escaped the understanding of a boy brought up with the classic ideals of antiquity.

In the 1930s a sharp contrast also developed between the Catholic clergy and National Socialism, which had meanwhile become the State Power in Germany and led inevitably to a national polarisation. Loyalty to my school at Eupen and to individual Belgian teachers whom I specially revered was pronounced, but a feeling of being 'different' from them became ever more distinct. The strong division between the Germans of my home province and their Walloon neighbours in the west, which had existed for centuries, contributed to it. The demarcation line ran between the former German border village of Herbesthal and the 'old Belgian' Welkenrath. On one side only German was spoken, on the other only French and the Low German 'Plattdütsch' dialect, liberally sprinkled with Walloon words. At my school there were students from this area with whom I never felt completely at one. This inner discord in a boy who tended to be uncompromising was bound to lead sooner or later to a grave decision: because I had been too young for conscription into the Belgian Army up to the time of the German invasion, luckily I was spared having to make it.

My parents were deeply rooted in their German lineage, but their strong Church indoctrination made them into resolute opponents of the National Socialist regime. I often heard my father say: 'Hitler means war'. When he was proved right in 1939, I transferred the blame from Germany to Great Britain, which – not only from my own understanding – had encouraged Poland to adopt an aggressive stance, leading in August 1939 to the murders of German townspeople at Bromberg and elsewhere in Poland. That Germany had prepared the disastrous escalation by demands supported by exultant, giant mass marches could not be denied.

Hitler ordered the invasion of Poland; Britain and France declared war on Germany, igniting the Second World War. I did not feel the least enthusiasm for the event but rather a growing feeling of anxiety and fear for the future. I was seventeen, therefore at a refractory age, and let my opinions be known. There was discord between my parents in which I was not involved – I showed consideration for the outlook of my father – and they expressed their views in conversations with acquaintances and neighbours. Here my father remained fairly reserved, but my mother spoke her mind, as was her nature, and this was to have serious consequences later on.

In April 1940 I had a strange experience, which I considered a paranormal augury. I was cycling from Walhorn to Asteret under a totally clear sky. Suddenly I saw a single cloud in the firm shape of a giant sword pointing to the west. I stared at it in shock and then rode the 100 metres home as fast as I could to fetch my 'Agfa Billy' camera. Alas, by the time I had got it the phenomenon had disappeared.

In the early morning of 10 May 1940 I was awoken by the drone of Luftwaffe bombers beginning the attack on Belgium. Shortly afterwards the Belgian Army remote-detonated the Hammerbrücke railway viaduct at Hergenrath a few kilometres away. It had been built in 1840 and resembled a Roman aqueduct, 40 metres high and 250 metres long. A number of soldiers of the Belgian security force were buried beneath the rubble, eight survivors came along the railway line to Astenet, bathed in sweat and distraught. I spoke to them in French, attempting to calm them down. Suddenly the first German soldiers appeared on motorcycles with sidecar; the Belgians took up positions in their trenches intending to resist. I convinced them not to open fire for fear of hitting women and children in the streets. A few seconds later the Germans disappeared, and in company with a neighbour we coaxed the Belgian soldiers to go into the courtyard of a nearby house where they would receive coffee and sandwiches. Soon a German formation came marching up: I acted as interpreter, the Belgians laid down their arms and were sent off to the east. They were probably back home again before long, for the Wehrmacht released its Belgian prisoners of war between June and July 1940.

On an impulse, my camera slung around my neck, I cycled to the Hammerbrücke just in time to take photos of the ruined bridge from the valley and the bridge ramp. The railway tracks spanned the abyss undamaged over the entire length: a short time later they crashed into the depths with a noise like thunder. The photos brought me my first royalties as a would-be reporter; they were published on postcards and in 1941 the railway managers at Cologne bought the rights for an exhibition on bridges. With the proceeds I bought a new camera, which I was to have with me throughout almost the entire war.

Everything changed overnight. Now we were Germans and my first feelings were of relief at my release from the dichotomy, which had entrammelled me as a child of two Fatherlands. But soon I became aware of how much I remained attached to the Latin world of my education. The Ancient Germans and Rome were and are contrasts, one always awakening emotion, the other tradition and rationality. People who grew up in the border areas of the cultural circles are aware that both have their sublime and their negative qualities. The repeated attempts to unite the concepts have always been unsuccessful.

At first school continued as before. Some of the teachers were no longer there, amongst the absentees being our much-loved Professor Bernard who took the Unterprima ('Lower Sixth') and was highly revered by me. The lessons were not what they were: my attention was also much drawn to the events happening around us. Columns of field-grey troops marched, soldiers were billeted, a giant railway gun sheltering in the tunnel at Hergenrath was brought out regularly to fire on the strong Belgian forts near Liége.

I cycled everywhere so as not to miss anything: I was the first person on the scene when a seriously wounded German fighter pilot crash landed, and I also spent a lot of time with the men of the heavy anti-aircraft unit along the railway line. Nobody tried to stop me taking photos and these brought me my first royalties from newspapers. Together with the ruins of the Hergenrath railway bridge my favourite subjects were German soldiers taking a break while marching and a shot-down Belgian aircraft.

In July 1940 the long school holidays marked the end of the Collège Patronné. We began the new school year in the 'Oberschule für Knaben' (Upper School for Boys) and found that the High School syllabus of Humanities had been discontinued. Whereas previously we only knew Mathematics in its philosophical-logical form, in order to prove to us the backwardness of the Belgian school system now we were taught the technical applications of Mathematics, for example the graphic representation of the phases of a three-phase AC motor. I soon got on top of it, which is more than I can say for the climate at the German school, best described as 'pre-military'. Unlike elsewhere in Belgium, where a scholar was rated by a clear points system, in the German school everything was based on the subjective appraisal of the teacher. I was never an opportunist: my school-leaving certificate in the early summer of 1941 was accordingly not well balanced. All in all, I liked the Belgian high school better.

A short time after the invasion, the German authorities set up shop, and in June 1940 we were made German by Führer-Edict, or more precisely 'assimilated in status to German citizens'. This was a second-class naturalization, for we were not yet 'Reichsdeutsch'. The 'Heimattreue Front' (The Front Loyal to the German Homeland), which had previously been illegal, formed the cadre for the National Socialist organisations and membership of the Hitler Youth for those of the right age became obligatory. I served willingly, mastered the theoretical knowledge from the organisation's books and within a few months became the HJ-Comradeship Leader at Walhorn. What we did was not much different to the Belgian boy scouts: the emphasis was on physical hardening by sport.

In the autumn of 1940, we sixth formers were canvassed at school for a career as a naval surgeon, a condition being that one volunteered for the Navy. I would have seized the opportunity, which I saw as a good prospect, but being under age I needed my father's counter signature on my application and he refused. Shortly afterwards at the end of 1940 I was summoned to Eupen for conscription and signed up for an artillery regiment at Düsseldorf.

After the war this conscription was found important by the Belgian military court trying me in my absence, for it meant that I had volunteered for the Waffen-SS to fight against the Soviet Union and had, thus, wilfully borne weapons against Belgium's ally. In the struggle for their own 'political rehabilitation', my parents had tried to mitigate this accusation and found support. Three of my former classmates, whom I had known for several years, prepared statements for my father that together with themselves and other boys born in 1922 I had been ordered to attend for compulsory conscription at Eupen. One of them, with whom I formed a close friendship from the 1970s, closed his letter to my father with the words: '. . . I wish from the bottom of my heart that you see Herbert again, or soon receive news from him.' That was in 1947, two years after I had re-established contact with my parents. For probably well-justified reasons, they kept this fact as secret as possible.

After the German arrival in Eupen-Malmedy in 1940 there began a period of uncertainty for my father. In 1920 he had been transferred from German into Belgian officialdom, had belonged to the local council and, as was well known, had at least a very reserved attitude towards the National Socialist regime. Overnight he was restored to his former position as a Reichsbahn official. In the summer of 1941 he was transferred to Gemmerich as station-master, but this hardly amounted to a promotion, for the area had not been German before 1920 and had therefore been annexed without any prior claim to be German: the local population maintained a very icy attitude towards the controlling 'Prussians' who besides my father included two teachers and two police officials.

My father was categorical on the point that he would never join a National Socialist organisation, and would not even become a member of the NSV (National Socialist People's Welfare organisation). Nevertheless, as the war neared its end and Belgium re-took Eupen-Malmedy, he was arrested for collaboration and thrown into Liége prison for several months, a fate which many Eupen-Malmedyers shared with him. Some had worse to suffer: my cousin, Lambert, conscripted into the Wehrmacht, was so hard on himself that he made a vow to enter a monastic order should he return home safely when it was all over. Afterwards he spent twenty years with a Franciscan Order in Formosa (Taiwan).

After the Germans came to my province, a more serious situation arose as regards my mother than was the case with my father. One day in March 1941 the NSDAP district leader summoned me and advised me as follows: everybody was completely satisfied with my 'political attitude'. My father and his officials were still a matter for discussion. Especially problematical was an utterance by my mother. On Sunday 3 September 1939, immediately after the war began, leaving church in conversation with three other women she had made a statement, as evidenced by depositions from witnesses, namely: 'This Hitler is a criminal!' I knew this to be a fact for I had heard her say it and it was clear in my memory.

The NSDAP official made clear to me that this was a very grave matter, and serious consequences could only be avoided by a very broad-minded course of action. It would be extremely helpful in this respect if I volunteered for the Waffen-SS and my father agreed. As I had already been notified of conscription and was awaiting my call up, it was not a difficult decision to make. As a result of this interview, and armed with an application form, I went home, discussed the matter with my father and he counter signed – obviously with a heavy heart. And I did not feel all that good about it either.

After receiving my school-leaving certificate at Easter 1941, in accordance with my career ambition I spent a few months as an unsalaried editorial employee with the *Westdeutscher Beobachter* at Eupen. At the beginning of September 1941 I received my induction order to the Leibstandarte Adolf Hitler. On 16 September 1941, less than two months before my nineteenth birthday, I took the through-train from Aachen for Berlin. My youth was at an end before it had really begun.

Chapter One

Recruit in the Leibstandarte

During the Balkans campaign in the spring of 1941, without waiting for the arrival of the artillery and panzers, which had been sent up in support, No. 7 Company/ LSSAH repeatedly attacked Klidi Pass, defended bitterly by the Greeks. When they finally took the Greek positions, there were only eleven survivors of the original fighting force of 120 men. The company commander received the Knight's Cross.

This was told to the young recruits of the Leibstandarte reserve battalion at Berlin-Lichterfelde. It was one of the typical stories which symbolised its *esprit de corps* and explained why the Leibstandarte – initially only a regiment, a brigade in 1940 and not a division until 1942 – required so many replacements. In that way the elite unit made its purpose clear to its junior arrivals: they were to die for the glory of the Führer.

I did not yet know this version of the ideal soldier when I passed through the barrack gates at Lichterfelde for the first time on 17 September 1941: I had quite the wrong impression of what awaited me. I believed that I had been chosen to serve as a member of the Führer's personal bodyguard, and was expecting special training in hand-to-hand combat and close-combat weapons, and further schooling in the 'world view' of which I had a basic understanding from the Hitler Youth. The reality was correspondingly very sobering: I had not come to join an elite troop as I imagined, but, by their own definition, a 'hotchpotch'. From my first impressions it

15

seemed to me that it was something between an organisation of German exiles and a foreign legion.

On my very first day at Lichterfelde I had to bury some of my illusions. In order to comply punctually with my call-up papers at all costs, and in impatient expectation of the great things that I was to experience, I planned my departure for twelve hours earlier than was really necessary. My parents accompanied me to the Berlin express, which left Aachen-West late on the evening of Saturday: I was due to report to the LAH barracks by noon on the Monday. I knew therefore that I would be in Berlin early on the Sunday morning, presenting myself at the barracks soon after. When helping me pack, my mother said they would certainly give me a midday meal and rations for later, but she would make me sandwiches just in case.

The train arrived on the dot, and at six on the Sunday morning I sat in the waiting room at Berlin Friedrichs-Strasse station drinking ersatz-coffee and eating my sandwiches, I would have needed food coupons for anything more. Because I had time on my hands and the weather was pleasant I decided to stroll around Berlin until I felt tired. I had never been there before. I was impressed by the scale of the city, but what gave me a feeling of displeasure, initially not clear to me, was the lack of substance in the buildings: no ancient Gothic churches of granite with great windows striving towards the heavens, no mixture of housing styles from all epochs, no great monuments from the distant past, no narrow medieval alleys. I missed the inviting atmosphere of the cities I knew: Aachen, Brussels, Ghent or Paris.

Towards eleven that morning I alighted from the tram at Lichterfelde and soon found myself standing before the LAH barracks, which until the end of the First World War had been an institution for Prussian military cadets. The sentry at the gate cast a critical look at me and my suitcase, inspected my call-up papers and said: 'Well, you seem to be in a mighty hurry! If you go around the block over there, behind it you will find the entrance to the office of the reserve battalion.'

I set off and found the office where an SS-Corporal was sat at a desk with a bottle of beer. He gave me a morose look and growled: 'What do *you* want?'

'I am reporting to the LAH, SS-Corporal, here are my call-up papers,' I stated eagerly, standing at attention. He read through the document and said, 'Yes, but look here, it says not until tomorrow, you're damn early!'

'I didn't realise that, Herr SS-Corporal.'

'Well you should have.'

'I wanted to make sure I arrived here on time. May I stay?'

'Well, I suppose so if you must.' He read through the document, flicked through some files and then said: 'You're with 4th E-Company. They will be in Block 5, it's the first building on your left when you go out. Room 14 is on the first floor. You'll be told more tomorrow.'

Less enchanted than when I arrived I found Room 14, bare and uninviting with two tall windows and furnished with seven two-tier field-bed type bunks. I put my suitcase on one of the upper bunks and decided to have a look round.

The barracks was an extensive complex of redbrick buildings. Between them were unpaved dusty exercise yards with a few trees. Along the northern wall was a new swimming baths, oversized and its front façade decorated with the huge relief of an LAH man in parade uniform with the long greatcoat. Since it was midday and I felt hungry, I decided to look for the kitchens: they were located in the main building together with the dining hall and canteen. I entered cheerfully and found where they were dishing up. Here I met the first soldiers and soon I was standing before a stout NCO ladling potato goulash on to great oval earthenware plates, so-called 'Hundeteller'. I gave him the most guileless look I could manage and pleaded: 'Please, may I have something to eat, *Kamerad*?'

'*Watt is datt denn*,' he replied 'Who are you to be calling me *Kamerad*? You haven't even got a uniform on, you nut.'

'I've been called up, but got here too early,' I explained.

'Yes, I can see that. Tomorrow the replacements get here, come back then, you don't get anything before. Next!'

I traipsed off, disheartened. Gone were the beautiful images of the great comradeship I had read about in the books of Werner Beumelburg and Edwin Dwinger. Much later I was comforted to learn that the comradeship of the front and that of the homeland barracks were two very different things. Here I was with the 'reserve hotchpotch', functionaries of all kinds from the rearward areas, office studs, training instructors and other shirkers who owed their safe positions to influential Party bosses or fathers, or other good contacts.

My judgement was premature, and later I had cause to revise it: SS-Corporal Hans Ebner from the Tyrol who had moved to Germany from Austria in 1935, so enthusiastic was he for the Reich, had been retained as a squad training instructor with the reserve company while waiting for his wound to heal. He was a great fellow in the best sense of the word. The same went for our company commander, SS-2nd Lieutenant Karck, and several others.

An idea occurred to me. My Aunt Maria whom I had met twice at Hergenrath was a cousin of my father. He had told me to call on her should the opportunity present itself, and I had been provided with her address. So I went back to the battalion office and asked the duty NCO in the most servile voice possible:

'I have no provisions with me for today. Please may I leave the barracks to visit my aunt? She will definitely feed me.' The SS-Corporal stood up, arms akimbo, and said in quiet, threatening tones, 'You seem to be nuts. Do you take me for an idiot? This morning you pleaded with me to inscribe you, now you want to leave. You have handed in your call-up papers and you won't get them back. Your first leave pass is in six weeks. And now piss off before I forget it's Sunday!' Back in the squad room I consoled myself with wise words from Lichtenberg's aphorisms, then I made another tour of the barrack grounds.

I spent the remainder of the afternoon sunk in gloom. Towards evening the other recruits arrived: by the time it got dark the room was full. We introduced ourselves to each other but only a comrade from Westphalia and I hailed from western Germany. I got friendly with Bernd Kloska from Oppeln and Sepp Brunner from Regensburg, both of whom had just obtained their school-leaving certificate (*Abitur*) and we stayed together until we got to the Eastern Front. The new arrivals had stocked up at home before leaving and in the evening the smell of cheese, sausages and boiled chicken wafted across to me, but despite my rumbling stomach I did not like to ask anybody for a share.

Next day we paraded in the courtyard and then for the first time formed a queue in front of the Company office on the ground floor of our block, No. 5. We would devote many hours of our lives to queuing in the years to come. One always had to queue when fetching coffee in the morning, before the midday meal and to receive dishes of cold meat; at the clothing store, the arsenal, for all imaginable examinations and registrations, to pick up leave passes and pay, and for many other things proving the motto: 'For half his life the soldier wastes his time waiting.'

For the recruits who had had their turn ahead of me all seemed to have gone well so far as I could make out. When it came to my turn, I had another unpleasant experience. I came across an 'office bully' of that despicable kind whom I only had the misfortune to meet on one other occasion, when I passed through the DDR border control from West into East Berlin after the war.

He bawled at me: 'Name?'

I answered as loud and clear as seemed suitable to make the best impression: 'Maeger, Herbert'. I have to point out that in my local dialect, this having been formerly that of the Duchy of Limburg, and also in Flanders, Brabant and the Lower Rhein, 'ae' in family and place names is pronounced as if it were 'ah'. Therefore my name is pronounced 'Mahger'.

'Do twenty knee bends!' he ordered. After I had carried this out with the best attitude I could muster he said, 'Now do you know what your name is?'

'Mahger, Staff-Sergeant, that is my family name in the Eupen district.'

'Do another fifty knee bends, you can't even pronounce your own name you stupid half-wit!'

After I had accomplished these he told me, 'Your name is

pronounced Mehger, is that clear? If you can't read and write German I'll note it down, you miserable excuse for a Beute-Germaner'.[1]

Weighing these first lessons in the balance I realised that in the days and weeks to come I was going to be subjected to a period of re-education compared to which my Belgian high school was like a summer holiday resort. And I also knew: for reasons I have already mentioned I had to come through it all, for there was no way I could ever call it a day and go home.

The experience was indicative of what lay ahead. The combination of SS-myth, Prussian tradition and hooligan mentality created a group identity with which the LAH through its *esprit de corps* made itself into an idol of its own isolated stamp. There was no room for the National Socialist motto 'One for All and All for One' in the Führer's elite troop, for its primary aim was to brutally grind out all individuality and so create a force as ruthless against itself as it was against the enemy. One of the by-words which did the rounds was: 'The impossible we achieve at once, only miracles take a little longer.' It was intended to be self-evident that the LAH was not only the best military unit in the world, but the best there had ever been. In principle all it knew was successful attack. Pulling back was not practised once even in training, something which was to have bitter results in the future.

In order to prevent any false conclusions being drawn from all this, however, I should say that we were given a thorough grounding in the rules of the Geneva Convention and the Hague land warfare ordinance, and therefore we were taught the valid international regulations as regards the humane treatment of prisoners and the civilian populations in occupied territories.

The military training was basically exercises in the field and weapons handling. The '4. E-LSSAH' (No. 4 Company Reserve Battalion Leibstandarte SS Adolf Hitler) to which I now belonged as a recruit, was the reserve unit of No. 14 Company of the LAH Regiment at the front. As a 'heavy company' it was made up of three heavy machine-gun platoons and one mortar platoon. Our special weapon was the rapid-firing MG 34 on a tripod. It had a considerable expenditure of ammunition, which had to be brought up by the other members of the gun team acting as runners. The cases contained belts with up to 300 rounds.

Normally a 'heavy' MG squad would have one gun: the No. 1 carried it, the No. 2 carried the tripod and sight, and apart from the squad commander the other seven men were ammunition carriers or in soldiers' jargon 'Schützen Arsch'. Their job was to carry up to four boxes of belted ammunition, each weighing 17 kilograms, and other equipment such as replacement barrels; if the MG barrel became red hot or non-operational due to damage or a blockage, it would be replaced using an asbestos glove. It was essential that everything was done with the greatest possible speed. The following also had to be practised in the terrain exercises: dismantling the MG while in a prostrate position behind it: jumping up with the heavy weapon and racing with it 50 or 60 metres to a new position: assembling the MG to the stage of readiness for rapid firing: according to the situation construct a camouflaged shelter or dig in with the spade. All this had to be done at the greatest speed possible *mit der Affenzahn* (like greased lightning) as the instructors used to say. This was to ensure that the LAH would always be quicker than any potential enemy.

Active service in the field put a great strain on even a well-trained crew. The LAH was something special, however: it had double equipment. Each squad had two heavy MGs, which therefore required that all the additional back-up material for two guns had to be hauled along by the crew. Because the squad commander and No. 1 gunner had to have their hands free, the ammunition carriers had to transport, in addition to their own infantry gear, four instead of two cases: even in training the No. 2 had to carry two cases as well as the tripod. The total weight would be as follows: MG tripod 22.5kg, plus two ammunition cases 34kg, the sight and other equipment including pistol, gas mask, tent canvas, haversack, field flask, steel helmet, spade, clothing and other components about 8kg – all in all about 64kg. The LAH would march for 20 kilometres bearing this weight and more, frequently in heat and cold, rain and snow.

The MG gunners carried a box with the gunsight on their chest. This had two purposes: as a telescopic sight on the mount for direct fire, and for indirect fire by adjustments vertically and horizontally using a spirit level. In this latter case the gunner did not aim at the target himself, but operated it from concealment using settings for the MG calculated on a trigonometric basis at a central fire-control point. This was a fairly complicated affair when one bears in mind that with our double load of equipment we had twelve MGs to calibrate. In principle it was the same fire-control system as was used by our mortar team and the artillery in general, if not employing sound-ranging. I was trained in this procedure but never saw it used at the front because it was too involved and time-consuming. Probably because I knuckled under too willingly, I had the doubtful honour throughout all my period of training in Berlin of being a No. 2 gunner. This caused me thick blisters on my feet because the smallest boots of the pre-war LAH had been size 45, and I took a 42.

My training at Berlin-Lichterfelde lasted two months and three weeks. Besides weapons training and drills I learned hardly anything which I had not been able to do much better for a long time before. In the summer of 1940 as the only graduate school leaver from Eupen-Malmedy, I had gone on a four-week course for Hitler Youth leaders at Blumenthal in the Eifel mountains. The course was run by Wehrmacht officers and the training was to make us into 'battle exercise leaders'. This qualified me as a Hitler Youth pre-military instructor although I was never active as one. Amongst other things I learned topography, military surveying and mapping and the various kinds of target recognition and description, skills never spoken of at Lichterfelde.

As a recruit they were not of much use and I was pretty soon aware that the important thing was to avoid giving the impression that I was cleverer than the NCOs whose main purpose was to treat us as absolutely stupid beginners who even had to be taught to walk and stand. Instruction was always given at the tops of their voices. Everything was done precisely as laid down in Army regulations, knee bends and push ups practised until they made us retch – and this methodology was to make us finally ready: apparently the purpose of the whole thing was to make the frontline seem a kind of relief. A speciality to encourage one's best performance in training at No. 4 E-LSSAH was called the 'Kalte Klamotte'. From the push-ups position the delinquent soldier had to spring up on all fours and while in the air clap his hands and click his heels at the same instant, repeating the exercise twenty or even fifty times as according to the humour of the instructor.

The endlessly-repeated training of MG crews could be seen as a sensible activity. Rifle exercises and in particular the drudgery to perfect the goose step were obviously intended for that glorious post-war victory parade before the Führer.

I found the harsh training excellent for my physical condition – never again in my lifetime was I so fit as then. Nobody in the company could keep raising and lowering the MG mount – weighing half a metric hundredweight – one-handed as often as I could, sometimes thirty times in succession, nor could any instructor hold the carbine by the barrel with arm outstretched longer than I. That earned me some plus points, as did the pre-military training I had picked up on the Hitler Youth special courses. Much of it, such as orienteering, recognition of targets and preparation of terrain sketches were, surprisingly, military skills which were not required: all recruit training was based on exercises and drills and other less-sensible barracks activities such as the 'correct way to pass superior ranks in taut posture'. The most useful of them were: moving about the terrain, weapons training and the rapid changes of location carrying the MG, something which we practised innumerable times.

Even snaking forward with the chest pressed to the ground could be seen as useful although it was torture when carrying all necessary equipment. The instructors were anxious that recruits understood how to keep the heels always flat on the ground, for in action they could be hit by rifle fire or shrapnel. This might possibly bring the gunner a highly-desirable 'Heimatschuss' – a wound which kept him in Germany for the duration. In all these exercises it was never clear to me whether the idea was to train the men for the field or simply to satisfy the evil whims of the individual instructor. In the end I concluded that both alternated in order to increase the effect, something which probably all armies intend should be translated into action in due course.

Something I found very unpleasant was the contempt for us common to the barracks' permanent staff – a few instructors and officers excepted. I had the following experience. When we received our field equipment in early December 1941 at the end of basic training, I was issued amongst all else with a pair of lace-up shoes several sizes too big. I went to the clothing store to exchange them. I placed them on the counter. The NCO tossed them back at me saying, 'Clear off, you bum. You don't need any others, at Christmas in Russia you'll have a cold arse!'

The Leibstandarte was not a homogenous troop. Its officers, nationalistic and more or less professional soldiers trained to think for themselves, were nearly all drawn from the former 100,000-man Reichswehr Army allowed by the Treaty of Versailles. The other LAH men were initially 'old troopers', usually of above-average build, hardly fitting the political-genetic image of the SS: they were nearly all men of the simplest origins and of little education, reared more in ideas of *esprit de corps* and lured by the rewards available to a professional soldier of this special kind rather than political ideas.

The entrants born in 1922, my own generation, included for the first time young wartime volunteers from bourgeois families – amongst them school-leaver graduates – which the LAH accepted very reluctantly. Because for the most part the 'old troopers' had by then been ruthlessly despatched for slaughter at the attack hotspots, after a short period of transition the troop standard became more 'intelligent' and elite in the better sense of the word.

All in all the training hardly met the requirements of what was needed to begin fighting in Russia just ten short weeks after induction. A programme embracing rifle and parade-ground exercises was as unsuitable as the equipment with which we were fitted out to be sent out into the raw reality of the Russian winter: cotton underwear, leather field boots high enough for wading and lace-up shoes, a cloth uniform, light cloth greatcoat, field cap, thin cap-comforter and light gloves. The inadequate clothing alone was responsible later for enormous losses due to the bitter cold. From the point of view of international law, to begin a war, even one defined as a pre-emptive one, with completely unsatisfactory clothing and inferior weaponry was a crime against one's own troops.

I found the Prussian 'sharpening up' methods repulsive. The purpose of these was to subject men to abusive treatment apparently with the aim of making them ready to follow orders without question, to suffer deprivations and to die slavishly obedient. Oppressive measures such as the so-called 'masked ball', in which the men had to parade in underwear, then dungarees and finally in uniform within a period of two minutes, and scrub the barrack floors with a toothbrush, featured amongst the regular exercises night and day which gave the instructors satisfaction.

Ultimately this engendered a kind of discipline which destroyed individual morale and the soldierly ethic of the German soldier that I had read about with such enthusiasm in Ernst Jünger's inspiring First World War classic *Storm of Steel*. The soldiers of the Leibstandarte learned to die, but they were prepared for battle with a mentality which in effect was the suicidal mechanism of a robot. As I saw and experienced it, the low-grade personalities of the NCO corps were decisive in this respect.

It was my personal good fortune when serving at the front to nearly always have officers over me who respected my individual abilities and gave me tasks appropriate to them. It may be seen as all the more surprising, therefore, that I refused stubbornly to become an SS officer with the LAH. This would have meant signing on with the Leibstandarte for a twelve-year term because it had only career officers. It was soon clear to me that my future did not lie in military service, and especially not with the Leibstandarte, and that the important thing was to come through this epoch of my life as advantageously as I could.

First I had to get my time as a recruit fairly well behind me. It lasted almost to the end of 1942 as a result of the special interest that a number of spiteful corporals showed towards me. After that, throughout practically the remainder of my service as a member of the LAH, I was to enjoy a certain special position. Leaving aside the episode of my two months at the SS-Junker School, Prague, I never had a rank higher than senior private, but after my first year of military service my company commanders maintained me almost constantly in a 'ZbV' (for special purposes) role. I never had to carry out an order against my conscience or principles, although in that I suppose I was probably lucky.

My motivation was clear: by upbringing and education it was impossible for me to order men to their certain death, something which an officer cannot avoid having to do. At the front, however, I always did my duty, also volunteered to take on risky jobs, for example to bring in wounded men. Somehow, in time, I developed a special talent for problem solving where there was nothing in Army regulations: later as a company commander's driver and therefore driving the leading vehicle of a whole convoy I got us to our destination with remarkable accuracy in a Russian blizzard. Similarly reliable was my intuition for finding something to eat or drink supplementary to our frugal rations. I became a sort of expert in 'organising' – a military concept for obtaining almost anything which one was having to do without. I will describe the context of that later in my story.

In Berlin it was easy to see how the bulk of the old LAH had been cut down in the campaigns in Poland, France, the Balkans and in Russia during the first four months in the East. Rumours reached us to the effect that the average fighting strength of the front units had been whittled down to 20 per cent of that authorised. It was obvious that the leadership had not taken steps to provide the necessary reserves. Apparently we had been led into the Russian adventure under the crazy impression that it would be a military stroll, another 'Blitzkrieg' in the chain of fast and successful campaigns. The rate at which trained replacements were now being turned out was proof that the correct inferences had not been drawn from earlier experience. The leadership acted as if nothing were more inexhaustible and cheap than 'human material', and that, moreover, in the face of a growing number of enemies across the world. 'My honour is loyalty' was the inscription on our belt buckles: a motto which the leadership for their part did not reciprocate in their ethical attitude towards us.

My personal attitude to the Waffen-SS may appear contradictory and is so because the Waffen-SS was an organisation full of contradictions. It was not unequivocally heroic with stainless shield but neither is it right to say that it showed ruthless harshness towards prisoners of war or brutality against the civilian populations in occupied territories, contrary to what has been said of it repeatedly ever since.

To be a soldier is a very personal experience. The uniform sets the tone and in the best cases one tries to make come true the positive ideals attached to it. In a military unit, moreover, there are not only the dynamics of the group, but people – individuals who are forced repeatedly to decide their attitude based on their personal responsibility.

The limited moral latitude which a soldier has in his dealings is determined by his disposition, talents and upbringing, but also by his experiences in the face of death. If he changes his personality, a new concept of duty will emerge towards others known as comradeship or – against a defenceless enemy – chivalry, and which one cannot abandon honourably.

That was the situation and community into which I was thrown from one day to the next. In the flippant definition of the time I was a 'booty Germanic', and I felt like one too. The man who has two Fatherlands remains a man of two halves, or he must decide totally and unreservedly in favour of one and accept all the consequences that go with it. I did that in favour of Germany, but the step from a strongly Catholic parental home and a Church High School in Belgium into the Waffen-SS was another thing altogether and not achieved without an inner struggle. My development bore the stamp of many experiences and events in the life of a child and youth.

Chapter Two

My Arrival on the Russian Front

When in mid-December 1941 the great day finally came and they read us our marching orders for Russia, we were poorly prepared as fighting men and miserably equipped for the Eastern Front. The Leibstandarte itself lay – we did not know this when we left – between Taganrog and Rostov, and on the way there we judged by the organisational state what heavy demands the Russian winter had made on the German leadership.

There was apparently no proper planning even behind our transportation. We went from Berlin to Cracow in a comfortable sleeping carriage coupled to a scheduled express train. After we spent a few days in a former Polish cadet academy at Cracow, we proceeded by stages to Vinnitsa in the Ukraine by local trains and spent a week there in barracks.

One morning we had to parade, were given a handful of dried fruit as rations and then set off on a march until evening over icy streets, finally being loaded aboard a goods wagon on a narrow-gauge railway. It rattled all through the night to Uman. Our morale was rock bottom in the icy cold until somebody began to sing a song which struck me as macabre:

SS marschiert in Feindesland und singt ein Teufelslied,
Der Schütze steht am Wolgastrand und leise summt er mit:
Wir pfeifen auf unten und oben, und uns kann die ganze Welt
Verfluchen oder auch loben, Grad wie es jedem gefällt.
Bei uns da geht's immer vorwärts, und der Teufel, der lacht nur dazu;
Wir kämpfen für Deutschland, wir kämpfen für Hitler,
Der Rote kommt nie mehr zur Ruh.

('SS is marching through enemy land and sings the Devil's song,
The gunner stands on the Volga shore and softly hums along:
We don't give a damn and the whole world can
Curse or praise us as they please.
We keep going forwards, and the Devil he laughs just the same;
We fight for Germany, we fight for Hitler,
The Reds will never know peace again.')

This song highlighted the dark side of a regiment made up of those assorted elements to which I now belonged. The other extreme was the crusader spirit in secular form transmitted from the time of the Order of Teutonic Knights of St Mary's Hospital, Jerusalem, with its asceticism and unconditional obedience. Murderers were always present in every crusader army; to judge by what we know of them, considerably more of them than in the Waffen-SS.

We spent a miserable Christmas at Uman in a barracks whose rooms were at least heated by giant wood-fuelled stoves. To pass the time there were diverse kinds of exercises in the nearby wood. It was typical of the many woodlands of crippled birch one finds all over Russia and the Ukraine. Its paltry cover had a very depressing effect on me.

Then – we were meanwhile more than two weeks on the move – everything suddenly speeded up. Ju 52 transport aircraft flew us to Mariupol, at as low a level as possible on account of the poor visibility and Soviet fighters: shortly before landing I saw through one of the small windows how during a snow flurry the pilot suddenly lifted the right wing to clear a water tower.

I remember that we spent about ten days in unheated barracks at Mariupol, chilled to the bone and given next to nothing to eat. After days of waiting, open lorries took us the approximately 120 kilometres to the LAH regimental command post at Taganrog. There we were divided up: I was attached with about ten others to No. 14 Company HQ occupying a house of upper middle-class origins in a kind of avenue.

Our company commander, SS-Captain Max Hansen, a picture-book blond SS officer, greeted us with a handshake and pithy words.

We were served hot millet gruel: we did not suspect at the time that it would be our staple diet for months. Next day we were issued weapons, ammunition and equipment: nothing was in short supply because the authorised strength of the company was four platoons of 120 men and it had only twenty. At dusk an SS-Corporal led our march to the front.

The route was marked out by stakes, which were difficult to see in the thick snowdrifts. An icy easterly wind swept through our thin cap comforters and light field caps, penetrated our greatcoats and the light cloth capes, which reached to our knees. Our feet were almost numb in our jackboots and in my simple ignorance I thought to myself: 'This can hardly get any worse.'

The front ran from about 18 kilometres east of Taganrog to the Sea of Azov following the small Sambek River, its valley formed of smooth treeless slopes. About 25 kilometres to the north of the German positions was the river Mius, which flowed into the Sea of Azov west of Taganrog. These were the most easterly positions of the German Wehrmacht in the winter of 1941. The Russians were opposite us on the east bank of the Sambek about 300 metres away. We inhabited squat earth bunkers dug out before the LAH pulled out of Rostov and the terrain froze hard as steel. Depending on the space taken up by equipment, each had room for four to six men lying or sitting, but not standing.

The access hole into the bunker was covered by a canvas curtain and linked to an MG position constantly manned throughout the long nights. The bunkers were situated between 20 and 50 metres apart. The company had to defend 250 metres of front with twenty men, the battalion as a whole was responsible for a stretch of about one kilometre. Communication trenches between the bunkers existed only as appendages, they had not been completed by the time the severe frosts set in. They were never finished during this winter. 'My' bunker, which I shared with three other men and 10,000 lice, had a special comfort in one corner, a small stove fashioned from a marmalade drum. It could only be used briefly because of the shortage of fuel, and only then at night or in snowstorms. In clear weather the smoke rising from the chimney would betray the position of the bunker and attract Russian artillery fire.

I was attached to the remnants of a platoon reminiscent of a team of lost adventurers. It consisted of a SS-Sergeant known as 'Marinus' for reasons unknown, SS-Staff Sergeant Gottwald from the Sudetenland, of stocky build with black hair and coal-black eyes – not at all the SS warrior type – and a lanky SS-Lance Corporal called Laban ('long streak'); he was the only one with whom I spoke on familiar terms because like me he was not an NCO. At the beginning there was a SS-Private but he moved out because our bunker was too narrow. This came as a relief for me. As the 'Schlips' (a person everybody treads on) I had the least desireable place directly at the bunker entrance: everybody had to trample over me to get in or out and I had to constantly sweep away the snow. I was the 'Schlips' from the very beginning and probably, as was made clear to me, it was not worthwhile anybody getting to learn my name because a 'Schlips' at the front usually had a life expectancy of only six or seven weeks, if that.

My presence brought an advantage for the whole bunker team. Besides my camera, which was of lesser interest, I had with me a clock that could be used for dividing up the watch periods. It was the only valuable item of its kind and lay by night near the MG. It never failed, and as was determined only later, nobody ever set it to read false and so shorten his period of suffering.

The neighbouring bunkers were reached across open terrain. This had to be done as fast as possible, as I was to discover. It was a clear, sunny day and I had to take a message to the next bunker. I took my time because there had been no shooting for several days. Something prompted me to get back faster; fortunately, for a Russian sniper who had taken up position meanwhile shot the death's-head badge off my field cap. I noticed that rifle rounds which pass close to the ear do not whistle, but make a loud report as though the weapon had been fired in the immediate vicinity.

This event had a positive effect for me: more furious with myself than shocked by the sudden attack, I ran to our MG and fired off a burst at the low bushes and small hill on the other side of no man's land where we assumed the enemy positions were. My aim was true, as could be seen by the spurts of snow where they hit. Marinus, standing in front of the bunker entrance, gave me a nod of approval and said, 'Not bad, now I'll help you clean the MG.' I had obviously passed my baptism of fire and reduced some of his doubts regarding my aptitude.

I soon grasped why the so-called replacements always had the greatest losses. The 'Schlips' were treated by the frontline veterans – with some exceptions – as pariahs. They were given the worst night watches of four hours, had to collect the rations and firewood under fire, and by day crossed the enemy's field of fire when hurrying to the next bunker with messages. The LAH Old Guard had plausible motives for their lack of comradeliness. Coming as a rule from simple origins, they had only a slim chance of making NCO or ideally obtaining a wartime commission to create for themselves a limited career opportunity. Now along came these young wartime volunteers, amongst them bright types with the school-leaving certificate, who presented a danger to their narrow-minded hopes of advancement. The 'Schlips' had therefore to be given no concessions.

Within a few weeks of arrival, of every five 'newcomers', in general only two would still be alive, these having survived by good luck or by virtue of a sixth sense for danger. These latter would have advanced to the first stage of being front veterans – *Frontschweinen* – themselves.

Our first great problem proved to be the clothing with which we new 'Schlips' had been sent into the Russian winter. The only item which was to some extent adequate was the 'llama coat' of simple cloth lined with fleece which reached to the ankles. One could not wear it to move about the terrain because it caused one to stumble constantly but for standing the night watches at the MG post near the bunker it was better than the issue cape of thin cloth best suited to a mild Central-European climate. After a few days none of us was thinking of heroics. Even the old *Frontschweinen* were mainly interested in getting through the frightful winter with its depriva-tions. Weapons and ammunition were also in short supply. We gave no thought to attacking, not even reconnaissance patrols were sent

32

out. There would have been no point to them, for in good visibility we could see the terrain up to the slope nearly two kilometres away. The Russian positions were well camouflaged in the undergrowth and hedgerows between the ruined houses. Ivan, being better fed than ourselves, was keener on undertaking some activity. The Russians attacked only now and again, however. Occasionally Russian assault parties would slip through the gaps in the German line under cover of a blizzard, overpower the sentries and drag them back to their own lines.

At night the highest state of alert and the regular firing of flares was necessary, for the Russians wore white camouflage suits and were often not spotted until dangerously close to our positions. When I stood watch at night – usually after midnight and before dawn – I would circle cautiously on the spot: by moving my feet constantly I protected them against unnoticed frostbite. Also at risk were one's nose, ears and hands. Whoever stood watch had to be at the MG. Only this weapon had the firepower to allow a lone sentry to hold off a party of attackers until his comrades made it out of the bunker to support him. We also had hand grenades, machine-pistols and entrenching tools ready for use. Because the MG was not totally reliable in the bitter cold and the attackers could also come from behind, I used to hold a hand grenade under my llama coat ready to throw, but luckily I never had to use one.

In the most forward positions nobody wore a steel helmet. Whoever had the chance got Russian winter clothing for himself. This was not without its risks, for only the Russians had the accessories one needed for survival – fur caps, quilted stuffed jackets and fur boots – and they did not let them go voluntarily. One therefore had to take them. In principle that was not so difficult. All that was needed was to creep into no man's land by night and take what one wanted off Soviet corpses. One had to bear in mind three things here: first, it could only be achieved after a Russian attack and before the dead Ivans froze stiff; secondly, Ivan liked to attack in snowstorms before dawn, conditions in which one could easily lose one's bearings after leaving the bunker; and thirdly, the captured items of clothing had to fit to some extent.

33

I found out that there had even been a raid, unfortunately not successful, for clothing by some of the young 'Schlips' from the first batch of replacements. They had crossed the Sambek and gone right up to the Soviet positions. The most desired booty was fur boots because the toes froze in German jackboots. This counted as 'self-mutilation' and could result in court martial and a barbaric punishment. In the first winter in Russia there were some exemplary punishments of this kind to 'keep up the morale of the troops', because too many soldiers preferred to lose a limb to frostbite and return to the homeland for treatment rather than stick it out at the front.

My bunker comrades had accepted me very dubiously at first but within the framework of their raw mentality had had to make survival possible for me from the outset. For standing watch Laban lent me his Russian fur boots and Marinus gave me a pair of extra socks in order to help fill the boots. During the first week I suffered dreadfully in the cold in my light cloth uniform.

Chapter Three

First Half of 1942:
Six Months on the Russian Front

It was early evening. I was gnawing at a slice of bread I had just toasted on the mini stove. Outside, Laban called out suddenly to announce that his period on watch was up. Gottwald, to his relief, stumbled over my feet and opened the canvas curtain at the entrance; at once a slurry of icy snowflakes swept over me. Seconds later Laban began climbing inside through the narrow opening.

At that moment all hell broke loose outside, the rattle of MGs competing with the lighter staccato of machine pistols while in between single rounds rang out and hand grenades went off with a dull explosion. We grabbed our weapons and tumbled out, myself leading. An icy wind greeted me, in the glare of the bursting flares I could see the snowflakes coming horizontally for my face. Gottwald positioned himself behind the parapet firing short bursts from the MG left and right into the slope behind us. Laban was feeding the belt to the MG straight from the ammunition case. I laid my carbine aside, pulled out a full case from the little depot we had dug into the extended trench and pushed it towards Laban, then took a couple of hand grenades and hurled them into the general area of the fray hoping for good luck.

Marius nudged my back and pointed behind me. I understood at once what he wanted and, re-armed with my carbine, I followed him to the anti-aircraft position behind the bunker. We got there not a moment too soon. The ground between our bunker and that of our neighbour was uneven with many small mounds and depressions from where the initial shooting had presumably come. In the diffuse light of the flares ghostly figures were running towards us. Marius raised his machine pistol and fired. I threw a couple of hand grenades, heard a cry and then it went dark again.

We went back to the MG position on our right from where violent firing was continuing, although in the open terrain and on the slope farther up nothing could be made out which might have been a threat. This wild shooting went on for a few minutes more into the magnesium-lit night then the furore abated to brief bursts of fire and the occasional single shot. On the slope below the position we heard a few muffled cries followed by several metallic sounds and then silence returned. Gottwald fired his flare pistol, after two 'plops' nearby, three flares poured their white light into the spraying snow. We saw nothing which might be the enemy but waited a few minutes to be sure that the Russian withdrawal was not a feint. I became aware again of the penetrating cold.

Marinus was the first to speak. 'We should have a look round, they always get vodka before they start these games!' Then he turned to me: 'With a bit of luck you might find something warm to wear. Let's go!' We did not have far to trudge. Barely twenty metres in front of our position lay a dead Russian, his steppe-jacket riddled with bullet holes. Marinus took the fur hat from the corpse, removed his felt boots and handed them to me. I was thankful that he did the honours, relieving me of the macabre task.

'I was wrong about the vodka,' he concluded, 'It was only sunflower seeds and machorka they had.' The latter was a substitute tobacco made from herbs. We returned to the bunker, where after Marinus had delivered his report on the partial success of our scavenging Laban said 'I'll have a scout around. "Schlips" needs a proper jacket!' He went down the slope to the river and came back a few minutes later with a fine warm steppe-jacket in excellent condition. 'Just one round through the head,' he said laconically, 'You've got some Bolshelvist lice as a present to go with it, so now you're a real Soviet *Frontschwein!*' I had very mixed feelings about all this but finally it gave way to a kind of satisfaction at having got away with it in one piece and no longer having to be so horribly cold.

As the only 'Schlips' in our squad I got all the wearisome and unpleasant work. I still got a break, however. In a neighbouring bunker there was an SS-2nd Lieutenant who had his men bring a sofa on a horse-drawn sledge from Taganrog. The sofa took up so much space in the bunker that the other men could only sleep sitting up. This bunker had been dug before the onset of winter and was impossible to enlarge because of the metres-deep permafrost, which was as hard as concrete. We worked daily in turns at a communications trench about 1.70 metres deep and 70 centimetres wide. Lengthening the trench by 10 to 20 centimetres after two hours' toil with pick and shovel was thought as good progress. The extension had proceeded so far in one month that one fine day the SS-2nd Lieutenant decided to exercise the four 'Schlipses' of the platoon. The Russians saw the flash of the bayonet blades and opened fire with their artillery. That was the end of the exercise.

There was very little one could do to keep warm. As despatch runner or fetching the rations one had the chance to get warm for half an hour in the farmer's cottage. This was located behind the slope over which the enemy had a full view. In the cottage our catering NCO Babucke ran the field kitchen assisted by the cook Löbel and two captured Ivans. It was a two-kilometre hike to get there, only possible by night or in a snowstorm. One always had to reckon on the possibility of sniper fire from the other side of the river, while the Russian artillery was very accurate and took a bearing on every individual man they saw clearly on the snow-covered terrain. Specially feared by us was the 'Ratch-boom' 7.62cm anti-tank gun with great penetrative power: its shells exploded before one heard it fire, therefore one had no chance to take cover.

Fetching the rations was one of my permanent duties. I was quite happy to do it for I could get warm in the cottage and often got a hot cup of tea there too. Every day the rations were the same: millet gruel, slippery bread and a piece of horse-sausage. It was as though we were on an island totally cut off from the Reich. The few transport arrangements still working were needed exclusively for bringing up ammunition. We received no change in the diet, nor any mail, until mid-April.

When I returned to the earth bunker, the gruel, bread and sausage would all be frozen hard as stone. They would all then be thawed ceremoniously on the marmalade-can stove. Warm toasted bread was a delicacy; and while eating the paltry rations our conversation would come to life. Our seclusion and deprivations led to there being nearly always only two subjects: Number one was women and the fantasies of frustrated infantrymen, ranging from romantic desires to perversions. Number two was food, in which the speakers would debate their preference for better quality or better quantity.

Especially for the 'Schlips' the time for chatter was short, for besides standing watch, fetching the rations and firewood, trench digging and weapons cleaning, it was necessary to sleep and also fight – against the Russians and against the lice, the latter being the more aggressive as I recall. They lodged in every fold and seam of dirty clothing and outer garments. I cracked thousands of them between my thumbnails without cutting down their numbers visibly. I left my vest on the bunker roof overnight in a temperature of minus 25° and found that even bitter cold was no deterrent to them. They were ubiquitous in masses everywhere, never stopped biting and gave us no peace.

In the bunker the cold affected everybody's bladder most unpleasantly. In a niche of the MG position near the bunker was a large tin to which we made frequent visits daily to lighten our load and tipped the contents over the parapet, to leeward, with the wind, if we could. The other business was done on to a spade emptied out over the terrain with the biggest swing possible.

Somebody shook my shoulder and I heard Marinus say: 'Up you get, my lad, it's a clear day!' It took me a while to understand what he meant. Then I got it: I was to fetch wood and pick up the rations on the way back. I had to set off in the early morning, for once the sun was up the Russians kilometres away could see all of the long flat slope on the west bank of the river where we were dug in. Their snipers had the sun at their backs and their rifles were equipped with telescopic sights. On the bright snow-covered surface, one had no chance against them.

I stretched myself, struggled upright and picked up the mess tins standing ready tied together. Despite my quilted steppe-jacket and fur boots I was stiff with cold, but the warmth of our bodies made the temperature within the bunker relatively tolerable, for when I pulled aside the horse blanket at the bunker entrance and stepped out, the icy morning air of the easterly wind struck me in the face like a fist. In the niche beside the MG mount were a couple of pieces of cord, which I took along to bind the firewood I was to fetch. At the end of the short communications trench which led up the slope I had a tinkle – in the cold one always had the urge.

I set off. I did not really get moving properly for a while because I still felt tired in my bones: I had stood the night watch at the MG from one to three o'clock and the day before worked to exhaustion digging the extension of the trench towards the neighbouring bunker in earth frozen hard as steel. I began to warm up only gradually once I had trudged to the top of the slope. Fortunately the snow on the track was not deep, the easterly storm having swept it into the gullies, but all the same I had to make sure always that I had firm ground beneath my feet and so conserve my strength. It was only five minutes to the crest of the ridge, and sheltered behind it was the farmer's cottage where our Gefechtstross[1] had its quarters with the kitchen: smoke full of promise rose from its chimney. When I opened the door below the porch roof overhang the snug warmth met me. SS-Corporal Babucke, our catering NCO was not around, but Löbel the cook grumbled to me, 'The food's not ready yet!'

'I'll come for it on the way back from collecting firewood,' I said, 'but how about a hot drink?'

Babucke and Löbel never made it themselves, two captured Ivans did it for them. One of these, Alexei, knew me quite well as the permanent rations collector for my squad. He handed me a half-full field beaker of what passed for tea. It was an indefinable liquid but hot and I thanked him for it. I left the mess tins on a shelf.

I had no time to lose and set off again. The path led north, along the safe western flank of the crest, and I made good progress on the crusted snow. On the way I ate my breakfast, a slice of pulpy bread brought with me from the bunker and stowed in my trouser pocket. After more than a kilometre I crept up high for a view over the landscape. In front of me was the valley of the frozen Sambek under a clear sky in which the stars twinkled, though already paler: in the eastern sky it was dawning.

Nothing could be heard for far and wide. The scene was one of the deepest peacefulness. To my left below me on the other side of the river bank I saw my objective, situated safely above the high-water mark, the village of Varenkovka. It consisted of thirty ruined houses, some of them charred by fire, others severely damaged by artillery hits. The village was reached through a fold in the ground on the rising slope: I could make out some recesses in the fold, which would give cover. Creeping back, I found the track a little farther on; it was still dark enough for me to follow it and I soon reached the upper edge of the village.

I was somewhat surprised to find that Varenkovka seemed abandoned even though its cellars between the houses and wealth of usable materials for bunker building were enticing. If any German units had set up in the vicinity there was no sign of them. The far bank of the Sambek, distinctly steeper and therefore closer to the river than the slope opposite our bunker, still lay in shadow as the sun began to rise. It continued peaceful and still, apparently neither friend nor foe had the slightest interest in this ruined village.

I could see that the houses had been abandoned in a hurry. Household goods lay strewn about: chairs, tables, broken utensils and even a mattress, a luxury in a Russian house. After some searching I found a few tools beneath the wreckage, including a hatchet, which would serve my purposes. Boards, small beams and even firewood was plentifully available and so I soon amassed a good supply; Marinus and the others would be pleased because the material was dry and would not smoke when burned, thus enabling us to keep the bunker nice and warm even during the day.

From the wood I had gathered I built a sledge with a base of two long skids. I was just considering making my way back through the gully to spend the day in the warm field kitchen when a deafening blow threw me to the ground. Recovering my wits, I found myself enshrouded in a great cloud of dust, which hung in the air almost motionless, there being no wind. I reacted instinctively and dived full-length behind the wall of the nearest house about ten paces away, then scrambled to another spot, which looked safer. While still checking myself over for any injury the next salvo arrived, three rounds close together, which landed right where I had been standing so unassumingly just a short while before.

The shells exploded without any previous sound of firing or howl from the incoming projectiles. From this I deduced that I was being fired upon by artillery with a high muzzle velocity and penetrative power, multi-purpose anti-tank guns to which we gave the respectful nickname 'Ratch-boom'. The single shell had been a ranging shot for the observer and was damned good. Therefore this Soviet battery were no beginners.

Normally two or three rounds would have been enough if the expenditure bore some relationship to the hoped-for result. I mean, it might have been justified to fire salvo after salvo to kill a regimental commander, but a simple German soldier, a 'Schlips' scavenging for wood, and all alone? Against all reason they kept firing at me with their anti-tank guns. Then they paused for a few minutes before resuming, following the procedure laid down in the artillery manual for a systematic bombardment of the village. It was by no means beyond the bounds of probability that I would not survive this: I therefore had to do better than keep moving from one area of cover to another, for the houses and the cellars were of adobe. I recalled having seen an abandoned Russian tank with its hatch open near the houses located at the edge of village close to the river. Thanks to the vast and ever-thickening cloud of dust thrown up by the artillery fire which now enveloped the whole village, I could not be seen. I reached my objective by working my way from one heap of rubble to the next and found the tank, a T-34 with a broken track but otherwise in good condition. I climbed in. The interior appeared to be in good order. The cannon was pointing towards the Russian slope, the shells were suspended neatly in racks along the turret walls. I thought about loading the gun and engaging the enemy battery but then decided against it: the highly-motivated Ivans were already worked up and might have concentrated all their available firepower on the village.

I was relatively safe in the tank. Now and again shell splinters pattered hard and sharp against the steel hull but only a direct hit would have been dangerous to me. After about twenty salvoes the firing slackened, and finally ceased altogether. The cloud of dust drifted off towards the slope and into the gully: that would have covered my withdrawal, but I could not get there safely from the tank. The Ivans were undoubtedly observing every inch of the village through good binoculars as the visibility improved: they were obviously unaware that I was sitting in the tank otherwise they would have fired on it at once.

Patient waiting was therefore advised, and now I looked around my steel quarters. The tank contained nothing edible, and I had not searched the cellars of the village for food. Water was not a problem, I had merely to stand below the hatch and collect snow from outside with my hands. As I got accustomed to my situation I found that it had its pleasant side. The sun had by now climbed quite high and was warming the interior. Furthermore, I found it increasingly enjoyable to be alone for the first time in weeks, and for as long as I wanted, or in any case at least for hours. That enabled me to reflect in peace; a luxury for a soldier which in principle and for good reason no army wishes to encourage.

My initial thoughts were directed to the question of why Ivan, usually sparing with his ammunition, had been so extravagant in my case. The answer had to be linked to the fact somehow that no other German soldiers were in the vicinity of the village. It was known to our units that the Russian gunners reacted with fury whenever they espied anybody scavenging in the villages on the Sambek. Perhaps the Russian observer came from the village or its neighbourhood? Or were the recruits to the Soviet anti-tank guns trained on the high and relatively steep river bank in well-camouflaged positions? Target practice against live targets, so to speak, a subtle psychological atavistic experience of hunting fever. After my short period at the *Westdeutscher Beobachter* in Eupen I was journalist enough to need to interview those comrades on the other side of the river regarding this matter, but unfortunately circumstances prevented it.

42

In any case I could understand the boys on the other side. Lyuba, the interpreter attached to our company command post at Taganrog, with whom I had had a conversation during one of my flying visits there, had explained carefully how they thought and felt. She had been trained in the Humanities, knew Latin and a little Greek and no doubt the Classics, including the sacrifice of the Spartans at Thermopylae besides: 'Wanderer, go to Walhorn, tell them there how you saw me lying at the Sambek, as the law ordered it . . . in a damaged tank as an allegorical tomb . . .'

Nobody would do so. A short notice in the Eupen edition of the *Westdeutscher Beobachter* perhaps: '19-year old Herbert M., before his conscription recently a troop leader in the Hitler Youth at . . . , has fallen on the field of honour on the Eastern front.' Hansen would send a letter to my parents: 'It is my sad duty to inform you that your son has given his life for Volk and Führer true to his oath of allegiance.' Marinus and the other bunker inhabitants would curse: no firewood and no rations, the damned 'Schlips' are all idiots, can't rely on any of them although this last one had seemed quite promising. Oh well, one of us veterans will have to do it again.

Otherwise, 'All Quiet on the Eastern Front'. Erich Maria Remarque (Uncle Joseph always maintained that the name was an anagram, he was really called Kramer) sends greetings. His Paul Bäumer, a High School pupil as I was, head stuffed full for twelve long years with grammar, vocabulary, mathematical rules and maxims, history, biology and geography: snuffed out in a split second by a little piece of lead within a copper jacket for better penetration, well aimed by an expert who had had his head stuffed full for twelve long years with grammar, vocabulary, history . . .

Suddenly I wanted nothing more ardently than a conversation with my Upper School teacher 'Professor' Bernard, a man from another world, a highly educated Jesuit of the noblest kind, an aesthete, tolerant, perceptive logician. Towards me, his pupil, always fair and correct. He never spoke a word of German and I never did discover if he understood any. But I venerated him like an idol from another star. On 9 May 1940 he held forth wittily about Horaz, next day the German Wehrmacht arrived. In common with various other teachers he disappeared suddenly and without trace; we knew that he was a major in the Belgian Army reserve, which did not exempt priests from military call-up.

In the confines of my T-34 I began to recite the prologue to Homer's *Iliad*. I did not get as far with it as I had hoped. I remembered Ovid better and also the list of the Kaisers of the Holy Roman Empire's German nations. Even the seven races, which in Caesar's time made up the peoples of the brave Belgians, I had not forgotten: the Nerviers, the Menapiers, the Eburons; Fräulein Maria Keutgen, who taught history at my first year of elementary school, would have been pleased.

Finally I brought out from my breast pocket paper and pencil and began to write. Slowly, carefully, in capitals, narrow and in tiny letters – paper was a luxury – I began to record what I had experienced since leaving Berlin: in most cases I even recalled the date. At irregular intervals the comrades on the other side let me have a 'Ratch-boom' every so often, sometimes into my sector, at other times into another corner of the small village. Probably they thought it important to remain on their guard, and in a curious way I felt honoured that they were taking me so seriously. Gradually it fell quiet until at last I could relax. I sat comfortably in the tank gunner's seat and found a spot to rest my head. Soon my enormous sleep deficit overcame me and I slumbered.

When I awoke, time had moved on: in the East it got dark early, not only for the season of the year but because all Wehrmacht clocks and watches kept Central European Time. Here at Taganrog, 3,000 kilometres from Aachen, in mid-March dusk fell at 4:30 in the afternoon: in addition, this place with its steep bank was already in the shadow of the setting sun while the Ivans on the eastern side of it had the sun in their eyes.

Now I could cautiously make my exit. Slowly I slipped out of the T-34 and, using all available cover, went from one ruined house to another until I reached the place where I had abandoned my firewood when the barrage started. It had survived the bombardment intact and I took the sled in tow, creeping to the gully, already deep in shadow. By the time I saw the first stars I had already reached the western slope and a little later the field kitchen. I hung the mess tins and rations sack on the strap slung above my shoulders and trudged back to the bunker.

When I reached it the moon had risen. Marinus examined my bundle of wood and remarked drily, 'Not so bad!' And then, 'So what happened?'

'I had a wonderful time,' I told him, 'Others should try it. I was in a T-34 until dusk and even managed to nod off.'

'Well, great,' Marinus replied, 'You can have the first watch!'

In quite recent history, wars were events held in the warmer periods of the year: if they assumed the character of limited field campaigns, the armies spent the winter in comfortable quarters. The First World War with its trench warfare in Northern France lasting for years was a new experience for staffs and troops. Yet what German frontline soldiers along the entire Eastern Front had to bear physically and mentally in the harsh winter of 1941 had no equal. The until-then unstoppable offensive was brought to an abrupt halt by the early and especially cold onset of the Russian winter, and now they had to dig into the hard-frozen soil for cover. This gave them only the barest protection against the better-equipped fresh troops brought up from Siberia, helped by a secret mutual Non-Aggression Pact signed with Japan.

The freezing German troops, dressed in uniforms suitable only for the Central European climate, worked at night for weeks and months excavating bunkers and digging communication trenches. After long weeks freezing under thin tent canvas they could finally get warm and set up an inter-connected, defensible front. Only with the mobilization of the last reserves was it possible to hold this front: yet despite all these adverse circumstances in the first weeks of winter before Moscow the Soviet Army failed to gain any ground worth mentioning.

The German advance had been seriously compromised. Against all tactical guidelines the mobile units were forced to stop and hold their ground along the entire Eastern Front because the infantry was insufficient to cover the wider sectors and the reinforcements coming up were too few. On 1 January 1942 the reduced German

Army in the East had then as before 135 divisions and seven and one-half Axis allied divisions of very limited fighting capability in twelve armies to face 328 Red Army divisions in forty-two armies.

The German leadership had to have known from its knowledge of Napoleon's campaign in Russia and the two-front war of 1914–18 what it meant to attack Russia, and additionally with an insufficiently equipped army. It was an irresponsible adventure, Russian roulette with six rounds in the chamber. The English military historian Liddell Hart stated in his book *The Defence of the West*:

> The first thing which strikes one about the 1941 invasion is the numerical weakness of the German forces. Not only the terrain but also the numbers spoke against Hitler, and from the very beginning of the campaign. On 22 June he launched himself into the immeasurable expanses of Russia even though he knew that his troops were numerically inferior to those of the enemy and that this unfavourable ratio would continue to deteriorate the longer the campaign went on. This fact is astounding. With regard to time and area, this game was more dangerous than any other waged by an attacker in modern history.

He continued:

> In the year 1940/41 the German Wehrmacht was more modern than any other. It failed to meet its objectives, however, because it had failed to assimilate the lessons experienced twenty years before. Even so, as things were, in the first summer Hitler might have been able to reach Moscow if he had given free rein to the panzers as Guderian had urged him. The older generals considered this to be a dangerously unorthodox plan and in this case Hitler sided with orthodoxy and so lost his best chance.

In January 1942, ninety-five Russian divisions faced thirty-seven German divisions of Army Group South along a 600-kilometre long front. Up to March 1942 the German Army in the East lost 1,107,000 men. Army Group Centre had only sixty-seven tired German divisions to face 190 Russian divisions along a defensive sector 1,000 kilometres long: Army Group North with thirty-one weakened German divisions faced eighty-six Russian divisions on 600 kilometres of front.

On all fronts therefore the Soviets were three times stronger than the Wehrmacht. That was true not only with regard to the number of men but also in a rather more favourable relationship of weapons. In addition: for every Wehrmacht fighting soldier there were nine in the 'rearward services', catering and transport units, depot and Army administration staffs and military staffs of all kinds. In the main, privileged personnel of definite origins established themselves in the rear, for the most part coming from the homelands of the old Prussian Army.

After six weeks at the front, I was able to go for the first time with four colleagues, amongst them an SS-Staff Sergeant, for a short three-day R&R to Taganrog. We set out at dusk, but after two or three kilometres we were overtaken by a violent snowstorm and strayed off the staked-out route. We tried to get a bearing by the direction of the storm, but had the impression it might have veered. After about three hours aimless wandering between high snowdrifts we were close to exhaustion.

Suddenly we stumbled across a snow-covered railway line. The SS-Staff Sergeant wanted us to follow the railway embankment to the right, but I was certain we should head left and so make west and south for the Sea of Azov and from there reach Taganrog. When I contradicted him, he reacted immediately in the very sharp tones of a superior officer. Eventually I was able to convince him and the others that to reach Taganrog we had to follow the railway line to the left and under no circumstances to the right because that way definitely led to Rostov and the Russian frontline to the east.

An hour went by during which we made better progress on the railway embankment, and then we came to a wood. A building stood between the first trees, presumably a linesman's house: a light was flickering within. I was first to reach the house and entered as cautiously and quietly as possible through a door, which was ajar. Inside was a kind of hearth in which the end of a man-sized log was burning: two men were pushing at it. They responded lightning-fast to my order 'Hands up!' My colleagues then arrived and we now tried to sort out where we were. This was not easy for the two dark forms wore Russian quilted jackets and fur hats though without any insignia. We saw no weapons.

The two grinned at us ingenuously and one of them stuttered finally: *'Nix russki soldat, germanski soldat otshin karasho!'* Then he offered us Russian cigarettes, which two of our squad accepted gratefully. We knew it was best to avoid tangling with this pair, although at the time we had no knowledge of partisans. After getting warmed through we set off again. At dawn we came at last to the suburbs of Taganrog and soon afterwards reached our destination: the house in which our company HQ was quartered. At Taganrog we slept on the hard floor but at least the rooms were heated; we could also exchange our underwear and shave. Even a visit to the theatre was arranged for us; I remember we attended the ballet although in my exhausted state I slept through most of the performance.

The German Army lost the war not least because its principal infantry weapon was the obsolete, unwieldy 1898-model carbine. It had a magazine for only five rounds, had to be reloaded by bolt action after each round was fired, and this meant taking fresh aim each time. The Russian machine pistol proved to be totally superior at short ranges with its spray effect and much greater firepower. In the 1942/43 Russian winter I captured a Russian machine pistol and used it subsequently throughout the war. I oiled my 98 carbine very carefully, wrapped it in a blanket and consigned it to the storage bin of my fighting vehicle.

One night I was standing watch near our bunker in a piercing easterly wind, which whipped the snow into my face, when I realised suddenly that I could no longer feel my hands, slapping my upper arms crosswise had no effect. In my panic I buttoned up my llama coat and placed my hands against my body inside it: they felt like slabs of ice. Gradually in this manner they began to thaw and I was able to finish my watch. My immune system had not taken kindly to the method however, and a few hours later began to revolt with vomiting and diarrhoea.

This brought me an unexpected benefit: next evening I was sent to the battalion dressing station at Taganrog. I set out with an older colleague who had a minor wound to the upper arm. We got lost in a blizzard and wandered for hours until finally reaching a solitary blacked-out farmhouse. It was soon opened to our resounding knocking and we found the anxious faces of an old man and a wizened old woman staring at us. We gestured for permission to enter, inside it was cosy and warm.

The wife prepared hot tea and we took out our frugal supplies, a crust of bread and a horse-meat sausage: my colleague even had a piece of bacon. I drank the tea with great relish but refrained from eating and pointed unmistakeably to my infirm stomach, offering the old couple my meagre ration. From that moment on the tension dissipated quite tangibly. The old man brought out some potatoes from beneath the floorboards: his wife disappeared into a side room and came back with a can full of milk; soon she had prepared a potato purée which we consumed with enjoyment, it had been weeks since we last saw potatoes. Then we had to lie down in the couple's bed, made up somehow on the floor, and we slept like logs until full daylight. What time it was we had no idea: we established that it was not far to Taganrog and set off. By the time I reached the dressing station the potato mush had almost restored me to health, but I was given a field bed and a hot meal all the same and convalesced for a couple of days before returning to the front.

I mention this experience as being normal and typical of the relationship between German soldiers and the Russian civilian population. I do so because in war films the Germans are depicted almost exclusively as looters and murderers. Basically we respected 'Ivan' and felt a vague kind of empathy with him because he couldn't help admiring us and was no better off in the field than we were. Russians who came across to us as defectors or in small groups to surrender were often simply mustered into the German forces.

The platoons of No. 14 Company LAH to which I belonged were made up of about 25 per cent Russians from time to time during the fighting. Generally they served as ammunition runners and this compensated for our high losses. Our MG 34 had a theoretical rate of fire of about 1,800 rounds per minute, while the MG 42 introduced into the LAH in the summer of 1942 could fire off 3,000 per minute. An ammunition box contained a belt of 300 rounds, each ammunition runner carried up to four boxes. From that it can be seen that the MGs in action fired off more rounds than the ammunition carriers could bring up. We were, therefore, always short of ammunition carriers and that led to the grotesque situation in which Red Army soldiers captured even in the bitterest fighting would rather fight, serve and die in the LAH than go to a prisoner of war camp. I never heard of a case in which one of them refused duty or deserted. In the winter of 1941/42 at the Sambek we were engaged in pure trench warfare and there was no room in our bunkers in the front line for Russians, but nevertheless as previously mentioned two Ivans assisted our cook at the field kitchen. I envied them, for they had it far better than we did in our holes. They sat in the warm and had enough to eat.

During those winter weeks something remarkable happened: at Taganrog a number of Leibstandarte men missing for weeks came back to us across the ice of the Sea of Azov. At the time of the massive Russian offensive at the end of October when their units had had to pull out of Rostov in great haste, they had been cut off from the main body and hid out in private houses. Surprisingly, they were kept hidden for months by their Russian hosts until the opportunity presented itself to slip back to the German lines, serving as further proof that German soldiers were by no means unpopular with the Russian civilian population. At the time Rostov was a Communist stronghold in the Soviet State.

In mid-March it got much less cold and the ground began to thaw, making trench digging easier. In the clear nights we could keep a good watch on the frozen river before us, and the Russians kept stolidly to their own side. Only the activity of snipers, artillery and their aircraft increased: Russian short-range reconnaissance aircraft, called by us 'sewing machines' on account of their rattling motor noise, visited us regularly at night to drop small fragmentation bombs on our positions. They flew slowly and it was quite easy to hit them with the MG, but their underbelly was armoured and one could watch the tracer rounds bounce off them. It would look like a rain of pearls, an almost charming firework display.

When at the end of March 1941 the sun began the thaw and the work digging the communications trench began to seem relatively pleasant, our company commander thought it would be a good idea to make proper soldiers out of us 'replacements' who had survived the winter at the front. Accordingly twelve men were selected from the four platoons and ordered to Taganrog. We were given quarters in the always-unheated classroom of a school and treated as raw recruits by an SS-Staff Sergeant and two SS-Corporals. From dawn to dusk we received a grounding in the basics again, but this time much more gruelling than at Lichterfelde. This period of re-training was obviously intended to make the front appear a desirable place to be, and with me it certainly succeeded.

In the school grounds was a slope. It thawed during the day and after being trampled by countless boots froze at night to form a surface of crunchy ice. Our training outside began every morning the same way. We had to run towards the slope bearing all our equipment and at the order *Hinlegen!* (lie down) were required to trundle down the slope on our stomachs. I used to carry the heavy MG mount on my back and this often slammed with full force into the nape of my neck.

How bad this training got can be estimated by a disappearance from our squad one night. Leurle came from a village in Swabia. He was constantly the butt of the instructors' spite. He told a friend that that he could not stand the torture any longer and was going to desert to the Russians over the ice in the bay. He believed more in their humanity than that of our slave drivers. His name was never spoken again.

In soldiers' slang, we all had it up to here. The singing of marching songs, normally a proven means for raising the morale of the troops, seemed to have been abolished. One of our squad who began singing a verse of the *Russland Lied* out of boredom during weapons cleaning found himself singing unaccompanied. That can be understood when one compares the lyrics to the reality of our situation. This is the text:

Nun stürmen nach Osten die Heere ins russische Land hinein.
Kameraden, an die Gewehre, der Sieg wird unser sein –
Von Finnland bis zum Schwarzen Meere -
Vorwärts! Vorwärts! Vorwärts nach Osten, so stürmen wir!
Freiheit das Ziel, Sieg das Panier,
Führer befiehl, wir folgen dir!

'The armies are now storming eastwards into Russia
Comrades, to arms, victory will be ours
from Finland to the Black Sea
Forwards! Forwards! Forwards eastwards we storm!
Freedom the goal, Victory the motto,
Führer give the order, we follow thee!'

Included in our training was weapons instruction according to Army manuals. SS-Corporal Wilms, the mentally most limited and evil of our three oppressors, led the class. Stupidly I could not resist making him aware of an error he made in connection with the 08 pistol. 'I shall bring that up with you later!' was his ominous reply.

It seems that he decided to finish me off using the regulations. After duty I was ordered to report to the instructors' room wearing my llama coat and bringing all field equipment, i.e. steel helmet, gas mask with case, cartridge pouches, haversack and carbine. The stove was glowing so hot the room was like a sauna. SS-Corporal Wilms ordered me to put on my gas mask and then he roared: 'Five hundred knee bends with carbine extended at arm's length! Each one according to the Army manual! And count out each one!'

This order meant that I had to perform each exercise precisely and as described in regulations, always keeping my arms horizontal, lowering my bottom to touch my heels each time. It was pure torture. After fifty knee bends I had back ache, after 100 in the heat and gas mask I could hardly breathe, after 200 I was tempted to murder Wilms by crushing his skull with the butt of the carbine, after 300 I thought of simply collapsing and taking the consequences.

'Louder!' roared Wilms.

Then I was overcome by the determination to deny the sadist his triumph. With choking voice I shouted through the gas mask, '311! 312! 313!' Somewhere within me there welled up besides my dogged rage renewed strength and indifference to the risk of collapsing unconscious or dead. It even got easier: I completed all 500 knee bends with blameless posture. After the 499th I tore off the gas mask, came to attention and shouted '500!' SS-Staff Sergeant Lenkwitz said drily, 'That's enough, Wilms!' That was the hour from which, more than my experiences at the front, I gained a consciousness of self and conviction that as a soldier I could come through any situation.

I was soon able to subject that to proof. We had been taught until we were blue in the face that on sentry duty we had to challenge any person approaching by aiming the carbine at him and calling out, 'Wer da? Parole?' Parole was a password changed daily by the district commandant and made known to us at evening roll call. If the person challenged did not respond to the second shout using the correct password, we had to shoot him immediately. Our Spiess[2] Nieweck who gave us instruction on it completed the session by telling us as cool as you please that we should aim to shoot dead the person challenged 'and make sure he never utters a word ever again!'

As we knew, Nieweck had his special method of testing recruits on watch. One night he simply approached the 'Schlips' sentry, tore the rifle out of his hands and gave him a week's jail. Some days after the knee-bends excess I was standing watch at night in the school yard. It was my custom to seek out a dark corner so as not to be seen at once in an emergency. Suddenly there was a movement at the school yard wall and somebody headed for me. I called out 'Halt! Wer da? Parole?' and received no answer. At a distance of eight metres I recognised Nieweck. After a second's reflection I made the second challenge and then fired into the air.

Nieweck sprang back and cried, 'You want to kill me, you stupid arse? You recognise me!'

I replied, 'Jawohl, Stabsscharführer, I shall shoot as ordered if you take one more step!'

Without a word, Nieweck spun on his heel and disappeared into the darkness. Meanwhile, the shot had alarmed everybody in the vicinity and my comrades came running up. I reported the incident and heard no more about it. After that Nieweck left me pretty much in peace.

In the yard of the school building stood a small house, presumably the dwelling of the headmaster. Somehow I got into conversation with the occupants, an elderly woman and her daughter. Tshura the daughter was a teacher and like most of her professional colleagues spoke passable German. While talking about this and that I heard for the first time the explanation in a nutshell which the Russians used to sum up their judgement of the invaders: *Germanski nix kultura*. Tchura spoke very frankly about the German occupation. Stalin's talk about the 'Great War of the Fatherland' to save the Soviet Union from the Fascist invaders had not missed its mark on her, but she refused to believe that the Soviet Constitution contained a Declaration of Communist World Conquest. She was a patriot and as such felt she had moral right on her side. She did not display her enmity towards me personally but ridiculed mildly my assertion that I was in her home town to free her from Communism. By her comportment she was much more self-assured than I, and this gave me cause to reflect.

Because our meagre rations continued to be millet, pappy bread and an indefinable sausage, I was now intent upon finding some improvement to my diet if the chance arose. In the neighbourhood I discovered a Russian family who to my surprise kept a cow in their dwelling in the Taganrog town centre. With them I traded aspirin or pyramidon tablets – I had brought both along to Russia as my private stock of medicines and had requested my parents to send me more through the field post – for milk, of which I drank heartily.

That must have been the way I contracted the illness which started with revulsion for any kind of food accompanied by stomach pain and expressed itself more fully a few days later by a yellow colouring of my eyes and skin. I was sent off to the hospital and quickly diagnosed with 'infectious jaundice'. As a result I spent six weeks in bed in a ward with a dozen fellow sufferers. We were given a watery soup with a few noodles three times a day. When I began to recover I got to know what real hunger was, but the radical cure did my sick liver good, although the after effects of the illness continued to make themselves felt years later.

With several other patients I lay in a large, bright room in a school, the convalescent unit of the battalion dressing station. We all suffered not only from our infirmity and the shortage of food, but also for months from the lack of female company, apart from close contacts of the most modest kind. In the effort to forget our hunger our endless conversations revolved around sex. Descriptions of sexual exploits, many based on pure fantasy, sprouted the most exotic blossoms. Some of my fellow sufferers even described details of which I failed to get the point. Not everything I heard appealed to my own sexual appetite or seemed desirable, but at least I understood what this war was depriving us of, and what presumably we would never have the chance to experience.

The war had become my destiny. I had plenty of time for reflection and these thoughts brought me some distressing conclusions. The reality with which I had to come to terms was light years away from the ideas and expectations which I embraced after reaching 'maturity' with my school-leaving certificate. The reality with which I now had to come to terms could not be more depressing as I drew up the balance sheet of factors. That I was shot at with the intention of killing me was nothing special having regard to how things were, and one also had to take into account the inhospitability of the land and the murderous cold. However, the fact that together with countless fellow sufferers I had had to survive malnourished for months because the lines of supply were practically non-existent; that in order not to freeze to death I had had to remove items of uniform from Russian corpses, and that I had had to come through a serious illness with neither medication nor sufficient food had nothing to do with the Russians, the Soviet Army nor its territories. Without a second thought I would have willingly sacrificed an arm or a leg to escape this misery.

It was not only I who had seen already that the war was lost. The causes of the catastrophe were obvious: the German political leadership, which had written the crusade against Bolshevism on its banners, and the Wehrmacht High Command, which had planned the attack on the Soviet Union, bore full responsibility for the whole wretched failure. Knowing the fatal historical defeat of Napoleon in 1812, they still sent the nation's youth into a campaign against Russia without appropriate winter clothing, weapons, equipment and adequate transport capacity for desperately-needed supplies. The losses amongst the fighting troops were enormous, the destruction of material immense. When as a result of this the collapse of the front loomed, draconian orders were issued. Since the soldier whose toes were frostbitten in his thin leather shoes risked being shot by firing squad if he reported sick, then in reality all the General Staff officers who had participated in the planning of the campaign up to the end of 1941 should have been court martialled.

It is typical of them that after the war this one or that had the cheek to conceal his criminal guilt by explaining that it was an early example of his planned resistance against the regime. Chief of the Army General Staff General Franz Halder maintained after the war that he had sabotaged the campaign in the East from its inception. The truth was that since 1940, therefore a year before it began, he had planned it in the most careful detail. Up to July 1941 he had placed an army of 600,000 men on the Soviet border without Hitler's knowledge.[3]

In his book[4] Halder wrote: 'It was very difficult for Hitler to make the decision to attack Russia . . . on the other hand there was a firm and not unfounded conviction that Russia was arming for an attack on Germany . . .'

The war against the Soviet Union had a remarkable pre-history. Between 1923 and 1933 the German Reichswehr had worked with the Red Army in the strictest secrecy in remote areas of Russia to develop fighting vehicles and train armoured forces. One of the results of this collaboration was the T-34 tank of which 12,500 were turned out in 1942, and 16,000 in 1943, being more than a match for German panzers and anti-tank guns. When the first T-34s were destroyed, it was discovered that many of them were fitted with the 7.62cm gun bearing the stamp 'Rh' for Rheinmetall. These guns had been rejected by the Heereswaffenamt (Army Weapons Office) in

56

the mid-1930s and released for export.[5] The Russian 'Ratch-boom' 7.62cm anti-tank gun was a copy of this weapon. Up to 1939 the German Army had only obsolete 3.7cm and in the East inferior 5cm anti-tank guns at its disposal. The victims of this circumstance were thousands of German anti-tank gunners who perished miserably, crushed to death by T-34s.

A million young German men were drawn into the war against the Soviet Union in the belief, continuously hammered into them, that it was their duty to help save Germany and Europe. They were reinforced by the knowledge of the terror-regime in the Soviet Union which already by the beginning of the 1930s had murdered millions. Confident in serving a just cause, they swore loyalty unto death to the German leader and many sealed this oath with the sacrifice of their lives. The Führer, the Government and the upper echelons of the military failed to reciprocate with the most primitive duty of care towards the fighting troops: thereby they broke faith and committed an unparalleled act of treachery against their soldiers and the Fatherland common to them all.

And that is not all. The brutal and disgraceful treatment of the Ukrainian people by the Party bosses and Army leadership, those same Ukrainians who greeted the Wehrmacht with bouquets of flowers during its fast advance, and unveiled the barbaric 'Crusade against Communism', in their blind arrogance calling the people 'sub-humans', almost forced them to become fanatical partisans. Thus were honourable and decent soldiers of the German Army deprived of their honour, which had been tied to the ethic of chivalry since the early Middle Ages and – as far as I could see – remained with some exceptions an absolute moral duty in this war too.

For my part, as a result of all I had learned, I decided on personal rules of conduct. I would only shoot at anybody, including the Russians, if my life or those of my comrades were in danger. Under all circumstances I would avoid having to send another to his death, and this meant renouncing ever being an NCO or officer at the front: wherever possible I would try to work against the spirit, which caused many officers and NCOs to treat their men more brutally than animals. I would do everything I could to be entrusted with tasks, which would help me in this aim; the most reasonable course of action seemed to me some activity with a medical unit. Something towards which I would strive wholeheartedly. I would always conduct myself fairly and decently towards the people in the territories we occupied and particularly the civilian population. And I would do everything in my power to survive this war staged by an irresponsible leadership. After just a few months at the front it was no longer my war – if it had ever been so. My loyalty was to my conscience and not to a criminal clique of incompetent, arrogant decorations-fetishists on the Staff.

Easter was approaching and a few days beforehand I was surprised to receive a Christmas parcel from home with less-than-delightful crumbly pastries and a Walther PPK pistol as a present from my uncle Josef. He was my mother's brother and at that time the cultural official with the German military government at The Hague. This uncle Josef had fussed over my mother's family for years. Originally a Catholic priest, he had left the Church after some kind of intrigue and discord, and at age forty resumed his studies at Frankfurt. He concluded these so successfully after two years that it awoke the interest of the regime. He joined the Party, married and became a Professor in Ordinary at Frankfurt University. In mid-1940 he was given the cultural post at The Hague. He died of a serious illness in 1945 at Herborn. While carrying out his duties for the German occupation forces in the Netherlands, he had been able to save the lives of a large number of Jews, and as a result after the war the Dutch Government invited his widow and two children to a long holiday of convalescence on the Dutch coast.

The starvation diet at the field hospital, though thoroughly unpleasant, worked wonderfully as a therapy and probably protected me against the later consequences of this insidious illness. As soon as I could stand and was able to leave for the first time I allowed myself a luxury, which I had again in Russia whenever the opportunity presented itself: I visited a hairdressing establishment for a shave. The service was substantial, carried out by young women and included not only a proper shave done twice over, but afterwards a pleasant hot facial compress: never again anywhere else did I experience such perfect treatment from tender hands.

When I was finally discharged from the battalion convalescent unit the winter was over, trees shone fresh green and only in shadowy corners could a little dirty compacted snow be seen. It was obvious that Taganrog lay on the Sea of Azov at about the same latitude as Burgundy. Somebody, my company commander SS-Captain Hansen, if not the company horror, Spiess Nieweck even, wished to assist in my recovery. I was sent off to re-convalesce with the security force at the Taganrog Rata works where Soviet fighter aircraft had been built before the German invasion. Rata aircraft were not taken seriously at first by the Luftwaffe because the fuselage and short wings were made mostly of plywood. This opinion changed very quickly once the Russian campaign began and the machines proved their extraordinary capabilities in combat by virtue of their light weight and compact design.

My new assignment was a real soft job. For the actual protection of the works Ukrainian militia were employed, armed with rifles and given their duties by us. There was nothing strange in this for up to that time there had never been any resistance to the occupation nor had we even heard of partisans. We had a heated room at the works main gate. In the framework of our monitoring schedule I could split up my day relatively freely. This gave me the chance to have a good look around the factory in which panzers and vehicles were being built for the Wehrmacht. I made the interesting discovery of whole rows of the most modern Siemens electro-turning lathes. The Ukrainian personnel told me that the machines had been traded for wheat in 1940 and were still being delivered up to mid-1941.

For this and other reasons, the works were a favoured destination for tours by higher ranks and HQs located in the vicinity. Because they were not fully occupied in their own duties, they binged almost daily while the front starved. I also got to see for the first time our brigade commander, SS-Lieutenant-General Sepp Dietrich and his staff officers, some of whom would later, including after the war, make headlines in contradictory reports.

Once on gate duty at the works I stopped a car in accordance with the strict regulations. Besides the Wehrmacht driver it contained a Russian female passenger in civilian clothes. She had no pass, and although the driver maintained that she had the authority of the competent district commandant, I refused her entry. As it turned out, she was the concubine of the commanding officer of a catering unit.

At the Rata works, bearing in mind the alternatives, I spent three pleasant weeks. Twice I even had weekend leave at the Taganrog town hall, which our commander had requisitioned as a comfortable command post a good 18 kilometres from the company's main front line on the Sambek. For the journey there and back through the town I took the perilously-swaying tramcars on worn-out rails also used by the forced labourers at the Rata works.

On one of these journeys it was already late evening and pitch dark. I had had to leave my works carbine behind for my relief. I was therefore in the tram, alone with at least three dozen figures giving me black looks, and would have been unarmed had I not had with me uncle Josef's pistol. I positioned myself on the platform at the rear with my back against the outer wall, advised my travelling companions to keep a respectful distance and as a precaution on the entire journey kept the pistol in my right-hand trouser pocket, loaded, safety catch off and with my finger on the trigger.

My tour of duty at the Rata works ended in mid-May. At my unit a new training squad had been formed to which I was promptly assigned. Therefore the same old oppressive measures and devilry as before. For me it lasted only a week for then I fell ill again, this time with bad throat pain and high fever. At the battalion medical centre a young assistant doctor looked at my pharynx and diagnosed an angina and ordered 'several days bedrest at my unit'.

There I grew worse daily, I could no longer eat nor drink and on the third day I could no longer speak. I writhed unstoppably with a high fever. My condition was so bad that eventually our Spiess was forced to send me to the military hospital. I was escorted there by my colleague, Bernd Kloska, from Oppeln with whom I had shared a common destiny since our first day as recruits in Berlin. It was more than a kilometre there, and I needed the last of my strength to make it.

At the entry hall to the hospital stood a SS-Major[6] who, no sooner than I had crossed the threshold called to me from a distance of at least five metres: 'Stand still and open your mouth!' diagnosed me from there and ordered: 'Diphtheria, 28,000 units of serum immediately!' In a trice I found myself in a field bed, received an injection and spent the next few days more or less unconscious.

I remember vaguely that the Russians launched an air raid against the hospital one night in which it suffered heavy damage: my bed was covered in dust and shards of glass. Next day I was removed to a village called Nikolayevka well behind the lines: its population of German stock had been deported at the time the invasion of Russia began. It consisted of neat houses with front gardens in the full bloom of spring, such as one never saw in Ukrainian villages. We were lodged in the school, which served as a field hospital with thirty places for the sick and wounded.

In the neighbouring bed was a 30-year-old comrade from a divisional rear unit who had been operated on for appendicitis. He was at first very taciturn and looked depressed. After three days he asked me if he could confide in me, and wanted me to swear not to repeat what he was going to say to any other living soul. I gave him my word. He told me that after the capture of a Ukrainian city – as I recall it was Odessa – at the beginning of November 1941 he was ordered with fifty other men of the HQ company of his unit to escort a column of over 3,000 Jewish inhabitants of the city. The walk was eight kilometres to an anti-tank ditch dug by the Russians where he and his colleagues were ordered to shoot the Jews – men, women and children. He confessed that he was deeply troubled by the incident. I was hardly less shocked. Even if previously and never subsequently did I ever hear of such a thing being done by frontline troops or by a rearward unit, from that day onwards after learning of the massacre my critical consciousness grew. And there also grew in me the sense of being threatened by an endlessly huge and inescapable calamity.

My next stop was a military hospital at Mariupol. This sprawling city on the Black Sea was the most beautiful I knew up to then in Russia. The experience of spring on the Black Sea made it difficult to believe that only a few weeks ago we had been in the deepest winter. I was at liberty to move around and had a couple of good weeks in which my health became noticeably better. My favourite dish was semolina made with milk and a blob of stewed apple at its centre: I usually got two portions because I got on well with one of the Russian nurses named Olga.

It was the end of June 1942 before I was discharged back to my company, which had been withdrawn from the front to the small village of Yegorovka, some billeted in farmhouses, the others in tents like a camping ground. We developed close contact with the villagers by trading now and again for an egg or some milk. Community life was uncomplicated. We lived in the houses and slept on the earth floor, the local people withdrew into their cellars, usually situated a few metres from the house, the location recognisable only by the steps at the entrance. These cellars were very functional. Their primary purpose was for the storage of grain, also 'kapusta' (sauerkraut), an anti-scorbutic very important for survival in winter, kept in earthenware pots or barrels, and sunflower seeds. The cellars were roomy enough to protect whole families during air raids or fighting, and big enough to live in them should the houses be requisitioned. And they would be undisturbed there, for we never had cause to go down into one of these underground dwellings.

It was almost like a holiday camp if one overlooked the garrison atmosphere. Reveille was at three in the morning when it got light because all clocks were set to Central European time. This meant that duty terminated at three in the afternoon in bright sunshine.

There were quite a few pretty girls in the village who soon became very friendly. Our colleague, Grulich, had an accordion, which he had been able to bring along as a lorry driver; he played, we conversed as best we could and as the mood advanced we danced. Incidentally, the first Russian words I learned on the way to the front were *payaustra* (please) and *spasiba* (thank you).

At first training in the terrain and the marches with heavy equipment were very exhausting for me: the effort caused my heart to beat very unpleasantly. I understood that my heart had not yet recovered from the serious infection, but after two or three weeks it cleared up and I was fully recovered. During the war years I was never out of action again save for a wound and a short bout of influenza.

Whoever knows war only from books and films may have the impression that it consists of an unbroken chain of battles. For the individual soldier this will only be true for certain periods of time in which he participates in concentrated operations of attack or defence. These periods of operations could last weeks and as a rule incurred heavy casualties; for that reason a fighting unit needed longish resting phases in which the losses in men and materials could be made good and the unit restored to battle-readiness. This applied even more to elite units, which were deployed at the hotspots of the fighting to achieve strategic or tactical objectives.

The Leibstandarte was an elite force: when it went into action it did so with a furious commitment from which no man could disengage himself and without any regard for the lives of its men. The Russians knew this, and sometimes it was sufficient for them to know that they were going to be up against the Leibstandarte to convince them to abandon a proposed attack. Thus in these weeks of early summer 1942 we were put on alert several times and took up our readiness positions, but rarely did anything ever come of it. We were not in a position to launch attacks being well below strength in men and having few fighting vehicles. The diversified life pleased us very much and I remember the hilly landscape south of the Donets as the most delightful I got to see in Russia.

Chapter Four

Second Half of 1942: France – Dieppe

A frontline unit on the Eastern front was more or less isolated. Everything coming through the field post was censored: anything official was given out in Company, Battalion, Regimental, Divisional or Army orders. Whatever remained was rumour, 'latrine gossip' mainly because it was hawked in those places where one tarried for the performance of the natural functions. Seated upon the 'thunderbox' one was undisturbed and had the surroundings in view so that certain things could be expressed, which supersoldiers with lace on their collars might have considered to be defeatism.

We were now left so long in peaceful and quiet Yegorovka that we began to wonder if the high command had perhaps forgotten about us. Maybe the war had ended and they had not thought to tell us yet. We knew that a few weeks previously the summer offensive had begun in the south of the Soviet Union, the advance proceeding at a tempo as if the winter catastrophe had not occurred. What reached us were victory bulletins in the old style, a little more reserved as to the numbers of tanks destroyed and Red Army men captured, but the tone was rather more shrill, with more talk of endurance and Final Victory brought about by fantastic operations and the joy of sacrifice. A rumour was circulating that we were soon going to be transferred out to France and re-equipped as 1st Regiment of an LAH now expanded into a division.

That summer the sun always shone in the Ukraine: our marching orders came to us literally out of a clear sky. Next morning all of us were loaded aboard vehicles, which all bore the scars of battle after ten months of the Russian campaign. After a couple of hours on the road we reached Charzyssk near Donets where a goods train was waiting for us in a small station. We set off towards the West, and as each hour passed the certainty grew: we were not bound for the central front at Leningrad, but for Germany. This put us in good spirits. We enjoyed the sparse straw on the hard floors of the wagons and the miserable rations from the field kitchen and even the birch woods along the way, which hitherto I had always felt to be a rather poor excuse for woodland. Like most of my comrades I spent the fine weather amongst the vehicles on the low-loader wagons.

On the morning of the third day the train rolled through Silesia. Woods in leaf and homely villages received us, girls stood at the level-crossing barriers waving to us: everything was clean, green and friendly and we had the almost unbelievable experience of rebirth after many months of fighting, cold, hunger and strangeness. As we continued onwards through Saxony, Thuringia, Hesse and Rheinland-Pfalz it all become much more obvious, and everyone waited excitedly to cross into France, land of cathedrals, 'demoiselles', haute cuisine and wine. The fathers of my comrades, veterans of the First World War, had apparently told their sons wonderful things about the country.

The reality which first offered itself to view was a disappointment: modest stretches of railway track with dilapidated stations and a monotonous landscape. Meaux, an eastern suburb of Paris where we de-trained, was a typical industrial 'banlieue' of the city and as such not enticing. We were accommodated in a school, where about fifty men of the 'reinforcements' who would bring us up to fighting strength awaited us. There were also new vehicles – mostly four-wheel-drive Opel 'Blitz' lorries – new uniforms and the new MG 42, whose legendary rate of fire had preceded it. It could actually fire 3,000 rounds per minute, but only in theory for the belt of 300 rounds contained in one ammunition box would last only six seconds, after that the gunner would be forced to pause.

We might have had to go through the usual grind in the terrain exercising with the new weapon but it did not come to that initially. After days of cleaning weapons, polishing boots and belts, washing underwear, darning socks and having haircuts, we had to turn out for show parades of all kinds connected to all these activities. One fine morning we were driven in a spotless convoy of vehicles into the centre of Paris where we had the proud experience of sitting to attention with bayonets fixed to be paraded along the Champs-Elysées for the generals. The citizens of Paris stood along the pavements and did not appear to show any hostility. That evening, in further celebration of the event, each of us received a half litre of red wine presumably chosen by a catering officer from the eastern Elbe, for that was what it tasted like; judging by my secret tastings of the mass wine as an altar boy the French product was far more pleasing to the palate.

A few days later we got to know the real France. After a drive 200 kilometres westwards we arrived at Boissy-lèz-Perche near Verneuil, an inconspicuous little village in an idyllic district of low hills. A castle-like manor house at the end of a driveway lined by giant chestnut trees within a beautiful small park, was to be our home for the next three months. It must have pained the owners, whom we never saw, to have had it requisitioned by the Germans, and particularly the notorious Waffen-SS. Nothing was ever damaged maliciously, the pavilion near the manor which had apparently been the library had been cleared out before our arrival, much to my regret.

The French summer had a calming effect on everyone, even the NCOs. The duty plan involved principally training with the new MG in the extensive fields, but also a lot of sports and so much free time that on the second day following our arrival at Boissy I had a bottle of wine and then went sightseeing. There was a tiny grocer's shop in the village; when I entered with two colleagues we disturbed the female owner and three young farmer's wives in their conversation. The four looked at us with such shocked expressions that we waited in silence, but after a few seconds one of the young women, the prettiest, had regained her composure and said: '*Mais ce sont quand même de beaux gens!*' – 'But despite everything these are fine men!'

I answered with a distinct bow: '*Merci, madame, pour le compliment, vous êtes très charmante!*' – Thank you, madame, for the compliment, you are very charming!'

Her stupefaction was a picture: the pert girl went red, but the shopkeeper gave me a sly smile and asked what we wanted. I interpreted for my colleagues and bought for myself a litre bottle of Muscadet, which she recommended. When I opened it later I recognised it at once: it was the mass wine which our old pastor Ernst preferred at the Astenet nuns' chapel. After that I often went to Madame Colette's shop for my purchases of the fruity dry Loire white wine, which out of friendship she let me have at a reduced price of two francs per bottle. Once we had our six morning hours in the terrain and lunch behind us, we were allowed a two hour break, which I dedicated to my Muscadet. It reconciled me for a while to everything, even to No. 14 Company of the LAH. It remained my favourite wine for years: after it could no longer be obtained in Germany, I would always bring back a small supply on my regular trips to France. I also gave it as a present to my guests which later, in my time at Krefeld, won me the reputation of an outstanding connoisseur of wine amongst the local political dignitaries.

Boissy was a place of transformation for me. I enjoyed every tranquil hour beneath the old trees of the park where hardly anybody ever went. Even the tedium of being on guard became a pleasure for me; whenever I made my rounds in the warm nights, the stars shaded by the trees, I breathed the warm air perfumed by the corn and flowers of the fields and enjoyed with all my senses the incomparable magic of what the poets call 'la douce France'. The poetry of this country, whose literature I had studied for years in my college at Eupen often more as an obligation than out of inclination, opened itself fully to me for the first time in these surroundings. It was like a homecoming into an unknown land of one's longing.

My linguistic abilities soon brought me into contact with the villagers. I came to an agreement with a farmer's wife: I attended her midday meal on Sundays with four colleagues. She served us a delectable meal, meat and fried potatoes, as much as we could eat, and that was saying something. I also used to talk to 'Père Sauvage', who lived opposite Madame Colette's shop with his grand-daughters – cute little twins; his son was an officer in the French Navy and was now with De Gaulle's forces, as he told me openly. He always had a glass of red wine for me and indicated cautiously one day that he could put me in touch with 'the other side' if I were interested in that kind of thing. I was not, despite everything and on principle, quite apart from the reprisals to which my parents would have been subjected.

In this connection it proved wise that out of instinct I kept my ability to speak French a secret from officialdom. One of my colleagues who spoke it as well as I and helped out wherever he could was suddenly transferred to Divisional HQ, where he was given some unpleasant duties such as the translation of interrogations. When he returned to the company, his position as No. 2 MG gunner had been taken, and he found himself back carrying ammunition, which gave him nothing to smile about. Most of the corporals were very much adverse to persons who had more intelligence than they did.

As interpreter at HQ I would probably have got to know Paris, but I went there by another route. I dislocated my right big toe in a football match on the great lawn in front of 'our' manor house. This brought me a few comfortable days in the dressing station during which the Battalion surgeon informed our paramedic Sepp Rist that all members of the company with foot complaints should make the trip to Paris for examination. I reported at once as being a chronic sufferer and shortly afterwards found myself whisked off to the French capital. There was no great urgency in the whole business, and it was drawn out over four days with three nights in a hotel requisitioned for the Wehrmacht.

The examination by the SS orthopaedic surgeon took place on the third day so that we had plenty of time to see the sights, and in bright sunshine at that. Sepp Rist and my squad leader SS-Corporal Gerd Hübner had latched on to me as a connoisseur of the 'ville lumière' because I could speak the language and had visited the World Exhibition in Paris in 1936 with my family: my father had used his right of free travel as an official of the Belgian railways for the purpose.

Rist, Hübner and I visited Notre Dame, the Eiffel Tower and Napoleon's sarcophagus in Les Invalides, walked along the

Champs-Elysées and enjoyed the flair of the incomparable city which, even though we were into the third year of war, had lost little of its charm. It was in the nature of things and in the Paris air that we wished to know the fabled charm of the girls of Paris, and that this would be no more than a fleeting contact. In the evening, therefore, we attended one of the popular establishments where business seemed good. The lady I came by provided me with a professional and anonymous service; it was my first experience of this kind and nothing about it merits further mention.

Almost unnoticed by us in our seclusion, a significant re-organisation of the LAH had occurred. The original LAH was a regiment which in 1940 had been expanded into a motorised brigade, and had now been further expanded into a division by the inclusion of an additional motorised infantry regiment, an artillery regiment, a panzer regiment, and reconnaissance, anti-tank, self-propelled (SP) gun, anti-aircraft and signals detachments. Our former No. 14 Company, 3rd Battalion LAH was now No. 9 Heavy Panzer Grenadier Company attached to 1st Regiment of the reorganised unit.

The idyllic days at Boissy came to an end in mid-August and we moved out to a new location in Normandy. The new accommodation was far less feudal and consisted of a number of barrack huts set up in front of the big railway marshalling yards. At their centre was a heavily trodden grassy surface with a flagpole where we paraded for roll call. The small village nearby was called Potigny and from there it was nine kilometres to Falaise, twenty to Caen.

We had hardly settled in than there was a night operational alarm which turned out, contrary to our expectations, not to be an exercise. The cause was the landings by Allied troops on the Channel coast at Dieppe, 140 kilometres north-east of Caen and fifty north of Rouen. We drove through the night with a couple of stops and dug in next morning at the edge of a wood. It drizzled unpleasantly all day and we saw no action. About 6,000 Canadians had been sent ashore for no obvious purpose, about 4,800 of these finished up dead or wounded, the rest were taken prisoner. We were transferred to the coast where we met the Canadians held in an open camp under guard but without other security measures. I gave one of them, a pleasant youth from Quebec, some of the rations from my haversack and chatted with him for a while in French until Spiess Niewek spotted this and stormed up with his obligatory roar to stamp out this fraternisation.

Boissy and Potigny were different worlds. With the new ambience came a change of weather and mood. The barrack huts were musty and dark, the landscape more monotonous and cool, and most of all I missed the muscadet because we had no local shops. In order to improve the meagre rations, every Sunday I bought a pound of butter from the farmers, which I mixed in a bucket with mashed potatoes and milk: the result was a tasty purée for my roommates Henze, Spethmann and Kälbel.

There was a certain indefinable ill-humour in the air. The weather was mainly responsible, which in October was dull, rainy, windy and at night also quite cold. We spent many nights in the open, lay on the damp grass and dug more infantry trenches into the muddy earth than we had in the whole previous Russian campaign. The only comfort was the many Normandy apple trees, which gave delicious fruit. When it grew colder, I learned to appreciate the coffee of the region: hot and served with a slug of Calvados.

At Potigny the whole stupidity of the soldierly life waiting around lay heavy as lead on our spirits. In the barrack huts the monotonous conditions of mass quarters dominated, and opportunities to escape the misery were rare. In order to create for myself at least the illusion of a private area, one day I began to fashion a small table of birchwood crowned with a table lamp with the primitive tools at my disposal. How I came by the materials for the lamp, the bulb and cable I cannot remember, and that I was successful seems to me astonishing in retrospect as was the fact that my highly unmilitary initiative was tolerated and none of my colleagues made fun of me for it. I suppose that they too enjoyed the modest touch of homeliness which the lamp spread during the evenings.

The everyday routine was dour, boring and stupid, but probably no different to what had been passed down from the army of Old Fritz. What we really enjoyed, for the opportunity it gave us to get some proper exercise while doing manual labour, was to be selected for the tree-felling party, which fetched wood from the nearby forest for the huts' stoves. One day when I was picked for it, a branch fell on my lower left leg causing fairly heavy bleeding, This earned me a few days rest in Sepp Rist's convalescent ward. This was located in the upper floors of the estate house where the officers were billeted.

One fine afternoon Rist appeared and announced with a grin: 'I've got something for you, a first-class girl from Caen – officer quality!' At once two sprightly girls stood in the doorway. One went off with Rist, the other one approached me with a look of determination. I was not keen on professional girls and made clear to her that I had no money. She gave me the once-over and then decided: '*Eh bien*, of no importance! You will do. For me it's the same as usual, for you, first class!' She got down to business at once, and I was gentleman enough not to protest.

Especially for me, the everyday routine was not pleasant. I had meanwhile become one of the 'veterans', which provided some relief because the notorious martinets concentrated on the intake of recruits who had arrived in September. Nevertheless two corporals, Wilms and Baldauf, who had made life difficult for me since Taganrog, quickly roped me into their dubious activities and treated me as a 'Schlips', which brought in its train nasty tricks of all kinds.

I was still usually No. 2 gunner on the heavy MG, occasionally No. 1 gunner, and had been promoted from SS-Mann to SS-Private (trained soldier). At Potigny I drew guard duty so often that many nights I only got six hours sleep, once or twice even only four. These types had little use for someone like me, who as a holder of the coveted school-leaving certificate had rejected signing-on for twelve years with the LAH and the officer's career path.

I was also a long-term candidate for the potato-peeling squad, and as a rule I was assigned this mind-numbing task when the others were off duty. Baldauf, who was often Duty NCO and liked it, used to turn up out of nowhere to examine the thickness of the peelings: if they were too thick then the offender got punishment sentry duty. I quickly made sure that he never got me for it, for I was soon more skilled with the potato-peeling knife than with a knife and fork. As Duty NCO Baldauf had a special delight for himself at curfew: he would burst into the barrack hut and shout 'prick parade' at which every man had to stand beside his bed and produce his penis with foreskin retracted for inspection. If he found anything not to his liking, there would be some kind of chicanery due.

If I really disliked someone I was never able to conceal it. Baldauf knew what I thought of him and that I deliberately provoked him by the way I carried out his orders and the manner in which I replied to him. He understood that in the latent antagonism with me he was gambling with his authority. In order to make an example of me he had to find something new and, devoting all his intellect to the task, finally he came up with something. For me this was to be an encounter with high risk, but unavoidable. And it was a matter of my individual and in consequence also my physical existence.

I knew that it was Baldauf's voice even before I was fully awake. In the early morning he stormed into our barrack hut as Duty NCO and roared *Aufstehen!* – All rise. Although I tried to make it as quickly as I could to the floor from my upper bunk, I was not fast enough for his purposes. Without wasting a second he shouted: 'Maeger, out into the open!' which I obeyed in accordance with my mood with some lassitude. It was early November, the day before my birthday; it was cold and still dawning, outside the barrack door the rain was falling into a number of dark puddles in the mud.

Baldauf roared: *Stillgestanden!* – To attention, then *Rechts um!* – About turn, which brought me to face a pool of water. He waited for about ten seconds until the rain had soaked the only item of clothing I wore, my shirt. Meanwhile a number of colleagues from the company who had been on the way to the washroom barrack hut had stopped to watch.

Baldauf's next order rang out. I was surprised that my body did not react to it. The order, repeated ever louder, *Hinlegen!* – Lie down – I perceived only as if from a distance. I felt as if something within me was slowly tearing. An impulse on the far side of reason and my drilled, apathetic senses, took over control of me.

An animal instinct must suddenly have gained the upper hand over me; I must have become aware: here you stand with your back to the wall, this is a duel between a brutal monster and your intelligence; the moment in which one way or another this is about your naked physical existence. Some time or another this swine will kill you. If you do not gamble everything on one card now, you will have thrown away your last chance: it will be over for you.

And I heard myself very loud, but calmly and coolly, reply: *NEIN!*

Baldauf fell into a state of dumb perplexity. Finally he gathered his wits together and said quite mannerly; 'Report yourself immediately to the office belted up and with steel helmet – *Wegtreten!* – Dismiss.

I returned to the barrack hut, dressed, put on my belt with sidearm and proceeded to the office in the mansion. The brawny office NCO, SS-Corporal Ziegler, always kindly disposed to me, noticed my entrance, looked at me and shook his head almost imperceptibly but significantly. I came to attention and waited. Spiess Nieweck sat at his desk and at first ignored me, then finally looked up, rose solemnly, drew himself up to his full height before me and stated in sharp tones: 'Three hours punishment drill for refusing an order! Today at 1400 hrs dressed for route march, four bricks in your field pack. Punishment ordered by Company commander! Fall out!' It was clear to me. That was it. I did an about-turn as smartly as possible and try to put on a demeanour in keeping with the significance of the moment.

My colleagues were still at breakfast when I went back to our room. Immediately an awkward silence fell, which I broke finally with the question, 'Where do I get bricks from?' Henze, No. 1 gunner in the first squad of my platoon, my neighbour in the next bed and a good comrade suggested, 'Go behind the barn at the midday break; you'll find some there.' And he was right.

Punishment drill was a serious matter and not often awarded. I had never done it before but had twice seen others subjected to it. This was the ritual. The delinquent had to present himself in full kit: dungarees and field boots, with carbine, belt and cartridge pouches, wearing a steel helmet and carrying the ominous bricks in the field pack. Regulations stated that an NCO had to be the bloodhound but in the presence of an officer. The delinquent would be taken to a freshly ploughed field, wet if possible, or to a similar terrain and there, for three hours without pause, had to follow the orders of the NCO, to run and crawl through mud and morass, practising *Auf-marsch-marsch!* and *Hinlegen!* as well as doing somersaults backwards and forwards. If he failed to maintain the required tempo he would be placed at once under close arrest for a military disciplinary hearing or, in wartime as according to the circumstances, court martial. In the evening free period he had to bring all equipment and clothing to a state of perfect cleanliness for inspection at a special parade called for himself alone. For the merest trifle he would have to repeat the punishment drill the following day. A speck of dust on the rifle, or a crumb of soil in the seam of a boot, which could be extracted with a sharpened matchstick as evidence, were sufficient. In my case it was Baldauf who would be running things.

The morning passed as if it were a procedure of no importance. Baldauf stood off at a distance. I carried through the business in the field and had lunch with my comrades: it was one of my favourite dishes, noodles with dried fruit.

At three minutes to two I stood in the prescribed get-up almost at the exact spot where the dramatic morning intermezzo had been played out. Baldauf appeared a minute later and looked at me without speaking: I had the impression that he was lewdly licking his lips. SS-2nd Lieutenant Köster, my platoon commander, who over recent months had changed his name from Kusakowski, arrived punctually at two. Amongst his important duties, of which at that moment I was unaware, he had to check that my carbine was not loaded, that there were no rounds in the chamber and that there was no other manner in which I could present a danger during the punishment drill, for there had been occasions in the past when the delinquent went crazy and shot his torturer dead. My carbine gave no grounds for complaint, being clean, empty and therefore harmless. Köster opened each of my three cartridge pouches right side, they were empty. 'Almost finished,' he said, casually opened the clasp of my first cartridge pouch left side, then the second – and suddenly he had a clip with five rounds in his hand.

Köster had decorations for bravery in the field, had distinguished himself in death-defying actions at the front and was therefore not a faint-hearted man. He stared at the magazine perplexed, gave me a sharp look and raised his eyebrows. I maintained a stolid expression and was equally dumbfounded. I had forgotten that I had these cartridges from my last evening on watch. Absolute silence reigned for a period of time, which seemed interminable.

Finally Köster turned to Baldauf and saw what I saw: Baldauf had gone white in the face and drops of sweat had formed on his nose. Köster turned to me and said curtly: 'Fall out! You will be hearing more about this!'

With great presence of mind, and – as was later to prove – it was the right thing to do in the situation I replied: 'I request permission to report to SS-Captain Anderlik, SS-2nd Lieutenant.' Köster showed no reaction.

'I will report it. Hold yourself in your room in readiness!'

For a good hour I sat in the corner on my field bed cleaning my field boots, belt and cartridge cases. Then one of the recruits arrived and said, 'You have to go at once to the Spiess.'

The office looked no different to how it always was. If I expected a drama there was no suspicion of one brewing. Ziegler, sitting in his corner, threw me a glance and quite contrary to my expectations looked as if he were enjoying himself. I stood at attention and silent, my chin under the strap of the steel helmet. Niweck rose and said: 'The punishment drill has been changed to three two-hour periods of punishment guard duty. The matter is closed. Dismiss!' I stood my watch literally, as the army metaphor has it, 'on the left cheek of my arse', that is to say I passed the hours, cheekily, self-confident and pig-headed as the experience had made me, in a totally forbidden manner: in the warm cow stall in the presence of its occupant seated on a crate of fodder.

Why the affair had terminated in the strange way it had I discovered a few days later from SS-Corporal Ziegler. A few months before, the unit had been advised of a Führer-edict expressly forbidding throughout the entire Wehrmacht any more punishment drills. The thinking mechanisms of a Nieweck, an Anderlik and of course a Baldauf came to the conclusion that this accursed Maeger quite obviously had personal knowledge of this curious order of the Führer, therefore he must have some obscure contacts which we do not have. That was how I was handled in future: the whole company had a new attitude of respect for me and, as I noticed – undisguised sympathy. Three days later the Führer-edict was announced officially to the company during evening roll call.

There was subsequently another incident tacked on to this new arrangement and which suited my purposes nicely. At morning roll call a week later, an order from Division was made known in which all weapons not issued by the Waffen-SS had to be handed in immediately. After Nieweck had read out the order, Anderlik asked: 'Who in the Company has captured or private weapons?'

I was the only man to speak. I came to attention and said, 'I, SS-Captain. I own a Walther PPK pistol.'

Anderlik replied: 'Report at once to me with the weapon!'

The Walther PPK pistol, (criminal police model calibre 7.65mm) was a very much sought-after firearm, especially by officers. Anderlik, as I had long been aware, carried only an ugly Czech pistol at his belt, undoubtedly from his time as an officer in that country's army. When I reported as ordered to his room in the estate house he asked, 'Where did you get the gun?'

'My uncle sent it to me, he is a SS-Major and cultural adviser with the German military government in the Netherlands.'

Anderlik gave a harumph and said, 'If it's all right with you, I shall carry the pistol myself. I will leave a receipt in the office stating that the pistol is to be returned to you should anything happen to me. Are you agreed?' Naturally I was and saw the opportunity as an additional trump card in my newly-begun hand.

Meanwhile, after the bulletins announcing fresh victories in the East, the raising of the German war flag on Mount Elbrus mountain in the Caucasus and the conquest of Stalingrad, forecast as almost certain, at the end of November news filtered through from unofficial channels of the looming disaster on the Volga.

76

Besides myself there was another character who could not handle drill. He was a West Prussian by the name of Kascmarek and was no shining light: his protest was neither intelligent nor efficient. If the chicanery got too much for him he would get up to silly pranks during the routine drills, dropping his rifle, on parade suddenly taking off his steel helmet to wipe his brow, on the exercise yard if the NCO ordered loudly 'To the edge of woods! Go! Go!' and then 'About turn! Go! Go!' Kascmarek would simply keep on going into the woods and disappear. Once he failed to reappear for half an hour. Woodentops like Baldauf would be beside themselves with rage and act as if possessed. It was obvious to them that Kascmarek represented a challenge to their authority not based against them personally but against blind obedience to orders. Besides Baldauf and Wilms there were two more of their ilk in the company.

Therefore, soon they got him for refusing orders and 'absenting himself without leave' by entering the woods without permission and alongside punishment sentry duty and confinement Kascmarek received the worst that could be done to him at company level, twenty-one days 'Bau'. This was a corner room of the estate house emptied of furniture, the windows boarded over: he stuck his head out between the gaps, called out to anybody passing by and sang obscene songs to them. We all felt sorry for him and many of us thought that Baldauf and his consorts had driven him crazy. Later, during my time at Giessen I often pulled duty on Sundays in the secure wing of the military hospital there, which had over a hundred certifiable Waffen-SS in it, and the presumption no longer seemed to me so far-fetched. They tried to have Kascmarek court martialled and he was taken off to Battalion HQ never to be seen again.

What I liked about Potigny was the opportunity to have regular, unlimited hot-water showers. We would march to a nearby colliery where there were the usual washing facilities and changing room in which the workers secured their clothing against theft by hoisting the garments to the roof on a pulley and chain, which was then secured.

We also marched, as a company without equipment, to a cinema now and again. We were required to march in step in a very close formation singing military songs at the top of our voices. We had to sing one of these until we were sick of it; presumably Niewek, who generally led us, had some memories of a girl with one of the names mentioned:

Frühmorgens, wenn die Hähne krähn,
Ziehn wir zum Tor hinaus;
und mit verliebten Augen schaun
die Mädels nach uns aus.
Am Busch vorbei wir ziehen,
wo Heckenrosen blühen.
und mit den Vögelein im Wald
ein frohes Lied erschallt:Von der Lore, von der Lene, von der Trude
*   und Sophie,*
Von der Ilse, von Irene und der Annemarie.
Schön blühn die Heckenrosen.
Schön ist das Küssen und Kosen;
Rosen und Schönheit vergehn,
drum nütz die Zeit
denn die Welt ist so schön.

'In the early mornings when the cock crows, we march
    to the town gate;
And with loving eyes the girls watch out for us.
We pass by the bushes where the dog-roses bloom,
And along with the little birds in the wood
A happy song resounds;
Of Lore, of Lene, of Trude and Sophie
Of Ilse, Irene and Annemarie.'
The dog-roses are beautiful when they bloom
We love to kiss and cuddle;
Roses and beauty fade away,
Therefore use the time, for the world is so beautiful.'

The song got on my nerves because I could not reconcile in any way whatever the supposed joyful life as a soldier with what I was living through at the present. There was also another reason for my frustration: when we marched out on our daily trudge carrying equipment weighing between 50 and 70 kilos per man for up to 30 kilometres, somewhere on the march back the order would always come: 'Gas masks on!' and then 'A song . . . two, three, four!'

We would then create a muffled bawl in the close-fitting mask and the most evil oppressors amongst the corporals, who had nothing to carry apart from their side-arms, would dash through the ranks checking with a quick grasp that one's gas-mask filter was properly fitted so that no more air entered the mask than intended. Anybody found using this method of trying to find some relief had to leave the column for an 'excursion into the countryside'.

The procedure was depressing and humiliating and hardly the sort of thing to raise the spirits of the troops or make them enjoy singing the happy song. It was not only adopted by the 'NCO sub-culture' but also as 'leadership style', for our company commander Anderlik, a black-haired bull of a man, declared his training programme to the assembled men one day with the threat: 'I shall make this company into a concentration camp!' I had the feeling when he said this that not only did he mean it, but he also had experience of what he was saying.

On a couple of occasions I had the chance to visit Falaise when I would eat in a small restaurant near the Gothic church. I was always accompanied by a comrade, for by that time we were not allowed to show ourselves in public alone and unarmed because the Resistance activities had begun. One Sunday two of us had covered one third of the nine-kilometre distance back to Potigny when we heard a vehicle approaching us from behind. I turned and waved my arm in a gesture to get the driver of the Citroën 2CV to stop and pick us up. He slowed at first, but then increased speed abruptly and drove at me. He would have run me down had I not thrown myself into the roadside ditch. I confess I dearly wanted to fire a couple of rounds from my pistol after him, but was then denied the opportunity.

I was so mad about this incident that I drew my pistol so as to be better prepared for the next customer. As we walked on, we heard the noise of another car coming up: I placed myself in an unmistakeable position in the middle of the road and aimed my 08.

When the car stopped I noticed the tactical insignia of the Leibstandarte, a 'Dietrich' (key) on a heraldic field corresponding to the name of the commanding officer, Sepp Dietrich. As I stepped up to the vehicle the door opened and I recognised an officer with an oak leaf on the left collar patch, the man himself, and then SS-Brigadier Witt, my regimental commander, his adjutant sitting in front of him beside the driver. Witt inclined forward and asked calmly, 'What's up?'

I collected myself swiftly, clicked my heels and reported: 'SS-Private Maeger and SS-Mann Weber proceeding from Falaise to Potigny, Sir! We wanted to stop a Frenchmen and he tried to run us down. That should not be allowed to happen to us again!'

Witt thought for a few seconds and then said, 'That satisfies me as an explanation. OK, get in!' He made space, we got in beside him and the car brought us right up to our accommodation in Potigny: some of our colleagues could hardly credit it when we got out of the car and smartly took our leave.

It was close to Christmas, but that gave us little reason to look forward to it. The *Sonnenwendfeier* – festival of the shortest day of the year which in the SS had taken the place of the Christian festival[1] – was once again a sorry occasion. Before a smoking fire in the drizzle we sang solemnly:

Hohe Nacht der klaren Sterne, die wie weite Brücken stehn
über einer tiefen Ferne, drüber unsre Herzen gehn.

('High night of clear stars standing like distant bridges
over a deep chasm, over them our hearts pass.')

Then we assembled in a hall in the village where our gifts awaited us: besides fine pastries half a bottle of Arrak blend from the Führer 'personally' and a whole bottle of Armagnac from Division.

Out of deference to the Führer nearly everybody started on the Arrak blend with the result that in no time at all the schnapps rotgut had got them all drunk and they now began to sing 'Silent Night' and 'O Tannenbaum' by mistake. The whole thing then degenerated into a booze-up which, having regard to the situation, was not necessarily a bad thing. Next day, most of my comrades had a fearful hangover; they were all so sworn never to drink again that I was able to obtain from them six bottles of the best, very expensive Armagnac.

The tension which we had all begun to feel over Christmas increased noticeably at the end of the year. Hardly anybody put it into words but it was clear to us that something terrible was about to happen; the tragedy of Stalingrad cast its shadow over our everyday life. The company spent New Year's Day 1943 cleaning weapons, clothing and equipment: a parade was ordered for the late afternoon. Because it was raining it took place in the barrack hut where each man arrayed before himself his 'Seven Things' so carefully prepared: the field pack, field blouse and trousers, camouflage jacket, steel helmet with camouflage covering, greatcoat, gloves, field cap, underwear – including long underpants which the regulations said had to be worn no matter what the temperature – lace-up shoes, two pairs of socks and one pair of slippers, pullover, one necktie; also the twenty-two other items of equipment, the most important of these being the assault pack, blanket, ground sheet with all accessories, gas mask and canvas cover (for protection against sprayed poisons such as mustard gas), mess tin, field flask, haversack and cutlery. We received camouflage jackets and camouflage covers for the steel helmet in the summer of 1942: these were gradually introduced afterwards throughout the whole Wehrmacht; today they form part of the standard equipment of all armies.

In the second week of January we received a new issue of winter clothing. This consisted of quilted fur-lined jackets with fur hood and reversible warm fur-lined trousers white on one side and of a brown-grey pattern on the other, fur boots and fur-lined gloves. White meant Russia, we could all see that. The performance of daily tasks within a military unit resting for a long period tends to follow a sluggish routine, but now it transformed into unmistakeable activity increasing to a hectic level; drills fell off and instead the duty plan concentrated much more on preparing equipment and vehicles.

After the new weaponry in November 1942 the company received more new fighting vehicles, sixteen Mercedes troop carriers with four-wheel drive and Kfz 69 six-cylinder motors for each squad, and these became the pride of our 'Schirrmeister' – harness master, a term surviving from the time of horse-drawn units. A curiosity of such service posts was the importance attached to the correct term for the officer's function both in the Waffen-SS and the army: only a SS-Captain could be a company commander, an SS-1st Lieutenant could only be a company leader, and at the front, depending on the circumstances, even a SS-Lance Corporal could be a company leader temporarily if he had become the highest-ranking survivor of the unit; he would then have full responsibility and the same power of command as the officer he was substituting for, his unit by then would be no more than eight to ten men in strength. Only a SS-Major or Colonel could be nominated to command a battalion or regiment respectively: any man of lesser military rank fulfilling his function as a deputy would be designated as 'Führer' of the unit. It must be pointed out scurrilously that the all-powerful Führer of the Reich, Supreme Commander-in-Chief of the Wehrmacht and therefore of all its commanders, Adolf Hitler, had only ever risen as high as Senior Private during the First World War. One will appreciate that I could not resist the temptation to make reference to this discrepancy.

We kept our distance from the inhabitants of Potigny. My contact with them was limited to obtaining milk, butter and potatoes. As we spent quite a few weeks in barrack huts at the edge of the village some of my comrades had another sort of contact, which generally began with the onset of darkness. One or other lonely country-woman would have no objection to a short visit by a handsome young LAH man provided he acted with discretion. If the ladies were appealing enough they would usually expect a gift while those less attractive would be quite satisfied to give themselves for free.

This kind of supply and demand has functioned since time immemorial wherever soldiers happen to be. In the midst of the boring routine of the duty schedule, however, there occurred something very unwelcome. At an evening roll call held before dusk

(LEFT) Berlin-Lichterfelde: No. 4 Company Reserve Battalion Leibstandarte SS Adolf Hitler paraded for roll call.

(BELOW) Berlin, the training group from Room 14, the author at the extreme left.

No. 4 Company Reserve Battalion LSSAH on the march during training.

Berlin-Lichterfelde: the author (sitting, left) with other recruits in front of the barracks swimming baths.

March 1942: the author in a captured Soviet uniform at an MG post on the main frontline, Sambek Valley, east of Taganrog.

In the bunker, SS-Quartermaster-Sergeant 'Marinus' and SS-Lance Corporal 'Laban'.

(ABOVE) Yegorovka, June 1942. Off duty with Ukrainian women. Left, de Boer (d. 1943); head turned to the side, Spethmann (d. 1943).

(RIGHT) Yegorovka: a small concert with two violins and a bass mandoline. Left, Uscha Hübner; to the right (without sleeve emblem and shoulder straps) a young Russian 'Hiwi' auxiliary volunteer.

The author during home leave, August 1943.

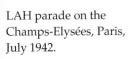

LAH parade on the Champs-Elysées, Paris, July 1942.

(ABOVE) The author as an MG gunner in preparedness position before the Canadian landings at Dieppe, September 1942.

(RIGHT) Excursion to Paris, September 1942, with Uscha Hübner (centre) and paramedic Sepp Rist (right).

In front of the Boissy 'manor house', from left to right: Wolf, de Boer, Schamper, Spethmann, the author.

A heavy MG group at the beginning of an attack.

Olshany, May 1943: the company collecting rations.

The Battle of Kharkov, March 1943: a meeting in front of an MTW (troop transport vehicle) KFZ 69 (Mercedes Benz).

and which all company members were obliged to attend, two German field-gendarmes appeared accompanying a middle-aged woman, a man and a young girl who were introduced to us by Spiess Nieweck as a French couple and their daughter. It was stated that the girl had been raped by a German soldier, and they were visiting various units including ours in the attempt to find the offender.

It was an uneasy scene. It affected us but we remained at attention, stony-faced. The girl went along our ranks and looked each man in the face, tears running down her cheeks. As probably most of us did, I tried to overcome the contradictory emotions I felt. I was ashamed for the crime an unknown German soldier had committed, perhaps a comrade, I felt indignation at being in a line-up as a potential rapist and I felt sorrow for the poor girl, no more than 16 years old. Nobody was picked out; we were relieved to get it over with. Even the cynics in our barrack hut refrained on this occasion from making the usual brazen remarks about the incident.

On 22 January 1943 the deceptive calm overlying the growing tension gave way suddenly to certainty: 'We're going back to Russia!' Our marching orders were read out at morning roll call and unleashed the usual frenzy: 'everything went round in circles' as we used to say. I had already got my Seven Things together and was contemplating where I should stow my six bottles of Armagnac when a runner came with an order for me to report at once to SS-Corporal Ziegler.

A message from Ziegler was never ominous, and so I went to his office directly. He gave me a friendly look and said: 'Three drivers have had an accident with an Opel Blitz at Caen, one is dead, two in the military hospital. It says in my files that you have a driving licence. The commander has ordered that you will take over a Kfz 69,[2] if you like with your former squad. Can you do that?'

Somewhat taken aback, I responded without much deliberation, 'Yes, of course. No problem at all!'

'Well, then, report to the Schirrmeister . . . and good luck!'

My driving licence was not what it seemed. In Belgium one could drive a car without a driving test or proof of competence. For whatever reason, the German authorities had allowed this situation to continue after they took over the country: I had taken advantage of the opportunity and on 11 November 1940, the day after my eighteenth birthday, I went to the district administration at Eupen and got my driving licence.

I had had my first experience of driving long before at Rheydt in Germany where my aunt Ottilie and uncle Franz had a wholesale haberdashery suppliers. They liked having me there for my holidays because I enjoyed helping out in the business. My uncle was a man who had little time for official regulations and directives and he would often make surprisingly spontaneous decisions. His Opel Olympia was an object of my undisguised admiration. One day when I was 14 years old he took me in his delivery van to Düsseldorf to collect some goods. On the way, between Mönchengladbach and Neuss, he asked me suddenly, 'Would you like to drive?'

Definitely I did. I slipped into the driver's seat and drove so skilfully that, at the end of the stretch he had decided upon, he let me keep going. I drove through Neuss and Düsseldorf to the main railway station: we loaded some parcels and then I drove the whole way back to Rheydt. As we arrived in the yard my uncle had a satisfied look: aunt Ottilie on the other hand, who watched me drive in, shook her head in disapproval and then, being a pious woman, looked up gratefully to Heaven. My parents were never told of this adventure, which gave me the experience that was probably to save my life years later.

At Potigny I left Ziegler and the office smartly and ran to the Schirrmeister SS-Corporal Köber. In less than half an hour I had passed a test drive and taken over my new Kfz 69, which had a big storage area at the rear where I put all my gear and the six bottles of Armagnac. And so everything had at least begun well.

84

Chapter Five

My Second Winter in Russia

T he uproar resembled the fire-brigade alarm for a major conflagration. Everything was done with the greatest possible shouting and running about without which any military activity is unthinkable. The orderly departure began before dawn on 27 January 1943 to Mezidon near Caen where with remarkable competence the previously unpractised loading-up of the eighteen fighting and eight rear-support vehicles went ahead. The two motorcycle sidecar combinations and single machine were easily stowed.

Immediately after the last rope was secured the train set off and kept going with only short pauses for food; it steamed through Flanders to Brussels and then Aachen. During the second night I slept through the stretch from Herbesthal to my native village, Astenet, then it continued via Krefeld, Duisburg, Hannover and detoured north surprisingly through Stettin to Königsberg, which gave rise to speculation: would we be going to Leningrad on the threatened central sector of the Eastern Front, which we had defended successfully for a year?

To be a driver brought with it, initially, more drawbacks than advantages. While my former MG squad travelled with the remainder of the company in closed passenger coaches, coupled behind the locomotive and steam heated, I had to sit in my vehicle with the other drivers. I could stretch out to some extent in the back of my Kfz 69 personnel carrier but it was devilish cold: the folding hood and the side panels with celluloid windows fitted into the low doors offered little protection against the icy January air and the wind as we steamed eastwards. I had organised a bale of straw for the underlay when we set out and this offered a bit of comfort.

At night I wrapped myself in everything I could find by way of warm clothing and blankets: luckily we now had fur-lined winter clothing. The six bottles of Armagnac proved a real treasure, each evening I emptied about half a bottle and then slept through until morning. This was against regulations, for we had been ordered to remain alert with the vehicles in order to protect them and the long train against partisan attack. That danger did not become more acute until we crossed the frontier into the former Lithuania. It made me reflect: on these unprotected low-loaders a handful of determined attackers with knowledge of the district could have shot us down like clay pipes in a shooting gallery before we even got to see them.

We were spared any such thing. We rolled and rolled so fast through flat Byelorussia under dismal grey skies that on the sixth day of the journey just before dusk and in snowfall we reached our destination – or what we thought it was. Shortly before we had rattled through Kharkov and so knew roughly where we were. What we did not know was that there was no frontline, after the disaster at Stalingrad in the final days of January it had collapsed over more than 500 kilometres of its length; the Soviet divisions had stormed the breaches, re-taken Rostov, encircled the Second German and Second Hungarian Armies between Voronezh and Pavlovsk and other sections of Weichs' Army Group, and were now concentrating massive forces for the attack on Kharkov.

During the train journey we had fitted the vehicles with snow chains. At unloading we were told of a problem which would have serious consequences for us throughout the entire winter: our new four-wheel drive Mercedes personnel carriers, in which we had invested such great hopes, would not start despite supplementary tanks filled with aviation spirit for ease of ignition. These tanks were located at the left side of the windscreen. After the vehicles had been pushed manually with great expenditure of effort up the unloading ramp, Harness-master Köber held a drivers' conference and revealed that the Mercedes motor of the Kfz 69, manufactured in the second year of the war in Russia, would only start if a pre-warming chamber below the radiator was heated with a blowtorch first. This procedure lasted ten minutes, after which the engine would start normally. This depressed us all, for in the conference with the illustrious manufacturer nobody had asked what the Russians would be doing while we spent ten minutes blow-torching the engines.

It was noticed that the Mercedes diesel lorries of our rearward section which had already been used in the campaigns in Poland, France and the Balkans got through the Russian winter fairly well: they had no all-wheel drive but instead were fitted with dual tyres at the rear and motors with high revolutions to assist turning. They were therefore superior to the under-performing six-cylinder petrol engine of the Kfz 69, particularly in mud. Over the next two months more than half the Kfz 69s were out of action due to damage to the motor and four-wheel drive. They were then cannibalised as much as possible, for spare parts could not be obtained.

Most of the other administrative vehicles were only operational to a limited extent and seemed to be under constant repair for this or that. The exceptions were the Kfz 70, an efficient car with a Ford engine, and the Kfz 15, a Horch V-8, always in service, absolutely reliable and good over all types of terrain. The qualities of this vehicle will be mentioned later. Also beyond criticism were the VW Kübelwagen car and the VW amphibious vehicle, a kind of bathtub with a hinged propeller: both models had only two drive wheels on the rear axle but in an emergency could grub themselves out of any situation and then be carried to firm ground by four men.

The first operational day after de-training on 4 February 1943 began chaotically. The company commander and platoon leaders had to orientate themselves and finally established that we were at a tiny railway halt near Voltshansk, north-east of Kharkov, which consisted of nothing more than a warped storage shed. There was a road near the railway line, recognisable only by numerous Kfz tracks in the snow.

Once all our vehicles had been unloaded and we had formed up into a column facing towards what we considered was the front, and were waiting for orders, as night fell over the landscape of low hills we saw a picture so ghostly in nature that at first we could not believe our eyes. Through the light snowfall a flickering light appeared on the horizon, which grew ever brighter: when we began to pick out details we saw that it was a giant convoy of vehicles. Soon its leading vehicle approached us. Anderlik had placed two vehicles so as to block the road, and a heavy cross-country vehicle came to a halt before them. A figure dismounted and opened his thick fur coat sufficiently to expose the red trouser stripes of a General Staff officer. He shouted: 'What is the meaning of this? Who are you? Clear the road immediately!'

Behind the leading car was an SPW[1] containing thickly muffled, dark-looking forms with machine pistols: field gendarmes, 'chained dogs', specially selected brutal types, privileged to serve at a safe distance behind the lines where they spread anxiety and fear. Stragglers separated from their units by the fighting and who were unable to furnish written orders were given short shrift by their field courts.

Anderlik considered it advisable to find out where he stood. 'SS-Captain Anderlik with No. 9 Company LAH awaiting operational orders. May I ask what . . .?'

'You may ask nothing at all,' came back the answering bark, 'I am the 1a[2] of Army Group B Staff. We are bringing to safety secret documents and material of the greatest strategic importance. Make room at once and protect my action with your men! That is an order!'

None of us was naïve enough to misunderstand what was being played out here. Members of the illustrious HQs of the 'best Army leadership in the world' were shamefully legging it and disguising their action with cheap phrases. Not only had they left the officers and men 200 kilometres to the east in the lurch, somewhere on the banks of the Don; they were depriving them of the food, ammunition and food they needed for survival.

In view of the threat uttered Anderlik had no choice but to clear the road. And then we saw with growing shock the extent of it. In two lines the whole quixotic assortment rolled and passed, a drive-by of all the makes of vehicle assembled in the hands of the Wehrmacht: German lorries and other fighting and rearward vehicles manufactured by Opel, Ford, Mercedes, MAN, Magirus, Büssing, Steyr, Stöwer: French Army vehicles from Renault, Citroën and Peugeot, individual British types, presumably captured at Dunkirk: amongst them all buses came lumbering, and ordinary civilian cars: Mercedes V 170, Opel Olympia, Adler, Audi, Renault – it was astonishing that they had made the way deep into Russia and then could have made the return journey to this point. Each vehicle was more or less loaded to capacity with cases, sacks, canisters, barrels, some also with individual boxes and bottles.

The apocalyptic cavalcade pressed and shoved onwards. Behind the front and side windscreens we made out ghostly pallid staring faces. A dead-beat car with a defect came to a stop in front of us, the vehicles behind simply ramming it aside. We attempted in vain to speak to the occupants in order to find out more about the whole business: the reaction was empty looks from panic-stricken faces. Their only desire was to grab a seat in another vehicle and continue their blind exodus; to the West, only to the West.

These were the caste of the arrogant 'Herrenvolk' – members of military Staffs and special units of all kinds, Army administration officials, commissars, Sonderführer[3] – nine of them for every front-line soldier, for fighting was not their speciality: they were competent for the issuing of orders, which sent hundreds of thousands of brave soldiers to their deaths, competent for the tirades of conquests on behalf of the 'Volk without living space' – this really meant the immoderate craving for booty in land, people and their property. Their war was not played out where Germans suffered, starved, froze and died, but in the comfortable regions behind the line where it was warm, to where the well-organised supplies of cognac, champagne and delicatessen flowed and where young women could be found with empty stomachs or threatened with deportation to a work camp and were thus available cheaply. All done under the cynical motto: 'Let us enjoy the war, the peace will be terrible!'

It took the convoy an hour to pass. The creepy experience left us bewildered and thoughtful. We had no orders from Battalion or any other HQ and so Anderlik decided sensibly to form a hedgehog around the station and so afford us all-round protection.

A few hours later contact was re-established by despatch riders from Battalion HQ. They were apparently having difficulty judging the situation and told us to stand by. Our squads hacked and shovelled shallow depressions into the ground, we drivers helped them. The situation had one saving advantage: our Quartermaster Babucke, who was usually to be found at a safe distance from the front, found himself obliged to put the field kitchen at the centre of our position and so we always had on hand hot coffee – or what passed for it.

Towards noon next day our movement orders finally came. After the unavoidable operation with the blowtorches our column set off back over the Donets bridge and then headed south. After a couple of hours on the latitude of Kharkov we turned east again, driving through a forest over eleven kilometres long to the west bank of the Donets where the steep precipice offered us the possibility of an excellent defensive position. This was so extensive that the four platoons which started bunker-building immediately had to guard a sector over three kilometres in length with approximately 110 men. Later we discovered that the Soviet armies had headed for Kharkov in a pincer movement from north and south and had practically cut us off.

With other members of the fighting Tross (administrative element) I assisted my platoon in the setting up of the new position. When night fell under clear skies, lights appeared again on the eastern horizon and became ever more numerous forming what seemed like an endless chain. These were the advancing units of the Soviet Army, now – we did not know this yet – equipped with an enormous and ever increasing number of Studebaker lorries with powerful engines and six-wheel drive on three axles. The United States is said to have supplied to the Soviets from the summer of 1942 a total of 434,000(!) of these, the most modern transport vehicles of the period.[4] What we had to offer, with the exception of the Horch V8, the Kfz 70 with the Ford engine and the MAN/Büssing, none of which were available in sufficient numbers, was ripe for the scrapheap.

The fighting Tross, and with it myself as a driver, headed off westwards through the forest. On this first outing in the dark I learnt the function of the Wehrmacht's very useful 'Convoy Night Drive

Equipment'. In a small box at the rear of the vehicle were four horizontal lights seven centimetres high by four centimetres wide arranged in two pairs set at right angles to each other separated by a narrow vertical crosspiece: the distance between them in the centre of the box was about three centimetres. A driver maintaining the prescribed distance of six metres behind the vehicle in front would see two lights, if he came closer he would see all four, if he fell back too much he would see only one. In this way visual contact within the convoy could be maintained relatively easily.

After a long drive we reached a village on the far side of the forest where we found relatively comfortable temporary billets. As on other occasions we arranged with the occupants a kind of understood symbiosis in which they slept in the 'upper quarters' around their warm stove and we had the dirt floor. Next morning, in bitter cold but glorious sunshine, we began our normal routine: care of vehicles, obtaining rations, ammunition and wood for bunker and latrine construction as well as firewood for the field kitchen and so on. In the late afternoon a heavy Büssing lorry arrived from regimental supply with the first deliveries of rations, ammunition and cans of benzene and diesel oil. They also brought blankets and in my opinion this all made life at the front much more tolerable than in the first winter. Besides that I enjoyed driving, and on the first stretch I had quickly got to grips with handling the MTW[5] in snow.

The repairs to the drive shafts for the front wheels were already necessary, the universal drives having failed to meet the exacting requirements. We were also short of other spare parts such as tyres, ropes and brake linings together with general equipment such as towing hawsers, lifting jacks, winches and so forth. SS-Corporal Stöber had been told by the Battalion Tross that on the north side of Kharkov, about 20 kilometres away, was a huge spare-parts warehouse. We compiled a list of requirements and then SS-Corporal Danninger, who had been in charge of the fighting Tross since loading up in France, drove with me in my MTW and one of the two car mechanics, Hampel, took the Opel Blitz in order to fill our needs from the warehouse and get whatever else caught our eye.

We found the warehouse surprisingly quickly, for Kharkov, the great supply centre for the entire central section of the Eastern Front, bristled at each road intersection with directional shields: here at least the jackasses of the rearward section had done a good job. We soon learned that German thoroughness was capable of reaching even higher standards of perfection. When we reached the compound, which consisted of a large number of barrack huts surrounded by a high wire fence, we found the wire-grilled gate without guards and locked. I drove up close, took out a crowbar from my MTW and had just set to work on the gate when three uniformed figures rushed out of the neighbouring building and ran towards us.

'What are you doing there?' the fattest of them shouted, gesticulating in excitement. If I interpreted his tinsel correctly he was something like an Army senior administrative official, equivalent to a Major or Lieutenant-Colonel.[6] Nobody in the Leibstandarte had any respect for this kind of soldier, and our esteem for him had fallen to rock bottom particularly after meeting the fleeing motorised mob at the Donets still fresh in our memory.

Without making any gesture to me to stop, Danninger responded curtly: 'We have orders to fetch spare parts for our vehicles as soon as possible! We are part of I Panzer Corps!' He brandished the requisitions docket: 'It's all written down here!'

Fatty adopted a posture, his chubby jowls turned scarlet, he took a deep breath and then snarled: 'You'll get nothing here! We have inventoried everything and prepared it for demolition! Clear off, or you'll be sorry!' At that his hand went for the pistol holster on his belt.

Danninger, a Tyrolean, was fast on the draw and both he and I had our 08s in our fists as slick as Buffalo Bill's Colt in his prime: Hampel jumped out from his cab at once with his carbine. Then we saw the funny side of the situation and began to laugh so loud that it was difficult to control our merriment.

Danninger was the first to pull himself together. 'And you'll be sorry too, you August plum!' he said cuttingly. 'Open up at once and give us what we want! If not, I shall place you under arrest for sabotage and bring you before our Divisional commander, SS-General Dietrich!' At that he opened the neck of his white steppe-jacket to reveal the SS runes.

This did the trick. Fatty's face went the pallid colour of Army cheese spread. After a few seconds he had recovered enough to bark a couple of orders to his subordinates. The gate came open, we drove into the compound, another three administrative assistants appeared from nowhere to offer help. And really it must be said that the warehousing was so orderly that all our requirements had been met within half an hour.

'Thank you, comrades,' Danninger said drily in parting, 'We shall recommend you to others!'

It was Danninger himself who intercepted me on my way from the latrine to my billet. He said at once, 'You're a smart fellow. We need someone like you to take the rations and ammunition up to the front. When it starts snowing, the route through the forest is not so easy.'

I felt privileged in my new post knowing how things were with my squad at the front and this gave me something of a bad conscience. 'Yes, of course! If I could do it in half an hour, perhaps my comrades would then get something hot for their mess tins.'

The preparations lasted a while: I loaded ammunition boxes for the MGs and mortars, firewood, bread, margarine and 'rubber sausage' made from horsemeat: the field kitchen poured thick boiling-hot pea soup into canisters wrapped in blankets.

'Adele' – nobody knew why he was never called by his surname Brennecke – was my co-driver. When we left it was almost dark but the stars twinkled and a large pale moon was rising on the western horizon. It was dark in the forest but no fresh snow had fallen and the well-worn tracks along the narrow road were easy to make out even in the light of the slits in the camouflage covers over the headlights.

We made good progress, and after a quarter of an hour we had covered almost half the distance when a shot rang out and glass splinters flew around my ears: a hole gaped in the left upper corner of the split windscreen. My reaction was instinctive and spontaneous: I raised the handbrake lever, opened the quick-release of the carbine mount to the left of my seat and in seconds was laid flat behind a tree. Adele had reacted similarly of the other side of the car and let me know in a low voice that he was also uninjured but had only his despatch-rider pistol as a weapon. We understood we should keep silent from then on so as not to betray our positions.

I looked and listened into the night, bright with snow. Nothing disturbed the threatening silence of the wintry forest, not even a breath of wind. Given what little I knew of the situation I tried to make a clear picture of it. The certainty was that somebody had fired at us and narrowly missed. It was unlikely that one man would have lurked in wait for us all by himself, but why had only one shot rung out? Two determined opponents armed with machine pistols could easily have taken us out. Improbable as it might seem, was the round that had shattered the windscreen one which had had some other target and gone astray? Or was there behind the ominous occurrence a carefully worked out plan?

The following was a good theory: a Soviet scouting party or a couple of partisans had the job of keeping watch on the only supply road through the long forest on the Donets: they heard a vehicle approaching and decided to stop it with a single round rather than great bursts of fire, which might set off the alarm. From safe cover they could observe how many Germans would leave the vehicle and then just wait until they either slowly but surely froze to death or tried to get back into the vehicle and save themselves by driving on. The third vague eventuality, that with hope born of despair we would try to escape by getting up and attacking the invisible enemy, promised little and would not change the outcome they were aiming to achieve. In all of these cases they would put an end to these 'Faschisti' at their leisure, by shooting or taking them prisoner and letting them live for the time being until they had revealed all they knew about the confused front situation.

My mind wandered through other variations. Then it struck me: the soup in the canisters was getting cold, and we could not count on help, for there was only our supply depot to our rear and our own company ahead of us, tied down to its position and waiting for us.

An uncertain period of time passed during which I became ever more aware of the cold penetrating upwards from the deeply frozen ground. Soon I realised that despite my analysis of the situation I had to establish whether, in the twilight of the forest, through the bare branches of which the stars shimmered, somebody actually did have eyes on us. My vehicle was near a tree. I lay behind the tree but my vision was obstructed by dense vegetation: a few paces to my left a thicker trunk stood free. I tensed, sprang up and threw myself to the ground behind it. Almost simultaneously a round whipped through the undergrowth, and to the right of me there was a flurry of snow. I thought I saw movement behind a bush about 20 metres away and fired back: Adele also fired from the other side, but I had no idea if he had aimed or fired wild.

A voice ahead of me called out something unintelligible, and to the left of it somebody answered, it sounded like *Iditje suda!* (come here). After a few minutes of silence I saw clearly a fleeting shadow, aimed and fired twice. Then all fell quiet again.

We had discharged four rounds and quickly I counted up the remaining ammunition: I had two in my carbine and Adele's 08 had seven provided he had had a full magazine to start with. In all we had nine rounds left, not much for an encounter even with only a few enemy: the pistol was not of much use for this kind of warfare. The whole business began to make me feel extremely uneasy, or better put, it frightened me. There seemed no way out of the situation. I wondered if I could cautiously creep to the path farther back and crawl along it to reach the right hand side of my MTW and Adele. There was a possibility that nobody was waiting in ambush for us there and we might then have a chance of getting free to the south together.

Knowing that I had no alternative, I made my way back to the forest road keeping as flat as possible. Just as I reached it I heard engine noises coming up from the west, gradually becoming louder. Soon the lights of two vehicles appeared. Those of the leader fell on my MTW blocking the path and came to a halt. It was an SPW half-track with SS-grenadiers aboard, machine pistols at the ready: a second SPW followed behind it.

I stood up from behind a tree. A figure arose beside the driver and snarled: 'What's the meaning of this? What the hell is going on here?'

I could not make out his rank and so, chancing to luck, replied, 'SS-Private Maeger and SS-Private Brennecke en route to No. 9 Company LSSAH with provisions, sir. We were fired on in the wood here!'

The commander gave a short order, about twenty men dismounted, swarmed right and left of the track and combed through the surrounding area. We heard several short bursts of machine-pistol fire from various directions. Then he turned to me again. 'We'll keep it at SS-2nd Lieutenant, and too right you were fired on. Only idiots drive without adequate protection through this partisans' forest. Everybody hereabouts knows of it. We are bringing orders from Divisional HQ for the immediate withdrawal of your unit. Get in your vehicle and keep up behind us. Let's go!'

The half-tracks curved through the undergrowth to the right of our MTW and roared off ahead at full speed. Feeling as if a millstone had fallen from my neck I got behind the wheel, Adele climbed in beside me and the motor of the damned Kfz 69 actually had enough residual warmth to start up straight away. In gear, release clutch and step on the gas were one single movement. Then the motor died and the accursed vehicle stopped as though it had taken root. I knew why at once.

When we were fired upon, without thinking I had applied the handbrake, the brake shoes and hot brake drums had cooled causing water to condense and frost over, blocking the system. For good reason I did not want to use the blowtorch. There was only one thing for it: start up, depress the gas pedal, engage the clutch and that would either force apart the brakes, clutch or the gearing. I had speculated correctly, the brakes gave in with a loud crack and I drove, drove like the devil rolling and shaking along the forest path, soon caught up with the SPWs which had not concerned themselves about us any longer and finally we reached our company command post. Everybody there was glad that somebody had come bringing the food. Anderlik even gave me a friendly slap on the back.

The SPWs roared off again at once. Anderlik and our squad got into my Kfz 69, we drove slowly ahead of the platoons making their way westwards on foot. After half an hour we met up with the other company vehicles, everybody on foot got into them and then we all headed to the west. On the way a despatch rider came with the message that the Russians had trapped us within a large encirclement. We were enclosed with the infantry regiments of the Division and lacking heavy weapons. The artillery and the panzer regiment were still on goods trains between Kiev and Kharkov.

In this way we learned the practice of, and what it felt like to be part of, an orderly retreat. It was a total contrast to the euphoria of the Blitzkrieg. And from it we were able to draw the conclusion that the leadership had drifted away from its strategic concepts: they had also lost their tactical inspiration. All they were doing now was improvising, and badly. In these chaotic days of the struggle to hold on to Kharkov we were short of everything: we came across food, ammunition and fuel more by chance than in an organised manner, and above all we needed artillery, reconnaissance, the pioneers and supply units, but especially our panzer regiment, which only a few weeks before had been the first in the entire Wehrmacht to be equipped with Tiger tanks. According to all the rumours trickling through, their armour would resist anything the Stalin tanks could hit them with, and for armament they would have the most efficient of all German guns, the 8.8cm anti-aircraft gun. Nobody knew where exactly the trains bringing them happened to be, not even the Divisional nor Regimental HQ had a clue.

The enemy had the initiative: he was stronger, had superiority in materials and troop numbers, and was gaining in self-confidence, offensive capability and battle experience. The phase of the war had begun in which Germans forces in the East were no longer fighting for victory, but with the ever-increasing certainty that they were going to have to make every sacrifice to keep their families and the Reich safe from Bolshevism, and all this in the bitter knowledge that the nations of the civilized world were helping the Soviet Union in every way they could. Furthermore it was a leadership which had forgotten its own duty, and through its amateurish politics and brutal conduct of the war in the East had brought about this situation from which there was no longer a way out. One wonders how much the increasing excesses by the German side against the rules of humane warfare in the East was the cause and how much the effect of this agonizing knowledge.

There is a German saying, 'When the infantryman stops griping, the situation is deep shit.'[6] The break-out and retreat from the Donets position went ahead in the deepest silence, all we heard was a couple of terse orders. The squad in my MTW was equally speechless during the journey out: nearly everybody was seated asleep leaning against the next man. Platoon leader SS-2nd Lieutenant Bast alongside me in the co-driver seat had his head covered by a blanket.

The weather was ideal, the visibility very good, the snow only drizzled. I had nothing else to do but follow company commander Anderlik's Horch, and I could see it perfectly. We kept heading west and after a short time reached the outskirts of Kharkov. We could tell we were approaching a large city, for all cities in Russia were laid out on the grand scale.

We were doing 40km/hr, my motor purred leisurely on the smooth, even road surface. Looking ahead I had to watch the lights of the Kfz 69 of the company troop, following Anderlik's Horch V8; keeping distance was child's play and required more wakefulness than watchful concentration. Suddenly I was alarmed by something to my left beyond my field of vision. At the end of a road branching off I had noticed some bright lights, and with a quick glance back I saw flitting shadows carrying heavy loads disappearing behind tall buildings.

Spontaneously, without any prior reflection, I spun the wheel round, accelerated and within a few seconds had arrived at the spot where this activity was going on. I found myself in front of a giant warehouse with a large sliding door half-open, and through it I could see in the interior huge stacks of cases and twenty Russians helping themselves.

As laid down in regulations all vehicles had instructions to follow the vehicle in front even if acting completely without orders. As a result of my sudden change of direction, the passengers aboard my MTW were all awake and without any explanation of the situation they knew immediately what we had before us: a German Wehrmacht warehouse, stocked to the rafters with what the administrative types had hoarded and then simply abandoned before the city was recaptured by the Soviets.

When we got out of the vehicle and went up the ramp into the building, the marauding Russians, some wearing uniform, were making a run for it through the expanses of the warehouse, a structure so enormous that one could not judge its extent even though the electric lighting along the roof was still working. We could not believe our eyes and had to pinch ourselves to make sure we weren't dreaming. Right in front of us were some open cases filled with fine wood shavings and expensive-looking bottles within: I picked one out and read: 'Champagne – Veuve Cliquot' and on another 'Hennessy V.S.O.P.' On the gigantic stacks towering behind them were other names worthy of respect such as 'Bénédictine', 'Bols', 'Chartreuse' and 'Cointreau'. This mountain of cases alone must have contained thousands of bottles. Ten, twenty, thirty metres farther on were other mountains of cases, cartons with more simple kinds of schnapps – meant for the likes of simple soldiers like ourselves – red and white wines from all the noblest origins, chocolate, chocolate creams, lobster, goose-liver paste in tins, tinned vegetables, salami, biscuits, cigars, cigarettes – and whatever else the palates of the Staff officers and their retinue could feast on – obviously all of the finest quality. Farther on yet towered up, one upon another, barrels of butter, cooking butter, cured meats, beer and dried vegetables.

We surveyed the vast collection of delicacies in awe until SS-2nd Lieutenant Bast warned, 'We have to hurry, only pick the best!'

We knew he was right; we could only load up so much, and cognac was better than champagne, chocolate better than biscuits, butter better than dried peas. We loaded up our vehicles with all they could carry, butter, salami and chocolate above all, while each man took his private stock of high-proof liquor and cigarettes.

We were just working out the best way to arrange the goods on my Kfz 69, loaded at least to capacity when, as I had expected the whole time and calmly prepared for it, a vehicle raced up, crunched to a halt, and out jumped Anderlik. I came to attention.

'Where were you?' he shouted. 'I was unable to carry out my operational order! I am having you court martialled!'

Not until he had said this did the situation gradually dawn on him. SS-2nd Lieutenant Bast opened his mouth to speak but Anderlik kept me in his glare: 'I am waiting for your answer! I hope something will eventually occur to you!'

Actually something had already occurred to me. 'I was following you, SS-Captain. When we got to the road junction we were shot at from this street. I turned away at once to protect the company. I thought that the driver of the company troop vehicle would have seen that.'

Meanwhile Anderlik had noticed the bottles lying around on the ramp.

'Is what he says right?' he growled to Bast.

Bast answered appeasingly, 'It was probably like that.' There was a murmur of agreement from several of my comrades.

'We shall look into the matter later,' Anderlik said, then turned to his driver and told him, 'Load up a couple of cases!' This was done in a trice. Everybody got back in; Anderlik led out the convoy and we carried on. We drove through Kharkov and finished up in the south-west of the city in a small village near Merefa. An interception position was set up there but with no flanking units. We got there in time, the Russians had not yet arrived.

There was no more talk about my action: when our paths crossed for the first time next day Anderlik gave me a grin and even Nieweck, who had been in the following vehicle, acknowledged me with a smirk. Babucke the quartermaster had a face like Father Christmas: we were obliged to surrender to him everything we had amassed, including the 'personal' items, and he so overloaded his provisions vehicle and the field kitchen diesel that the springs distorted.

Nevertheless there was a good cartload of the booty left over. Somehow Babucke managed to wheedle out of Battalion – presumably in exchange for gifts from the 'cognac compound' – an additional Ford lorry for the remainder of the wares and guarded them like Cerberus; he only let the Company have the meagre provisions which the rear sent up.

As it turned out the company's illegitimate requisition was decisive in helping us hold out through the difficult days that followed. We drew on it for weeks: at Easter the field kitchen used the remainder of the cooking butter to make a gigantic baking tray full of cakes for everybody in the company.

I held on thriftily to some tins of Schoka-Cola and bottles of Bols orange-bitter, which I liked the taste of, and whose high alcohol percentage was a real help in the cold. In the company I had won myself considerable respect, as a successful independent interpreter of authoritarian structures and as an 'organiser' with a nose for unusual opportunities.

With my coup I had unintentionally stepped on the toes of somebody who, since our hotchpotch had come into existence, had held an unassailed special position in the true sense of the expression: SS-Corporal Babucke, the quartermaster, responsible for the food supply to the unit. He was the most remarkable character in the company, had a surname to suit ('Big Baby'), and as befitted his office he was well nourished, rosy and well rounded. Moreover he had an amiable disposition, always had a self-satisfied smile on his fat face, never looked at anybody directly with his small, cold eyes but never shouted using the SS-Corporal vocabulary, which his colleagues did.

The cook, SS-Lance Corporal Löbel, was devoted to him like a dog; the pair of them originated, as did most of the others in the rearward Tross under the rule of Spiess Nieweck, from Brandenburg where many were recruited for the rearward services. If he survived the war, which I consider likely, he probably found himself a warm nest in some cadre somewhere.

Babucke was a man of firm rules, which included the principle that soldiers should not be offered a good meal too often, rather it should be the exception so that they would learn to hold the quartermaster in high esteem. On the other hand he was always on the lookout for sources of food and so made himself indispensable.

He had few contacts and was not liked, with the exception of a certain species of Russian women whose scent he could sniff out with admirable certainty. Wherever and whenever we spent a day or – during the rest periods – set up quarters in a village for a longer period, in no time at all Babucke and Löbel would have found a roof under which lived an accommodating 'Matka'.

In our billets there were often enough pretty but absolutely cool girls and young women. We were all naturally interested in them but I never knew a case in which one of us got his way. Babucke, on the other hand, looked for and found suitable to his taste the fuller-figured, more mature and correspondingly more realistic and accessible partners who knew how to use his military position to their own advantage. If he did not find what he was looking for in the village where we had stopped, we would recognise the fact by seeing him flit along the village street with a package under his arm, heading off to some more distant place.

It was clear to me that we had to watch over the treasures in our 'cognac compound' like hawks if we wanted to retain for ourselves at least a share of them. Babucke belonged to the species which, given a chance, would have no scruples about stealing whatever he could lay his hands on from our sumptuous store and make off 'home' with them, or set off the royalties he was duty-bound to provide to his numerous lady friends. And I made sure never to let neither the three vehicles in which we stored our delicacies, nor him, out of my sight.

Our new operational base north-east of Merefa was a nest with only a few houses. As far as we could make out these were untouched by war so far. Our still fighting-fit platoons set up their positions a few hundred metres from the eastern end of the village. We, the fighting Tross, occupied the houses and came to the usual arrangement with the owners. Our company commander had ordered that the kitchen and QM vehicle were to remain with us; Nieweck and the supply Tross had already left for safety's sake for a new destination westwards, 160 kilometres away at Poltava.

In this God-awful hole of Merefa, Kiehn and I had double watch. This meant that not only did we have to keep our eyes constantly on the billets and vehicles, but also observe the open country to the south and west. In the confused frontline situation Russian scouting parties or even larger units could suddenly turn up and present a danger. Just to be safe therefore we excavated infantry trenches and an MG position in which the members of the fighting Tross could defend themselves, given a bit of luck.

Ede Kiehn was one of the oldest men in the company. He was the driver of the company troop vehicle and a real character. As the butt of all friendly fooling around he had earned himself several nicknames: Kazimir Krautkopf, Rasputin and also Molotov. There was some basis at least for the latter, for he said that during the signing of the historic German-Soviet Non-aggression Pact in 1939 he had met the Soviet Foreign Minister Molotov in some connection or other.

Around us was all silent and still. The night was still young and although the sky was clouded over we had good visibility across the snow-covered terrain. While making our rounds we regularly passed Babucke's three loaded lorries parked close to the farmhouse in which he had temporarily set up residence. I had long been aware that the becoming lady of the house was to his taste.

I dwelt constantly on the problem of what could befall our booty of food, drink and delicacies. Babucke was not a person who could assess risk and had stayed here with us in this unusually remote and unsafe outpost because he had not sized up the dangers. As soon as he realised the situation he would grab the first favourable opportunity to get himself and his two QM vehicles to safety and as far behind the lines as possible. Only the field kitchen and Löbel would remain behind together with some modest supplies of food. If we wanted to keep back some of the delicacies on his lorries, we had to fix the time of his flight ourselves so as to put him under pressure and impose our conditions.

The conclusion was simple: we needed a plan and we had to carry it out. I set about the task as I had a thousand times at my Belgian college. *Hypothesis*: Babucke would make a run for it within a couple of hours and take the QM lorries with their comestible treasures with him. *Thesis*: The latter had to be prevented, and we would have to create a chaotic situation forcing Babucke to leave behind a proportion of the goods in the 'cognac compound', which were ours by right under the circumstances in which they had been sequestered. *Outcome*: We would achieve our goal in purely material things and obtain the satisfaction of having tricked Babucke, whom we all disliked, in such a crafty manner.

When the mood took him, Molotov, a Berliner, liked to sing the folk song *Die Krumme Lanke*. On that night too he was humming softly to himself:

Und so sass ich mit d'r Emma uff de Banke,
Über uns sang so schmelzend een Pirol,
Unter uns floss so still die Krumme Lanke,
Neben uns ass eener Wurscht mit Sauerkohl . . .

'And so I sat with Emma on the bench,
Above us sang sweet and mellow an oriole,
Below us flowed so quiet the Krumme Lanke,
Near us someone was eating sausage with sauerkraut . . . '

For my plan to succeed I had to ensure his collaboration. 'Speaking of sauerkraut,' I began harmlessly enough, 'a piece of fine salami or a tin of Schoka-Cola would go down really well, or even both . . . there's plenty on the lorry!'

Molotov licked his lips. 'But we couldn't,' he said doubtfully, 'Babucke watches it like a lynx. And he's also got a padlock on the tarpaulin at the back. You couldn't take anything without it being easily noticed.'

'Look at it this way. Ivan fires a couple of mortars at the sheds here or an MG burst. In a split-second the whole place is in uproar, led by Babucke; he will want to be out of here in a flash . . . but we won't let him before he has unloaded enough from the lorry!'

'But there is no Ivan here,' objected Molotov.

I had to make it clearer for him: 'Man, Molotov, you're such a dumb Berlin boy! Who can tell the difference between a Russian and a German mortar after it explodes?'

'Ah, now I get you . . . man, that would be really something!'

Molotov was now showing great interest. I explained my plan, and our respective roles. To carry it through was child's play and would last only a few minutes. It would be easy with the weapons we had to hand, especially the rifle grenades,[7] of which we had quite a few left because we preferred the much greater explosive effect of hand grenades. They were very suitable for our coup since they could not be distinguished from small artillery shells when they exploded.

We began by separating. Once Molotov had disappeared from sight, after a few seconds I heard two sharp explosions at the south end of the village, one after the other, and then his machine pistol rattled – the general alarm signal. I had three of my grenades at readiness and now hurled them one after another in a high arc to straddle Babucke's quarters and explode at more or less the same instant, the acoustic effect being that of a salvo of three.

Even for us, the stagers of the spectacle, the effect was pheno-menal. The first thing we heard was a loud scream from Babucke's dwelling, then the other houses became noisy with comrades tumbling into the open with their weapons, an MG somewhere began to rattle – the gunner swore to God later that he had fired at fleeting shadows – then Babucke's front door was flung open, he hobbled over the doorstep, jerking up his trousers with one hand while holding his buttocks with the other and crying, 'Start up the lorries at once and let's go! Ivan is getting our range!'

And then: 'Paramedic! Paramedic! I'm wounded!'

Our paramedic Sepp Rist was in the forward positions. I looked at the wound, gave Babucke a pad soaked in cognac to disinfect it and a field dressing. It was a four-centimetres long splinter from a rifle grenade, which must have come through a window, then lodged between his right upper thigh and buttock. At the time Babucke who would have been in bed face down and bottom up, a strange position to adopt for sleeping. But I would prefer not to speculate about that.

When the general hullabaloo began to assume some orderliness, the following picture of the scene emerged: around the location of the event the wide-awake men of the fighting Tross had now gathered. The motors of the QM lorries were running, the drivers were at the steering wheels and Babucke, with an additional cushion to spare his bottom further distress, was attempting to climb into the co-driver's seat of the leading vehicle.

Just as he ordered, 'Off to Poltava!', several men blocked his path.

'You surely don't think,' Harness-master Stöber growled threateningly, 'that you're going to take all this stuff away and leave us with the emergency rations, do you? Unload!'

'OK, OK, I'll see to it,' Babucke nagged, but this only reaped mocking laughter. I gave Stöber, who was standing next to me, a gentle nudge, withdrew far enough away to lob a hand grenade some twenty metres behind the house in front of which the crowd was standing, and this promptly had the desired effect. When I returned slowly and unnoticed, Babucke had already opened the rear flap of the box structure and had thrown out one case.

'More!' chorused various voices. And when I shouted, 'Schoka-Cola!' others took up the chant: 'Schoka-Cola! Salami! Tins of paté!'

With reluctance Babucke pushed out two more cases and some cartons, then stated in plaintive tones: 'That should be enough!'

Kiehn had meanwhile become so fascinated by the goings on that he also fired off a grenade from his rifle. This exploded close to the back of the house. Babucke became visibly nervous, but we stood our ground resolutely until an impressive stack of supplies had been piled up at the roadside, which would last the fighting Tross for at least two weeks. And the field kitchen lorry also stayed back with us with its normal consignment of rations.

Officially there was no reason to question the story of an attack by Soviet artillery. What had actually happened that night could obviously not be kept secret for long though, and Kiehn soon spilled the beans, enjoying his claim to heroic action. Years – decades – later the tale was repeated with much laughter and thigh slapping and probably grew in the telling. This is the true and correct first-hand account. If this burlesque seems unlikely in a time of such death and horror, it all goes to show that in war besides great inhumanity there is also much that is human and often comical. It was Babucke himself who closed the chapter on the whole affair. He submitted a statement describing how he had received 'his wound during a Soviet artillery attack'. For this he was awarded the Black Wound Badge, and he wore it with pride.

In the lower command strata, orders from HQ were rarely kept secret for long. The motor pool superintendent and the rest of the company troop – paramedic, radio operator, despatch rider, the man who operated the rangefinder – were usually as well informed of plans as the company commander himself. Soon we were all in the know, therefore: we had the tactical responsibility of holding out at our isolated interception point until as many men as possible of the dispersed German main front had reassembled. The other main unit in our sector was a horse-drawn division, which like us had been hurriedly put together in France: because of the total leadership chaos caused by the HQs taking to their heels prematurely they had been unloaded at a village within the operational reach of the Red Army.

The latter had apparently been so surprised at their own success that they had still not been able to develop a strategic plan. Although they had hurled massive motorised forces at Kharkov, they had still not mastered the German tactic, successful since the Polish campaign, of penetrating through gaps in the enemy front, of which there were plenty around Kharkov. Scarcely had our company installed itself in the Merefa position than the Soviets persisted in making frontal attacks on it, which caused them serious casualties in the open terrain. They could have gone instead one kilometre north or south of our interception point and under the guidelines of modern warfare comfortably rolled us up.

Naturally the Soviet HQs did everything they could to strengthen their attack spearheads: it was only a question of a very little time until they would have sufficient forces to follow up their spectacular success at Stalingrad with the Battle of Kharkov. Therefore the situation for us grew more dangerous by the hour, particularly since no supplies reached us after the second day.

The Russians in front of our interception point were clearly superior in numbers and maintained their attacks regardless. In the open country their losses were enormous, but we too sustained casualties every day. We had to bury our dead and bring back the wounded, only possible at night, and take them across unsafe territory to the battalion dressing station of whose location we were often uncertain of from one day to the next. In the four days at Merefa our company lost four men dead and had eleven wounded: to transport them I used my Kfz 69 on five occasions.

One of the duties of the fighting Tross was the burial of the fallen, no easy job in the deeply-frozen ground. I was spared the pick and spade but instead Danninger got me to do the inscriptions on the rough wooden crosses sent up with the rations. I did this with a sharpened square steel bar heated red-hot in the field-forge of the repair vehicle. I also had rags and the asbestos gloves used for handling hot MG barrels. With the improvised tool I burned into the bar of the cross the name and details of the deceased in Gothic script and everybody expressed satisfaction with the result.

We dug three graves near the church in a village close to Merefa and some kind of papal figure came, gave his blessing and spoke a prayer. On the following night the Russians attacked and occupied the village: when we re-captured it shortly afterwards we found that the graves had gone, replaced by fresh tank tracks.

The task we had at the Merefa interception point is now military history. There were controversial orders regarding its conduct or better said its feasibility: those from the Führer, who ordered us to hold out at all costs, and those of the Commanding Officer, I SS-Panzer Corps, General Hausser, who gave the order for a limited withdrawl on 15 February 1943 in order to stabilize the front with reinforcements brought up from France and prepare for the reconquest of Kharkov.

For all that, No. 9 Company LSSAH holding out at Merefa had the desired success. At dusk on the second day the sentries reported many figures heading for the village from the south-east and avoiding the company position. We set up our defences without delay but then saw to our astonishment that it was an unarmed crowd the first of whom, when they got within shouting distance, called out. 'We are Germans, comrade! German soldiers! Don't shoot!'

108

At least 500 men hastened past us calling out repeatedly: 'Perunye' Ivan is coming!' and could not be stopped. Some of them pleaded: 'Have you anything to eat, comrade?'

We gave them Army bread in exchange for confused information. From this we learned that they were members of an infantry regiment of the Herz Division,[8] conscripts from the easternmost part of the Reich, already under pressure from Soviet advance units as they unloaded. They had abandoned their equipment in panic and had taken to their heels. We did not like to ask what had become of their officers and other units of their division, and finally we were quite happy to see them hare off after the main body of their fleeing mob.

This incident reinforced our feeling of being an island in an uncontrollable flood which could overwhelm us at any moment, and concern became mixed increasingly in our tension. It was not only the knowledge of the precarious situation that contributed to it but also the instinct of the front soldier sharpened by experience. The enquiry by the company commander almost hourly to Battalion Staff always had the same answer: 'Hold the position! We are sending more men!'

Holding out finally paid off. On the morning of the day after, almost 40 hours after the fleeing horde of infantry, there appeared in clear weather on a hill to the east a column, which approached us in a quiet and orderly manner. When the head of it came to the village we saw horse-drawn artillery in the finest condition with men in regulation dress and correctly armed, some of them securing the transport at a measured distance to the left and right.

We went up to them, and as we reached the column it stopped and an Oberwachtmeister[9] asked straight away: 'Please, may we stay with you, our officers suddenly disappeared as we were unloading and our infantry simply ran off and left us to it!'

In view of the impressive sight of the regiment's great length the Russians laying siege to our command post withdrew hastily. This had enabled Anderlik to get away and join us. He answered the Wachtmeister: 'I would like nothing better, comrade, but I have orders to send you farther back behind the lines, they are waiting for you.'

From a few questions and answers it turned out that this was the artillery regiment of the Herz Division, its men were all from Westphalia. I felt something like pride in my countrymen and distributed amongst them as much Schoka-Cola as I could lay my hands on from my MTW. The men of the Herz Division with their guns were the last who could be saved out of the chaos of the collapse. That they had done it with so much bravura gave us a lift. After our depressing experiences of the preceding days they had proved that the German Wehrmacht had not all become a band of cowards, and they had shown that a confident and undaunted unit could still hold the Red Army at a respectful distance.

A few hours later our fighting platoons disengaged from the enemy in the gathering darkness. During this withdrawal SS-Captain Anderlik was seriously wounded. For several days, more or less disoriented, we headed west through a hilly landscape with many gullies. During the day we would set up defensive positions in the scattered villages, by night we drove on to new venues with neither names nor directions because the orders kept changing. The roads frequently led through the steep-walled gullies often made unpassable at night due to falling snow. This made the greatest demands on the men, who hardly had the chance of a few hours' sleep, and the vehicles.

Scenes of the naked brutality of war have remained with me from that time. A convoy was passing: in the light coming through the headlight caps I saw a soldier lying across the road with arms at an angle, whether he was Russian or German was not possible to tell. Every time a wheel drove over him, the stiffly frozen upper torso sat up. It looked as though it were making a desperate gesture for help. I could not get the scene out of my mind until the broad tracks of a panzer crushed him and left only a dirty red trail behind.

The following scene was also an example of the new dimension of tragic fatalities which the war began to bring about. In a narrow depression we met a detachment of Tiger tanks. All vehicles were driving so close together that it was impossible to create road space by manoeuvring. Right in front of me the driver of a motorcycle sidecar combination had attempted to make more room for oncoming traffic at a very narrow bend by steering as close as he could to the steep road edge and drive through the deeper snow there. Because the roadway fell away steeply his side, he could not get free. An oncoming Tiger panzer was set to pass the spot but began to slip on the angled icy surface. The panzer driver stopped two metres short of the motorcycle combination.

The panzer commander, standing up in the turret hatch, and in the relatively bright lights of the massed vehicles distinctly recognisable as an SS-2nd Lieutenant by his collar patches, shouted to the motorcycle driver,

'Make room at once!'

'I can't,' he replied, 'I am stuck fast. I need a tow to get free. You cannot come past without pushing me over!'

'You will see what I can do!' the SS-2nd Lieutenant replied and gave an order below through his radio mouthpiece. The panzer rolled forward, for a moment lost road grip and slithered with a crash against the motorcycle. The driver's left leg was a crushed, bloody mess up to the hip. The panzer engine died and for a second there was a ghostly silence, not even the injured man made a sound. He looked for a few seconds at his crushed leg, drew his pistol and shot the SS-2nd Lieutenant, and then shot himself in the head.

Even more memorable events happened. In one of our temporary positions we secured a village along a long road and on high ground. It was a bright day, and from our quarters in the farmhouses we could see far and wide towards Ivan, but there was nothing to be seen of him. Nevertheless outlying sentries were posted and for two hours I was one of them. In order to pass the time I drew my 08 pistol and fired a series of practice shots at a tree stump some distance down the slope. After that I followed regulations by removing the round in the barrel, secured the weapon and had a lie down for a while.

After I had had my nap I decided to clean the weapon. Apart from me in the room were three men of my squad enjoying the rare opportunity to laze, and the lady of the house sitting in a corner darning a sock. Suddenly the absolutely peaceful idyll was shattered by an explosion, glass tinkled behind me and I was the first to realise that the powerful shock had come from my hand holding the large-calibre 08 – 9mm; in comparison, the carbine round had a relatively modest 7.62mm calibre.

We all knew that the 08 was a capricious weapon. Differing from the slide action of other semi-automatics, it had a barrel and toggle assembly locked together. This assembly would travel back due to the recoil of firing, and then move forward under spring tension to load in the next round from the magazine. To make the gun safe, any round in the breech had to be removed, the magazine had to be taken off and the barrel and toggle lock disengaged. If there was a round 'up the spout' the sprung return of the locked barrel and toggle assembly could fire it.

This happened to me, the bullet went through my trousers at hip level, narrowly missed the head of my comrade Kälbel and hit a cabinet with a glass front. We were more puzzled that shocked, and then relieved because Kälbel had not been hit and I had only a light graze from the bullet. Our Russian housewife began to scream and shout, ran from her corner through the front door into the road and disappeared extraordinarily fast. We never saw her again. After-wards I felt really sorry for her.

It transpired that while I had been having my nap, one of my colleagues had inspected the firearm, loaded it and then after applying the safety catch, but not unloading it, had put it down again. When I went to clean it I assumed it was in the state in which I had left it. All the same, it was my weapon, I had responsibility for it and I had infringed Army regulations, which laid down clear instructions about weapons handling including an important reference to the 08. If it had been something worse than a close shave the consequences for me could have been very bad. In the event, however, I heard nothing more about it.

The new MTWs were causing problems. It was not only the heating up with the blowtorches, but also the six-cylinder engines were not up to the strenuous demands being made of them. They were a so-called side-steered type with a camshaft not fitted in the cylinder head but right above the crankshaft: this required long tappet rods to work the valves hanging in the cylinder head with rocking levers. The relatively weak motors had to be run constantly at high revs, which led to strain and in consequence to overheating and broken tappets.

My vehicle was the second to break down at night in a convoy after ten days of operations. The sudden engine noise was so alarming that I turned it off in annoyance. Cars were always objects of the greatest technical interest for me, and therefore I always gave them my personal attention. I investigated engine problems personally: they irritated me very much and I was unforgiving about poor design.

My Kfz 69 caused me great annoyance to put it mildly, and worse, Kiehn had to take me in tow with the company transport vehicle. My mood was not improved as I was dragged behind him up a narrow road on a slight rise when suddenly everything in front of us came to a sudden stop. By the circumstances of the tow my vehicle now stood more at the centre of the carriageway than was correct in principle.

Nothing happened for quite some time, my squad, all sitting up, were asleep behind me. I was also just about to nod off when a car horn sounded loudly and this soon turned into an unpleasant permanent noise. I was not in the mood to be impressed by it, and as soon as there was a pause I turned round and shouted 'Lick my arse!', quite a common army response in such situations.

The effect was considerable: seconds later a man appeared at the side of my driver's seat. I recognised him at once by his small stature, unusual for the LAH, his expensive general's furs with the insignia of his rank, and his face, which I knew from our earlier meeting in the Rata Works at Taganrog: our Divisional Commander Sepp Dietrich.

'So what are you telling me I should do? And why don't you move your vehicle?' he grumbled. I sat to attention in the driver's seat as prescribed: 'I beg pardon, Obergruppenführer, but I cannot move aside, my damned engine is kaputt!'

Sepp Dietrich proved himself to be a man of the legendary calibre much spoken of amongst the men. In a flash he had the occupants of my MTW on their feet, got a few more men from behind to assist and no sooner said than done, my MTW was to one side. Before he got into his car and roared off he took his leave of me with the words: 'Make sure you get that motor running again soon!' To this I replied with the platitude: 'By all means, Obergruppenführer!' The problem was neither resolved by all means nor in accord with the familiar motto: 'We do the impossible immediately, miracles take a little longer!'

At daybreak, SS-Corporal Stöber, car mechanic Hampel and I got to work. I took off the bonnet and the defect was visible straight away; the tappet of the outlet valve of the second cylinder was broken.

'Well, you can do that by yourself,' Stöber said, 'there's nothing more for us to do here.' Thus I was left with the problem. There was another Kfz 69 alongside the workshop vehicle. It was easy enough to remove a tappet rod from it as a replacement, but after inserting it into my MTW I found that it was several millimetres too short. I called Stöber over and we tried various ways to fix it. Most of the time I was in disagreement with his methods and finally motor mechanic Hampel took over. He thought the steering chain had parted, which was a job taking another six to eight hours.

'That is not my beer!' Stöber stated, 'You and Maeger stay here, take the parts you want from the workshop vehicle and repair it! We are leaving now!' This meant more or less, 'If you get it done we shall see each other again, if not, that's your problem!'

Luckily Hampel understood what he was doing. He took screws, bolts and another tappet rod from the cannibalised Kfz 69, we removed the radiator and then the front motor cover, and Hampel heaved a great sigh of relief to see that the steering chain had not parted: the problem was a broken bolt, leaving us now only with the dilemma with the tappet cup: after removing the camshaft cover we found it where it did not belong, stuck between the housing and the camshaft.

The rest was just routine but had to be carried out in the open in a temperature of minus 25 degrees. We were in no particular hurry and went into a nearby house to warm up before we started tinkering with the MTW again: in addition we felt uneasy about the

114

two of us moving off alone towards a lost outpost of the city especially since we kept hearing bursts of MG fire and the occasional rifle round in the distance.

Hampel and I were just on our way to warm up once more when suddenly a hail of shells and missiles of all kinds and calibres bracketed our village. We sought cover in a trench alongside the house wall, but since nobody fired back from the village it quickly fell silent and soon numerous vehicles appeared on the crest of the distant ridge, some of which broke away from the main group and sped towards us. We recognised them as German PSWs[10] and revealed ourselves. After some palaver, also involving in the crews of two other PSWs, which rolled up from between the village houses to reach us, the following was established: unknown to us, at the far end of the village an armourer and two men from our company had stayed back to repair an MG. When testing the weapon the burst of fire had reached a column of reconnaissance vehicles of our division, and had pattered down against their armoured sides without causing damage to armour or vehicle. The column had then returned fire from all barrels before approaching to ascertain the cause and results. After this adventure came to a satisfactory end, the PSWs went on. We finished the repair to our MTW, blow torched the coolant to the required temperature to start the motor and – wonder of technology – set off at last for the few kilometres to our company, arriving just in time for hot pea soup. Stöber had been right after all: it was a day in which I actually had learned something.

All orders that day were more or less confusing. This was caused by operating the still weak German defensive forces with the tactic of elastic resistance to the attacking enemy, and annoying him with fast changes of troop positions: this could only be improvised with the efficient use of motorised vehicles. The historian Peter Young explained it as follows:

The last and greatest operation of the Soviet winter campaign of 1942/43 began north of the Don. On 12 January four Soviet fronts broke through the German lines on a broad front between

Orel and Rostov and attacked Army Group Don in the south and Weichs' Army Group B. The Soviet goal was Kharkov. On the right flank the Soviet tanks flowed westwards in the truest sense of the word, encircled elements of the German Second Army and forced the remainder to fall back behind Kursk. Kharkov was liberated at the beginning of February by the Soviet Fourth Army and Third Tank Army. In the south the Germans fared slightly better.

By a tactically superior operation of his reserves, von Manstein succeeded in bringing the Soviet advance to a standstill. Despite a numerical inferiority in the ratio of 1:7, he then went on the attack. He recaptured Kharkov and, as a result of was able to eliminate the vulnerable Soviet forward front and set up a stable German frontline before the onset of the spring thaw along the Donets.

Despite Manstein's success, in their winter offensive the Soviets had struck the Germans a decisive blow. There are no exact statistics, but it is estimated that the 1942/43 Russian winter claimed 100,000 German lives. Some sources state that the Soviets destroyed or captured 5,000 aircraft, 9,000 panzers and thousands of other vehicles plus 20,000 firearms. Their losses were probably as high as those of the Germans but they had the satisfaction of having recaptured all the territory they had lost in 1942: moreover they knew that they were stronger than the Germans and on their way to victory.[11]

The almost daily movements to new positions with inadequate and slow-to-arrive supplies made the greatest demands on the unit. At night we drove or marched and at dawn the men had to dig in or attack. In the best cases all they had to do was perform security tasks, filling gaps in the front or acting as cover on the flanks, but as a rule a 'heavy' company with greater firepower would be sent to the hotspots.

Except in fast offensives to win territory, mobile warfare demands a much higher tribute in dead and wounded than static warfare with its protective bunkers and trenches. In the first days after we unloaded from the train our company's losses were slight, but in two short weeks, between 16 and 28 February 1943, we lost almost fifty men, and the worst was yet to come.

Sunday 28 February 1943 was sunny. It was also the black day of No. 9 Company LSSAH. It began with a relatively mild frost, and the rising sun transformed the countryside into a sparkling surface of snow visible for miles. After a long night march, the company had selected a new position in the upper reaches of a long flat slope, which descended to a hollow valley, presumably the snowed-over course of a stream, in which some huts and bald trees huddled together. We began at once with the laborious business of digging in: as previously we had no cover on the flanks. A position of this kind on a slope facing the direction of the enemy was always dangerous because it could be seen clearly from a long distance and offered no possibility of retreat into a less visible and therefore safer position. I believe that this tactical principle of the LAH caused many unnecessary losses; insofar as I had any influence on later decisions, I always argued for digging trenches and bunkers behind the crest of a ridge with two MG positions situated on the crest of the slope.

About two kilometres behind the frontline platoons the fighting Tross had found billets in a village distinguished by a remarkable number of hens. These were capable of flight and so intelligent that they kept to the roofs of the cottages and were thus out of our reach. Even for a disciplined force in the fighting zone with a monotonous diet and little enough of it, poultry were not taboo.

To the extent that the radio system actually worked it was only of use to contact Battalion HQ. The fighting Tross had no equipment of that sort. Unless a messenger brought us special orders we followed our set routine. After we had supplied the fighting element with weapons, ammunition, equipment and cold rations, if possible under cover of darkness, the MTW drivers would pull back to the best available cover, as a rule the nearest village beyond the range of enemy infantry weapons and out of sight of enemy artillery spotters. If visibility was limited or we did not expect to come under direct fire we would then set out several hours later, therefore by day, in vehicles suitable for the terrain taking hot food and tea in thermo-canisters to our freezing comrades in the advanced position. If this were not possible by reason of massive enemy activity we would have to wait until evening to take up ammunition and bring back the wounded and – unfortunately often enough – the dead.

That 28 February was so quiet all around that during the morning SS-Corporal Danninger, who had commanded the fighting Tross since Merefa, instructed Löbel to cook potato soup to take forward. Really I should have taken it but because of the excellent visibility none of the big Kfz 69s were suited for the operation, and the much smaller VW amphibious vehicles with lower profile, which almost disappeared from sight behind the big heaps of snow along the well-worn track were detailed for the job instead. They were driven by the smallest and youngest boy in the Tross who had come to us at Olshany from the Luftwaffe and was nicknamed 'Bobbel'. Danninger turned to me and said, 'You're the best man to go with him. Have a very good look round before you get to the top of the slope!'

Bobbel and I drove off. It was like a Sunday outing. In a few minutes we reached the height behind which we would find our men and surprise them with hot soup. Barely had Bobbel rolled over the crest of the height, which had been cut at an angle to the track, than he braked sharply as several artillery rounds exploded loudly on the far side of the crest. The VW stood favourably against a snowdrift, with our ever-ready entrenching tools we shovelled up a wall which almost hid the VW. In accordance with regulations Bobbel stayed with the vehicle, I crept and crawled carefully to the edge of the path until I had a good view over the descending slope.

What I saw made my blood run cold. Two T-34s were rolling at full speed towards our company's position. It was 150 metres in length and our squad had so far only been able to hack out a limited number of bunkers and trenches in the hard ground. In their fast approach the two tanks opened fire with all barrels from long range but they were rocking and shaking so much that it was difficult for them to take proper aim.

Bobbel suddenly appeared behind me. 'Drive back,' I shouted to him, 'and try to fetch help!' He made off as fast as he could. I

118

remained where I was, the helpless witness to the horrific spectacle unfolding before me. The steel colossi separated to either flank of the position and then began their cruel methodical work of killing. Without firing a shot at close range they turned along the incomplete infantry trenches and MG nests, rolled over them, going back and forth over every hole and every man until their broad tracks had crushed everything. They were thorough and took their time, and eventually there was nothing left to see but the deeply churned, fruitful, black soil of the Ukraine.

None of our company had run: it would in any case have been senseless, for the tanks' MGs would simply have mown them down. The survivors of No. 9 Company LSSAH now saw their chance in the unequal battle. Their light weapons useless against the T-34's, with grim determination and cold calculation they stood their ground but keeping to the blind side of the viewing slits and MGs of the monsters, jumped up and waltzed at the last second to one side, keeping clear as best they could of the tank tracks. In such desperate attempts to save their lives, many had the good fortune to get away with it.

I also saw how one after another they were squashed to a bloody pulp. It was a nightmarish scene, and I was overwhelmed with despair that I could do nothing but experience each death stricken with horror. I saw how three of our men, moving in the relatively safety of close proximity to one of the tanks, were gunned down by the MG's of the other. I also saw a tank commander in the open turret hatch with an MG, waiting to finish off my squad comrade Spohn: every time the Russian appeared, Spohn forced him back down with a pistol shot: the scene was repeated four times and Spohn survived.

Later there were many questions about how this catastrophe could come about. Why did the company have no limpet mines? Answer: there were none available, and it was very doubtful if they could have been used successfully, for it meant that the carrier had to jump aboard a tank in motion: the Russians knew the danger and would make constant abrupt changes of direction to prevent it: their new types could apply forward drive to the track one side and

119

reverse drive to the track on the other, something which no panzer could yet emulate.

These two Soviet tank crews ran a high risk. To attack without accompanying infantry was a bold stroke, particularly since they had to expect German anti-tank weaponry: that none was present counted as a stroke of luck for the Russians, for at any moment anti-tank guns or tank destroyers[12] could appear. By insisting on literally playing cat-and-mouse to kill individual men cost them time they could ill afford to lose.

The end came as surprisingly quickly as it had begun. To my left on the height of the slope the tall silhouettes of two tank destroyers appeared, and the T-34s immediately took flight. They had got about 150 metres away when the guns of the tank destroyers fired one after another. One T-34 was hit and blew up. In the attempt to escape the other zig-zagged spraying up clouds of snow: a round from a tank destroyer hit the rear of the tank which burst into flame. The turret hatch opened and a crewman attempted to get out, but the fire below spread too fast and caught him. The Russian fell to one side and within seconds became a flaming torch. He gave one long scream of agony before falling silent. After all that had gone before it was a comparatively undramatic conclusion.

I ran as fast as I could to the company position followed by members of our fighting Tross who had driven up in three Kfz 69s and the Horch. We came across the exhausted survivors, amongst them SS-2nd Lieutenant Müller, who had taken command of the company after Anderlik was wounded. We counted up our losses: before the attack the platoons had seventy-two men. Three wounded men had been brought up, sixteen men had fallen in the hour it lasted, fifty-three men came though. Under the protection of the tank destroyers we began at once on the work of rebuilding the position.

In the end not much was spoken about the incident. We learned that worse had been avoided by Bobbel having stopped and given the alarm to the two tank destroyers on the road ahead of the village where the fighting Tross was stationed. We also heard that there were three anti-tank guns in firing range at readiness south of the village, but these had frozen solid into the ground facing the wrong way and so were not operational.

More difficult days were to follow. In the early morning after Black Sunday, the company was ordered two kilometres to the north-east into an area which had been in Russian hands all day. When we were driving the platoons there we had to keep to a road staked out by the pioneers because all the surrounding area was mined. The enemy had a good view of us as it grew light forcing our men to cover the last stretch on foot, but at least they had protected new positions. These consisted of some buildings, presumably a small collective farm, partially gutted and ruined. The fighting Tross returned to where we came from since there was nothing more suitable.

All we heard from the position throughout the day was the sound of fighting. As soon as dusk fell I set out for the new position with the rations. I found the men in sombre mood: news had somehow filtered through that despite the bleak personnel situation they were to join I Panzer Corps in an imminent major offensive. The Red Army must have got wind of it for their infantry kept up attacks all day with artillery cover. After the reinforcements rushed up from France had arrived, the worst of the gaps in the frontline had been plugged. The Soviets too were constantly bringing up fresh troops; apparently they had discovered where the Germans had their greatest firepower and therefore the most dangerous offensive potential in the front line: our 'heavy' company's MGs and mortars. The hardest-fought day was that when the Soviets attacked with thirty-six tanks. Thirteen of these were destroyed with limpet mines.

As a sign that the German front was increasingly taking shape with the reinforcements from France, on the day before that the vehicles of Nos 7 and 8 Companies had arrived at the village. We had less room in our billets, but we were cheerful all the same at being in close touch with our neighbouring units in the battalion, and felt safer than before when we had been lonely and lost in no man's land.

It was obvious that the decision would be taken to coordinate the supply runs to the front units. Danninger agreed with the competent

SS-Corporal of No. 8 Company that one MTW from each fighting Tross would go forward together to the two company command posts with ammunition taking the No. 8 Company paramedic. The joint run was delayed because the MG and mortar ammunition was not delivered from the rear until around midnight, although when it did come it arrived in good quantities. The two vehicles set off and we pricked up our ears: the veterans felt in their water that the coming day would be no piece of cake.

The old Matka lying upstairs near her warm stove had rheumatism. At night whenever she made a false move and pain got her she would wail loudly. I noticed it this time because Grulich, sleeping on the earth floor near me and three others, gave me a nudge because he had to go outside. As with most men in their first winter in Russia, he needed to empty his bladder frequently when he had been at the bottle in the evening, and we still had many bottles from the Kharkov cognac compound.

Before Grulich came back, Danninger appeared in the doorway and said loudly, 'I need a volunteer!' I gave him a questioning look. 'The two Kfz 69s didn't arrive, they blew up, and one from the 7th as well! Damned Ivan mined the road over the last three hours. A man from Battalion HQ brought the report.'

Impulsively I commented: 'There can't be many mines in such a short time.'

'Three men should be enough, you just have to know what you're about and pick the right places.'

'I'll go!' I said, 'We can't leave the platoons in the lurch! I ought to take a couple of bottles and some chocolate as well.'

'OK. Heat up your engine.'

Danninger turned to the others in the room. 'You people load the ammunition at once! There's enough of it there!' and again to me, 'You should drive over the open country to the right of the roadway, the mines can't be as thick that side. Take Grulich with you. Good luck!'

I knew he was right: it was our only chance. The snow was superficial and so we would not get stuck, and visibility was passable; furthermore over the open and flat surface we would take the straight and therefore quickest route. That was important, for the night was ending and once it got light the Russian artillery would make mincemeat of us. The risks? That we had to drive through a minefield was a fact and not a theory, and even if we got through we could still go astray and finish up with Ivan. There was nothing for it by to grit one's teeth, set off as quickly as possible, step on the gas, get everything possible out of the crate and trust in whatever guardian angel or lucky charm one believed in during the evil minutes.

We left in such haste that there was no time for further reflection. As we drove the tension grew: to me it felt like I was driving a barrel of gunpowder with a burning fuze. With motor howling we drove over humps in the ground and furrows hardened by frost, behind me the mixture of ammunition cases rattled merrily.

Having reached the halfway point without incident Grulich tapped me on the shoulder and for the first time I took a deep breath. Just at that moment came a flash and a thunderous crack under the front wheels, and the MTW came to an abrupt halt. Something dark flew through the air describing a high arc to the right of me. It was a few seconds before we ascertained that we had sustained no injuries and that our explosive cargo lay silent and peaceful behind us. I got out to inspect the damage and found that the left mudguard was missing and the bonnet right side was hanging off.

Everything else was in place: the front wheels seemed intact, even the engine: I had stalled it in my natural reaction to stand on the brake pedal. All I had to do was replace the bonnet, resume my seat, restart the engine, depress the clutch, put it into first gear, depress the accelerator pedal and go. And the MTW moved off sweetly as though nothing had happened. Grulich and I knew enough about Russian mines to understand what had gone on here: we had run over a so-called 'infantry mine' made of wood, lacking any metal parts and thus undetectable with our search apparatus. They could kill a man but not inflict much damage to a vehicle. Our assumption was confirmed later when I found a hardwood splinter in the protective panel between the engine and driver's seat.

Minutes afterwards we reached the company command post in the ruined collective farm. We were not expected and despite all the misery of their present circumstances they greeted us with beaming smiles. After the heavy losses I had brought both hot and cold substantial rations for the platoons based on the pre-disaster complement and these were shared out between all in a trice.

SS-2nd Lieutenant Müller, on duty all night and who looked exhausted, gave me his hand and said, 'We have two seriously wounded who have to go back and we are also desperately short of mortars and limpet mines.'

'Will do, sir,' I replied without a second's thought, 'I shall drive back over my own tracks and bring what's needed.'

After loading the wounded aboard, Müller came to my car door and said, 'We have to expect more wounded. Tell Danninger that we need more MG ammunition. If you get here again, there is cover for you behind the wall.'

The drive back was child's play. The Russians did not notice it or had other things to worry about; our artillery, which had meanwhile been brought up, gave them a barrage before our regiment attacked. Carefully keeping to my own tracks in the snow, I considered mines to be a minor danger in view of the circumstances.

At the fighting Tross I loaded up the required ammunition as quickly as I could with Grulich's help and then we went back at a leisurely pace. On our arrival, SS-2nd Lieutenant Müller merely said: 'You'll get the Iron Cross for this!' He fell that same afternoon, and belonged amongst those whose passing was a great pity.

When the company attacked I made a third tour across the minefield because there was no other connection to the fighting Tross and I had to bring them the order to move up. When Spethmann of the HQ platoon, who had heard SS-2nd Lieutenant Müller's promise, told Danninger a couple of days later, he just laughed and said, 'Drivers don't get the Iron Cross, the most they can expect is the Kriegsverdienstkreuz (War Service Cross)'. But I didn't really care all that much one way or the other.

By midday the pioneers had cleared the road. Careful to keep within the cleared area, we followed behind all the vehicles of the fighting units, which won territory quickly in their attack. All came through unscathed except for the last, Bobbel with his amphibious vehicle, which suddenly turned a somersault inside an explosive cloud and landed on all fours. Bobbel looked around in bemusement before stepping on the gas and driving on. We wished the Soviet wood industry and infantry-wooden mine production a long future.

Meanwhile the Soviet offensive, which had begun on the Don at the beginning of January and by 11 March had pushed forward over a 450-kilometre stretch to the north of Poltava, was brought to a standstill between Stalino and Kharkov by the determined attacks of First and Fourth Panzer Army from the south, and II SS-Panzer Corps from the north. This relieved the German front and meant for the LAH, whose infantry regiments west of Kharkov had been encircled and decimated, and also for our battalion, salvation from the greatest danger, for it enabled the division to finally bring up its tanks and artillery. That fifty kilometres occupied only by Russian units lay between these heavy units and ourselves was something we did not know until later.

The Battle of Kharkov during February and March 1943 has gone down in history as a success for the German military command which, with forces much inferior in numbers, not only prevented the Red Army from extending its victory at Stalingrad into a total defeat for the Wehrmacht on the Eastern Front, but converted a difficult defensive situation against an enemy force seven times greater into a major offensive, which ended with the re-conquest of Kharkov and stabilised the German front in the whole central sector for months.

That this came about was only made possible by the commander of I SS-Panzer Corps, SS-General Hausser, who ignored Hitler's stupid order to hold firm where he was, and with consciousness of his responsibility and great tactical skill won back the trust of his troops, which had to a large extent been lost. Hausser had the task of halting the Russian advance westwards over the Don, of mastering the dangerous situation threatening the entire German southern flank, particularly the Army Groups of Manstein and von Kleist, and striking a heavy blow against the strong and far superior

Soviet forces advancing on a broad front between Slaviansk and Kursk. Before the Panzer Corps had assembled however, Soviet First Guards Tank Army had already crossed the Donets at Isyum and other powerful groups had broken through the weak German forces north of Kharkov. Thus the situation for Panzer Corps Hausser was extremely critical.

On 12 February Hausser's troops were still east of Kharkov. The enemy at his back controlled the Kharkov–Poltava supply road and was in the act of cutting off the SS-Panzer Corps from its connections to the rear. Nevertheless, on Hitler's express instruction, the army ordered Hausser to remain in Kharkov and hold the city under all circumstances. Two days later the SS-Panzer Corps was close to being encircled and wiped out. Despite this, Army Detachment Lanz, under whose command the Panzer Corps was subordinate, insisted that the Führer's order be carried out and that Kharkov must be held 'come what may', and re-confirmed the order on the afternoon of the same day.

We all now faced the same threat of being encircled and wiped out by far superior enemy forces, as had Sixth Army at Stalingrad under General Paulus for our panzers and artillery were still on the transporter trains coming from France. Hitler in his hubris ordered once more: 'Hold firm without regard to casualties.'

SS-General Hausser, commander of the SS-Panzer Corps, whose military career had begun in the 100,000-man Reichswehr army allowed by the Treaty of Versailles, was not cut from the same wood as Paulus. He was the embodiment of that kind of officer who proved to the contrary all the criticisms levelled against the Waffen-SS up to then: brave, determined, free from the traditional unconditional obedience to authority of the authoritarian-oriented army. There were others, the narrow-minded, ideological men of the political machine, but these were not be found amongst the fighting troops. Hausser was also not the deplorable kind of military commander who – provided with cognac and other pleasant aids to survival – would await his end in a safe bunker and then, wearing with all his decorations, sally forth to offer the victor his dagger.

Two years later, in the heavy defensive struggle in Hungary, Sepp Dietrich, commander of the Leibstandarte, also provided an example of his awareness of responsibility towards his men when in March 1945 he ignored Hitler's senseless order to defend his positions 'to the last man', broke out of an encirclement and so as its commander saved Sixth SS-Panzer Army and with it the Leibstandarte. Hitler ordered that all members of the LAH had to remove from their uniforms the cuff title with the silver embroidered inscription 'LSSAH *Adolf Hitler*', which was done. Unconfirmed is the rumour circulating in the Waffen-SS at the time that Dietrich and his Staff officers tossed their cuff titles and decorations on a fire at the same time.

These foregoing events prove that the representation of the Waffen-SS as a force blindly and unconditionally devoted to Hitler is not correct. As early as 1943 amongst the Leibstandarte it was being said quite frankly: 'If we want to win this war, we have to first have a thorough clear-out at home of the Party bigwigs and "gold pheasants".'[13] In 1999 I met a senior Bundeswehr officer who had been a young lieutenant in the Wehrmacht during the war and told me of his surprise at utterances of this kind made within his hearing by SS-Leibstandarte officers. Because I was not in Hungary at the time, I ignored Hitler's order as a curiosity: I belonged to the few Leibstandarte members who continued to wear the cuff title to the end, even after my transfers to the medical training establishment at Bad Aussee and to the Waffen-SS Medical Reserve Battalion at Stettin, and finally on the Oder front with Division Dirlewanger.

It is unfortunately a fact that important details about wartime events are likely to be withheld for years after the conclusion of hostilities until one or other of the former belligerents decides to release documentary material through its public archive. Many details of the Battle for Kharkov, for example, were only made accessible to Western researchers after the Moscow archive was opened as a result of 'Perestroika'.

In his untenable situation, and in agreement with the neighbouring corps Raus, to which *Grossdeutschland* Division was subordinate, Hausser ordered his divisions to evacuate their positions and fight their way out. Towards 1300 hrs Hausser reported this decision to Army Detachment Lanz: 'In order to prevent encirclement and save material, orders given to fight way out behind Udy sector on city outskirts. Fighting presently going on. Street fighting to the south-west and west of the city.'

After Lanz had replied by repeating Hitler's order to stand firm, Hausser reported: ' . . . on 14.2/1645 hr order to evacuate Kharkov and elude behind Udy sector night of 14.2 given simultaneously to Korps Raus (General, Cdr.6.Panzer-Div). Assessment of situation in writing to follow.'

Eyewitnesses stated that Hitler was livid with rage when he saw the report of the disobedience of his SS-Panzer Corps.[14]

This withdrawal fanned the flames of the Soviet attacking spirit. Nobody on the German side could have anticipated or assessed the enormous psychological effect which the evacuation of Kharkov had on Stalin and his General Staff, as is now revealed by the Soviet documents. The liberation of Kharkov not only inflated the Soviet sensation of triumph: Stalin also saw in it a confirmation of his guess that the German strategic intention was a general retreat. After all, why would Hitler's 'Praetorians' have abandoned Kharkov if no general retreat was under way?

On 21 February 1943 the following appeared in the Red Army's War Diary report No. 307:

The consequences of the loss of Kharkov and the collapse of the German improvised Donets Front have been assessed in the OKW as catastrophic. Since 17 February the units and remains of more than forty German divisions have been imperilled, cut off, crushed in hopeless defensive battles, wiped out in fruitless counter attacks or overrun by attacking Russian masses for subsequent annihilation. Almost half the panzer troops and panzers which the German Army and Waffen-SS still have left are numbered amongst these . . . indifference and fatalistic hopelessness is now very noticeably and rapidly weakening the fighting ability of German troops everywhere in the south of the Front, even amongst the German reserves which have still hardly fought at all, but who foresee their doom in the improvised rearward areas.

The Soviet Army's euphoria paved the way for their defeat in this battle. It was very quickly appreciated how correct had been Hausser's decision for a planned withdrawal. Two indispensable, fully battleworthy panzer divisions, experienced in the Eastern theatre, and the Panzer-Grenadier Division *Grossdeutschland,* had been preserved for the decisive phase of the defensive battle. In a few days the tide turned, When the SS panzer and artillery regiments finally arrived from France, the counter-offensive began at such a tempo that its success surprised the attackers as much as the Soviets.

The Red Army leadership lost control of events and was misled as to the true situation for days. On the late evening of 24 February they understood finally that the tank group of Army General Popov had apparently been beaten back while Sixth Soviet Army was in extreme difficulties, large sections being cut off and encircled. On 28 February the German 7th Panzer Division reached the Donets south of Isyum. Popov's tank group was wiped out. On the evening of 28 February XL Panzer Corps reoccupied the positions at the Donets, which they had been forced to abandon during the Russian winter offensive in January. Hoth's Panzer Corps pursued the fleeing Russian units, encircled them and wiped them out south of the Donets. The German losses were slight, those of the Soviets considerable. Six armoured corps, ten infantry divisions and a half dozen independent brigades had been either destroyed or were no longer battleworthy, 615 battle tanks, 400 heavy guns and 600 anti-tank guns had been destroyed: the Russians had over 77,000 wounded and 23,000 dead. Only 9,000 were captured; the German forces were not numerous enough to close the major pocket, and large numbers of the Soviet divisions poured through the gaps and saved themselves by crossing the frozen Donets, leaving behind their heavy weapons and vehicles.

II SS-Panzer Corps, the Leibstandarte and other units attacked Kharkov. In a brave attempt at improvisation, the Soviet High

Command sent two tank corps and three infantry divisions from Army Group 'Voronezh-Front' to protect the city against the SS-Panzer Corps. The group became entangled between the defensive fronts of the Leibstandarte and the two other SS-Panzer Corps divisions and were enclosed in a pocket from which only elements managed to escape annihilation by taking to their heels. At the beginning of the offensive the Panzer Corps had to shovel through chest-high snow and then the thaw came. Hausser had a clear path after wiping out the Soviet Third Tank Army's battle group. On the orders of General Hoth he was ordered to bear back on the city and on 8 March was once more at its western suburbs. On 11 March the re-capture of Kharkov marked the end of the offensive, which had begun five days before.

On the morning of 4 March alongside the entire SS-Panzer Corps, and supported by endless columns of heavy weapons, we had set off for the attack on Kharkov and demonstrated – probably for the last time in this war – the striking power of the legendary 'Blitzkrieg'. The Russians, apparently fearful of now being encircled themselves, offered no opposition at the approaches to the city. In order to use this situation to the best advantage we followed in hot pursuit but soon realised that even with troop carrier vehicles we had no chance of catching them up and offering battle.

Instead we found ourselves in a very remarkable battlefield. Rolling forward over mainly flat terrain we found it strewn with Soviet Army equipment relinquished in the typical sequence of a rapid flight. Next we came upon a zone of abandoned weapons and ammunition containers of all kinds; one kilometre farther on the field was littered with blankets and belts, and finally the fleeing hordes had literally left behind the last of all they had in their desperation to escape, for now we found only haversacks and greatcoats and last of all fur caps and lined boots.

Not until we reached the outskirts of Kharkov, which we approached from the north-west, did we find Soviet troops dug in and offering stout resistance. Because of the speed of the Russian retreat and our own arrival, they had not had the time to prepare a closed defensive line. When we received fire in open country we turned away and entered the city from the north. Bitter fighting in the streets and house to house ensued for two days. Finally on the third day our battalion captured the city centre, Red Square, surrounded by what looked like concrete citadels designed by a Soviet confectioner, a prestige project to demonstrate Stalinist might. After that it was renamed 'Platz der Leibstandarte' for the next few months: our battalion commander, now Max Hansen, received the Knight's Cross.

For some days we were able to rest in the tall blocks of flats. It was not pleasant, for we were forced to share with the remaining occupants, exclusively the wives and children of high functionaries of the regime, who looked upon us with fear and undisguised hostility. They found a very intelligent solution by mapping out the areas which were theirs, and they left the rest to us. The flats of these prominent people were equipped with a bathroom of a luxurious kind never previously seen in the Soviet Union, but our joyful expectations could not be fulfilled for although the water piping *into* the bath worked, the tubs had no drainage. Therefore the occupants used them to store sacks of coal.

In these tall concrete structures we felt, not unreasonably, trapped. In the case of the alarm being raised it would have taken us ages to make our way down the long staircases to get to our vehicles. Therefore we were glad to be withdrawn from the city, which lay within Russian artillery range, and obliged to find ourselves alternative living accommodation in open country.

I do not share the opinion of authors fascinated by the idea that with the sea-change which the re-capture of Kharkov brought about, the German offensive could have been extended to the 'Voronezh Front' on the 'Kursk Bend'. The troops were too exhausted, and that was proved in the subsequent fighting in our unit's new operational area, the region around Kasatshya-Lopan north of Kharkov. It was there that that curious form of warfare without a plan was continued, which had begun for us when we were unloaded east of the Donets in January.

Our battalion's fighting troops were very much less than the strength required to establish a stable frontline. Contact between the

131

units was maintained only with difficulty, the forward fighting troops and the supporting Tross had not only to work closely according to the rules and usages of combat – the drivers and vehicles intruded repeatedly and unintentionally into the battlefield itself. Since the campaign began, the transport capacity so important for changes of position and the supply of the troops had been always inadequate, and the unavoidable losses made themselves felt. These losses in men and materials were not made good, insufficient replacements of both came through only sporadically.

The situation was characterised by general confusion. Our leadership had no recognisable planned strategy, while tactics relied heavily on improvisation to suit the rapidly-changing circumstances. Two things gave us comfort: the enemy facing us was substantially greater than us in numbers but had only the same amount of food to go round, while on the other hand we had so much alcohol from the Kharkov compound that it kept our moods buoyed up to some extent. My personal supply, stowed under blankets in the back of the MTW, still consisted of some bottles of Bols orange-bitter. The contents of a bottle made even a night drive in a snowstorm more tolerable.

I did not get much rest or sleep. Because of my good sense of direction I was ordered ever more often to undertake supply runs to the forward lines and bring back the wounded. I would usually have a co-driver, but there would still be only two of us and we always had to be alert to the possibility of Russian scouting parties or groups of stragglers. That happened several times, but because we kept our eyes open I got us through each time by accelerating fast with determination. At night we had to rely on luck. If the front line was desperately short of men we would occasionally have to do a watch as simple infantrymen.

I lay pressed hard to the ground, close above me bullets hissed unceasingly. When I cautiously raised my head I saw behind the glittering surface the dark confusion of tree tops swept bare of snow by the wind, and the roofs of the low dwellings between which the Russians had set up their positions. Only the camber of the field behind which they were hidden protected me from the fire of their MGs.

132

At the moment when we had reached the top of the low crest and the silhouettes of the farm cottages and trees appeared before us, a massive and withering fire had overwhelmed us. Two men to the right of me fell dead at once, one of them was Ullrich from my company, carrying an MG and whom I had accompanied with two ammunition boxes; I did not know the other. Before it had a chance to fire, the Panzer IV close by received a direct hit. It stopped abruptly, there was an explosion and then bright flames licked out from its hull. Nobody got out.

Another tank which had advanced farther to my left went at once into reverse and withdrew with howling motor into the cover of the depression. I saw that I was alone and I felt abandoned and fearful. After pulling myself together, I crawled to Ullrich's body to retrieve the MG and one of the ammunition boxes, then I crept back to the others in the nearest safe refuge. Our improvised attack had come to nothing.

The disaster began as a rash reaction to an alarm situation. Towards midday a motorcycle despatch rider from Battalion HQ arrived at the small village in which our Tross had set up. His orders stated that every available man with all weapons to hand were to follow him to join the fighting reserves of our battalion at a high state of alert. It appeared that a strong Soviet force had outflanked our company and positioned itself in its rear.

The whole battalion had meanwhile received instructions to pull back to new positions in the rear because of the threat by a numerically superior enemy to its unprotected flanks. The other companies had already begun to disengage from the enemy. No. 9, which had to defend itself against constant frontal attacks, was therefore in an extremely dangerous situation.

In a very short time twelve men of the fighting Tross had assembled with carbines, two MGs, a number of ammunition boxes and hand grenades and followed the despatch rider in two MTWs. Ullrich carried one of the MGs. He was a SS-Lance Corporal from the old permanent staff of No. 9 Company; I was his 'team' with two ammunition boxes and a replacement MG barrel. After less than two kilometres we came to a shallow valley. Here there were two Panzer

IVs and a hastily-assembled group from the battalion reserve. The troop was forty-five strong with four light MGs. A young SS-2nd Lieutenant apparently straight from Junker school was attempting to bring some order to the troop, which had divided up automatically into its individual units. It was difficult to decide how the problem was going to be approached, since we knew next to nothing about it: nothing about where the enemy had established himself between ourselves and No. 9 Company, nor about his strength and armament. It was obvious that we had to act, and do so without long consideration if we were not to be bottled up together with the rest of the company without any prospect of salvation.

'Therefore, there's nothing like attacking!' an SS-Staff Sergeant from Battalion said, and everybody got into open formation and moved off, Ullrich with the MG leading, I was following a few paces behind. We advanced two hundred metres tense and ready without coming under fire. Then, at the top of the ridge, we were subjected suddenly and with devastating effect to massive fire.

Upon assembling in the valley we counted five men short: three wounded had been brought out; these were loaded into a field ambulance and taken off to the rear.

Our first attack had proved a catastrophe, but it had also yielded two important items of information: we knew now where the enemy was, and that he was stronger, apparently better armed and had plenty more ammunition than we expected. Moreover we had received reinforcements: another panzer had arrived, which was an important factor given our numerical inferiority and the unfavourable attacking situation.

The experienced SS-Staff Sergeant had quickly made the right course of action sound plausible to the young SS-2nd Lieutenant: a new frontal attack bore no prospect of success; we should divide into two fighting squads each supported by one panzer; in a wide arc either side of them we should go around the Red Army men located amongst the cottages and then attack them in a pincer movement from north and south.

With our lack of numbers we would be operating without contact between the two squads against all rules of tactics, a considerable

134

risk, but one in circumstances unavoidable. The SS-2nd Lieutenant took command of North Squad, which had cover for a good part of its advance. I belonged to South Squad led by the SS-Staff Sergeant and had been appointed No. 1 MG gunner for the fallen Ullrich; Reimers, who had come up on the last supply run, was my ammunition carrier. Kolb, the fighting Tross's armourer, carried a second MG. We had to take the longer way around a low hill, which would conceal us until we reached the knoll and the slope descending to the Soviet position.

Our eighteen-man squad covered the first stretch, over 600 metres long, in a loose file, hidden from Ivan's sight, then made a quarter-turn left: on the treeless, wide, snow-covered ground, glittering in the sun, our lonely band must have looked lost rather than threatening. The tank held back cautiously. After the violent end suffered by the other one this was not only understandable, but even without discussing it with the panzer commander it seemed sensible and desirable: the panzer was decisive for the success of our operation and therefore irreplaceable. We, the infantry, had to ascertain what awaited us behind the knoll; whether, where and how Ivan had posted protection on his flanks and above all what anti-tank weapons he had. Then we would have to wipe out the protection as quick as possible and attack the main Russian position under the covering fire of the panzer's cannon and MGs. We could only hope that there would be some cover for us on the downhill slope.

We reached the flat knoll, SS-Corporal Kolb and I took the lead with the two MGs. Doubled low and creeping over the last few metres we obtained a view over the terrain. The group of cottages was closer than we had expected, at most about 150 metres. On the slope leading down were some bare trees, wooden fencing and a couple of bushes. I saw light smoke rising from behind a spindly bush – probably somebody smoking machorka – and after studying the scene we counted four Ivans with a plump, antiquated Russian heavy MG, its barrel fitted with a water-cooling jacket and resting on a small chassis with wooden wheels. This type of gun was so heavy that it required two men to move it.

The eight or so cottages and the trees surrounding them in the otherwise bare landscape formed a flat ellipse, about 100 metres east of them we could see a lightly curved elliptical gully, a deep incision into the terrain. The four Ivans with the MG were obviously not expecting trouble. All their attention was concentrated on the upwelling of violent fighting on the far side of the cottages where North Squad, which had a shorter approach, had gone straight into the attack.

Our ammunition runners came up with the boxes: Kolb and I loaded in the belts and cocked the MGs. Kolb gave me a low whistle and pointed to the cottages, then turned to his left and raised his right arm with clenched fist upwards three times, the sign for our squad and the panzer to take up position quickly on the knoll. Immediately afterwards we opened fire. Kolb shot the four MG sentries while I combed short bursts into the Soviet main position starting from the edge of the hamlet. Kolb turned his MG on the cottages while the panzer, which had meanwhile taken up a good firing position, opened up with its quick-firing gun and two MGs. The remainder of our squad rained down fire from carbines and machine pistols. It was an impressive display of firepower.

It came as a surprise for us not to receive defensive fire. It was soon clear why. The Russians had panicked, swarming out of the cottages and making for the protection of the gully. To get there they had to cross open country, all 200 or so of them, running for their lives under a hail of bullets. I aimed my MG and fired without any reflection or thought, filled with a killing rage, which was totally foreign to me, against these Russians who had killed Ullrich and the others and tried to kill me. After I had exhausted my remaining supply of ammunition from the single box I had with me I realised that I had fired on – at that time unarmed – fleeing soldiers, and I was overcome by a sobering sense of shame and the knowledge that it was a reaction to the overly tense situation and my own fear of dying. I had experienced that strange thing, the personal 'state of emergency', which the First World War frontline veteran Ernst Jünger declared to be the sublimation of the experience of blood, battle and horror, for which he employed the term 'heroic nihilism':

136

less intellectually gifted authors speak of the 'mythical rage of the berserker' and *Furor Teutonicus,* or merely content themselves with the word 'bloodlust'. Whatever it was it affected me deeply. It was a new experience for me, and one which I never repeated.

Once the main group of the Russians had reached the gully, seventy of them were left lying in the open ground. The survivors took up a position in the gully: for the first time we observed that it had been defended by Ivan from the outset and that he had been firing at us: we had a re-count and decided there must be more than 150 of them holed up there. By virtue of the increasing fire coming from their new position, and the uncertainty what anti-tank weaponry they had in there, we withdrew behind the knoll. We were relieved to discover that we had achieved our considerable success without loss. This was doubtless due to the almost incredible coincidence that North Squad had attacked the Russians and distracted all of them at precisely the moment when we were ready to fire. The enemy must have expected a well-planned concentric action by a strong German force. What we had achieved with our risky ploy was not logical.

The business was not at an end, however. The force established in the gully was about four times the number of our two squads combined: they were well armed and had plenty of ammunition although they used it wastefully. Our South Squad held a short council of war, which decided it was best to repeat our proven method. This meant that we would circumvent the gully under the protection of the high ground between us and it and then turn in from the side, if possible at an oblique angle from the rear.

Three things had to be borne in mind: time was pressing, for the winter sun was close to setting in the west; North Squad, which we could make out clearly from the knoll, had no chance of getting to the gully from the north because of the open country they would need to cross, and thirdly we did not know the nature of the gully the Russians would be defending.

We had no choice but to set out in the way we had done so often in field exercises and see what happened. After a short while we reached a point where from the eastern slope of the hill we could see down into the gully from a distance of about 200 metres. It was a boot-shaped depression about 100 metres long and 20 broad on a north-south axis. The Russians were grouped thickly at the edges of its western side where it curved sharply. They were engaged in firing with all barrels at North Squad, which had meanwhile occupied the cottages: they were returning fire but we could not see it, or in any case not its effects.

The chances of North Squad achieving anything were slim and in the next few seconds disappeared altogether, for while we were surveying the situation there occurred a clear, violent explosion, and immediately afterwards the tank accompanying North Squad stationed between two cottages burst into flames. Kolb and I, watching prostrate, quickly saw the cause. At the centre of the long row of Russians we saw a man with a weapon which I had only heard spoken of and was called a 'Panzerbüchse': it had a two-metre long barrel, supported towards the muzzle on a bipod stand, which fired anti-tank projectiles of about 30mm calibre with high muzzle velocity and great penetrative power. Our Panzer IVs treated them correspondingly with respect.

We also saw something which imbued us with new courage. The ground between ourselves and the gully was as flat as a table top but covered with gaunt maize shrubs the height of a man, a phenomenal stroke of luck for us. Our own tank stood hidden by the slope. After a short talk with its commander, whom we informed about the Panzerbüchse, we set off through the withered vegetation.

At the edge of the field of maize we looked over the ghastly arena: 50 metres away and lying a few metres deeper than our own position, was the gully from where the Russians were firing incessantly. In front of it the white field with the seventy Russian corpses, farther on the cottages sheltering North Squad and their smouldering panzer. Dusk was falling and we had only minutes left. Our panzer moved through the shrubbery into position with great circumspection. In order that it should not be noticed by the Russians, the panzer commander did not use the main gun but began firing with his two MGs. The Russians could not hear the rattle of the MGs because of the racket they were making

138

themselves. The first of them to come into the crosshairs was the gunner operating the dangerous Panzerbüchse who slumped down suddenly, the barrel of his weapon now aimed to the pale heavens. Then with careful and deadly precision the panzer gunners sprayed fire into the long line of Russians from the centre outwards, and then from outwards inwards. We others did not fire, I had no more ammunition for my MG and was really quite happy not to be part of the grisly butchery.

The panzer wiped them all out. It was just a cruel slaughter and had nothing to do with the myth of heroic fighting man against man. Repelled but yet fascinated I watched the bloody theatre, played out according to the ruthless, inescapable barbaric logic of warfare: we or you, you or I! The inferno seemed to have no end, but probably lasted no more than a minute. Then suddenly an almost unnatural silence fell. We went down into the gully. Everywhere warm blood steamed in the cold air. The Russians were all dead, the panzer men had done their work well.

I went to the dead Panzerbüchse gunner to have a look at the weapon with which he had destroyed two of our panzers and their crews. It had a kind of telescopic sight so as to pick out vulnerable spots in the armour: the man, a young, powerful soldier apparently knew his trade. He must have enjoyed a preferential position in his platoon for he lay between two political commissars, the red Soviet star on the lapel of their greatcoats. I took the machine pistol from the slack hand of one of them and hung it over my shoulder, then drew my 08 and set out to scout the fissured rear area of the gully. I found a cleft running at a right angle and had followed the path a few metres upwards when suddenly out of nowhere a figure arose in front of me.

Instinctively I raised my pistol and shouted *Ruki vyersh!* (hands up!). Before me stood a young Russian, no older than myself who looked at me with wide eyes full of fear and raised his arms.

What happened next I experienced in a split second yet like a film in slow motion: before I could say anything else a shot rang out from behind me: I saw the trace of hope in the eyes of the Russian fade in unbelieving horror and then he collapsed.

139

In a fury I turned round to see Reimer, his carbine still at the ready. 'You absolute idiot,' I shouted at him, 'Was that necessary?'

In his eyes I saw bewilderment and dismay. He seemed to be searching for words; finally he came out helplessly with: 'I didn't mean to!' Deep within me I realised that I believed him, this young man experiencing for the first time the horror of war.

I turned and continued along the path for another twenty steps, and then a deafening report threw me forward and all went dark. 'So that's it, then,' was the first thing that occurred to me, but then I noticed that I was continuing to think and could move my limbs. I had no pain. As everything was still black when I opened my eyes I touched my head and felt my steel helmet covering the upper half of my face. I took it off and found that the machine pistol I had taken from the dead commissar and had been wearing by its strap over my shoulder had been loaded and cocked. Somehow the trigger had become entangled with the MG which was also hanging around my neck: the machine pistol fired, the round hit the rim of my helmet at the rear, forcing it forward and throwing me to the ground. I had been very lucky: the round had travelled along the inside of the helmet and exited at the upper curve: it could equally as easily have been deflected to hit my face.

I checked myself over and went back to the others. As a squad we returned to the point from where our operation had begun, passing the many dead Russians and our twenty comrades who had attempted to make a frontal attack on the group of cottages and had fallen before reaching them. The wrecked tank was still smouldering, several metres farther on lay five or six more dead and the young SS-2nd Lieutenant with a round hole stamped through the centre of his forehead. It was not bleeding: the Russian Panzerbüchse gunner had been a first-class sniper in life.

The return did not take us long, the direct route to the vehicles was less than a kilometre. After we had assembled we established that from No. 9 Company Ullrich and another man were missing. We ten survivors got into our two MTWs and drove at top speed to the fighting Tross where the rest of the team were waiting for us anxiously. At once we heated up the other vehicles to leave. As Ullrich had fallen and another driver had to take over his vehicle, we poured benzene over a Kfz 69 with a damaged front axle and set it alight.

A messenger from battalion brought us orders to bring out our fighting unit from near the cottages west of the gully. When our surviving five MTW's arrived there, night had already fallen. Soon after we received our frontline men, who had managed only with difficulty to disengage from the enemy's persistent attacks and get clear under cover of darkness. In the morning the head count, including the reinforcements which had come up a few days before, came to thirty-six men. We had drawn up the vehicles in a semicircle and by the light of their headlamps we counted thirty-eight exhausted men, amongst them eight not from No. 9 Company but apparently stragglers from our neighbouring No. 8 Company. We worked out that our Kfz 69s could take thirty-five men if they all sat pressed together as closely as possible.

The platoons climbed into the vehicles. Only now did I notice that amongst those I had assumed to be stragglers were two men who stood isolated in the midst of the others: Russian prisoners, awaiting their destiny with bowed heads and sunken shoulders. The stragglers were shared out amongst the MTW's: two of our own, an SS-Corporal from 8.Company and SS-Corporal Hübner from our second platoon waited by the Russians on the illuminated white trampled ground. Nobody spoke, fresh snow had begun to drizzle down in the silence.

'We can't take them with us,' Hübner said finally.

'One can lie along my right mudguard,' I offered.

'The other can ride on mine!' Grulich called out from the vehicle alongside me.

Seconds went by. Then suddenly Hübner's machine pistol rattled: the two Russians sank down without a sound. Hübner broke out into shrill, hysterical laughter and slung his weapon around his shoulders.

The No. 8 Company SS-Corporal looked at Hübner, spat and said, 'You miserable lousy swine.' Hübner went over to his platoon and the No. 8 Company SS-Corporal found himself somewhere else to sit. Then we drove off.

The strain of this new kind of warfare told on us all. It was the feeling of being exposed to events, of not being able to dictate them in the fluid situation, but having to play the role of the underdog: instead of exercising some control over them, we were increasingly only reacting to them with a growing risk and questionable success, and this preyed noticeably on our morale. The self-confidence of the men gave way ever more to a doubt in the myth of their superior fighting power and tactics, the backbone of their self-belief. As was the case with all other German combat divisions, Leibstandarte *Adolf Hitler* was reeling, and as in every military unit in which the attacking spirit is transformed into one of delaying defence, this has consequences: the élan of the Wehrmacht was broken, and in the Soviet Army the inferiority complex which had crippled it for fourteen months vanished, to be replaced by the knowledge that the Soviets were on their way to victory – and before us the spectre of defeat loomed ever more threateningly.

Amongst all the other problems we lacked sleep. The constant changes of location forced on us by the fluid situation meant that we grabbed two hours' rest at a pinch; because of the numerous special operations I had to carry out with the MTW I was affected more than most.

For almost all my four years as a soldier, with the exception of the weeks which I spent on leave or at a military hospital, those moments were the worst when I was awoken suddenly to fresh awareness of the bleak reality in which I found myself. The best case would be the roar of the Duty NCO in a dormitory; the worst a sudden artillery barrage or the loud cry of a frontline comrade in an alarm situation. No nightmare can be more depressing than that of awakening into a reality which has horror, deprivation and fear of death without end.

In those chaotic March days of 1943 I only ever got two or three hours sleep per day. In the deep snow, the motorcycle despatch riders, even those with a sidecar and differential drive of both rear wheels, often could not get through; the most serviceable and reliable vehicle, the only one to be considered for important missions, was the company commander's Kfz 15, a Horch jeep-like vehicle with a V-8 motor, which had the necessary turning moment and a robust four-wheel independent drive. It was difficult to drive because in order to avoid heavy vibrations on the gear housing caused by the powerful motor it did not have synchronised manual transmission. To change gear the driver had to double de-clutch, i.e. shift transmission to neutral, press the gas pedal to obtain exactly the correct rpms, then move into the chosen gear, depressing the clutch each change. It had to be done very fast, for during the procedure the vehicle would have practically no power and could stick in mud or snow within seconds. If that happened, the procedure to restart was much more complicated. If it was not handled with the necessary skill, the gear mechanism would protest with an awful grinding noise, if it reacted at all.

SS-Lance Corporal Schubert was the official driver of the Kfz 15 and its only authorised driver. When he reported sick with a light wound, aspirants were called for very hastily to replace him. On my test I got the de-clutching business right at the first attempt and was offered the job. Within a short while I had perfected the difficult gear change by not releasing the clutch and using only the gear lever and gas pedal lightning fast during the gear change. This piece of artistry brought me some plus points, especially from SS-Corporal Danninger. I had previously been in his good books and his goodwill, which developed later into a true friendship, was to be of great importance in my military career.

My first run with the Horch was almost my last. I had to take a seriously wounded man to the regimental dressing station, my co-driver was Grulich. The journey there went off without a hitch, but on the way back we got lost in the dark and a violent blizzard. After hours of searching for the marker posts on the snow-covered road we found a lonely farmhouse. An elderly woman invited us in and provided us with a mug of hot tea, then dog-tired we stretched out on the floor and fell asleep at once. I felt that hardly an hour had passed when I awoke from my leaden sleep to find our hostess tugging at my arm with both hands. She shouted at me loudly: '*Pan! Pan! Bistra! Bistra! Russki soldatt!*' (Sir! sir! Quick! quick! Russian soldiers!). Grulich was also awake, and we raced to our vehicle. The night was now clear, and over the bright snowy surface we could see at a dangerously short distance a number of figures stamping towards us. The Horch started up straight away and I drove off without lights until out of danger. Sometime during the night we reached our Tross.

I had a far worse experience a few days later. We had to re-establish contact with our neighbouring No. 8 Company to our left: I drove northwards cautiously with four up, all with weapons at the ready, the weather was misty. In a depression we came across six corpses lying together in the blood-soaked snow. We drove up and dismounted. The corpses were Waffen-SS, bestially mutilated. Their eyes had been extracted, ears slit away and sexual organs cut off and crammed in their mouths. We could see from the gigantic pool of blood in which the corpses lay that they had slowly bled to death.

The war in Russia was not a 'humane' war. From the outset the Red Army conducted it with the brutal harshness characterising Bolshevism in the Soviet Union, which had previously sacrificed many millions of its own citizens. The Soviet Union was the only major nation not to have signed the Geneva Convention, and in war it acted accordingly: medical personnel of all grades and ambulances bearing the Red Cross on a white background were a priority target for the Red Army. This led to medical staff no longer wearing Red Cross armbands and the emblem on ambulances being sprayed over with camouflage paint. The pitiless manner in which the Soviet Army fought promoted the crusader ideal of the Waffen-SS in exactly the sense that Reichsführer Himmler had planned it. The experiences in war and the flow of volunteers from European countries, however, frustrated its instrumentalisation. The composition of the Waffen-SS was multi-layered and international: in the thirty-eight Waffen-SS divisions Austrians, Sudeten Germans, around 500,000 Germans and 350,000 Scandinavians, Dutch, French and Belgians served.

In addition between 300,000 and 410,000[15] Volksdeutsche from Romania went into the making of the *Prinz Eugen* division and a series of 'foreign racial' Waffen-SS divisions: two Latvian, one Estonian, the Hungarian divisions *Maria Theresia* and *Hunyadi*, one

Slovenian, the Ukrainian-Galician and the Russian division *Rona*, also exotic units such as the Croatian *Handschar* and *Kama*, most of whose volunteers were Muslim. In the last months of the war there were even minor SS units from White Russia, Bohemia-Moravia and Italy.

Not until recently has the subject of the Waffen-SS been treated with more objectivity. Of particular note are observations by the historian Bernd Wegner[16], which I quote here:

What [. . .] Himmler's concept of an Order [. . .] threw into sharp relief was on the one hand its fanatical biocentric character combined with an imperialist aim, and on the other hand the considerable degree of its organisational realisation.

Even though concrete historical examples of the SS Order remain unrecognised, or at least are not examples *per se* argued dogmatically, partially valid historical examples have been used, stripped of their historical context in individual elements to fit the bill, and given a new meaning corresponding to the needs and interests of the SS model!

This is most clearly shown by the 'unofficial' models such as the Jesuit Order. This example is on the one hand stylized as the proto-typical incarnation of the clerical arch-enemy to the 'Nordic-Germanic' way of thinking, yet it is proposed repeatedly as the source influencing Himmler's own understanding of the SS as a 'counter-Order'. Of course, the apparent contradiction is easily resolved: Precisely because the *Societas Jesu* as regards its hierarchical structure, its function as an avant-garde body with a new world view and its principle requiring the individual's total submission to the Order was so exemplary, supposedly it won in the eyes of the SS a degree of dangerousness necessarily forbidden to bourgeois-liberal organisations.

The official model for the SS-Order was the Order of the Teutonic Knights of St Mary's Hospital Jerusalem.[. . .] This was the ideal model for the SS resulting not only, as in the case of the Jesuits, from the inner structure of the community, its ideas of virtue and concept of service, but beyond all that it suited the National Socialist concept of a 'political soldiery' [. . .].

145

Above all, however, the recognition of the Teutonic Knights as a model had its connection the process of colonizing the East. This seems to be the plausible point of co-incidence for the reconstruction of historical continuity avoiding the need for the transposition of historical ideas.

At first sight the extent of the resistance to be found amongst the 'Germanic race' Waffen-SS volunteers may come as a shock. B. de Wever gave an example of the Flemish volunteers. In this case, the political differences between the 'Greater Germany' politics of the SS Main Office and the nationalist-oriented Flemish National Confederation (VNV) led to a real opposition movement, which found its most spectacular expression in November 1943 when hundreds of volunteers refused to swear the SS oath of loyalty to the Führer; similar events had occurred in the months before amongst the Dutch volunteers. The journalist L. Reichlin is another author to have used the experiences of individual volunteers of the 800 to 900 men recruited from Switzerland to demonstrate the motives and expectations of Western European volunteers to the Waffen-SS. This was a theme long taboo in Switzerland. That the subject of research into national minorities in the Waffen-SS is making only slow progress is not surprising due principally to the traumatic experiences which the countries involved had during the war and occupation involving the stigma of collaboration: political persecution after the war also caused psychological and political blocks to form, which may only be finally pulled down in the fullness of time.

Bernd Wegner concludes that

> . . . as a result of the academic and philosophic puzzlement still surrounding the Third Reich, an analysis of the Waffen-SS in the Germany of today would probably identify it to a considerably greater extent than previously as a bizarre product, treating the stubborn enduring myth of the elite troop enclosed within itself *ad absurdum* and concentrating on the theme of the nationalist, professional and ideological angles of the extraordinarily heterogeneous nature of the Waffen-SS.

146

What united the Waffen-SS to a great extent was the common motive of uncompromising struggle against Bolshevism. The manner in which the Wehrmacht conducted itself in many cases can also be judged in this light. In general National Socialism is seen as the more criminal of the two systems on account of its motivation and results. However, the question of whether Communism or Nazism was the worse evil can only be decided on the basis of individual experiences and characteristic features. Thus the Nobel Prize winner Alexander Solzhenitsyn answered the question based on his personal experience in his book *Gulag Archipelago*:

> These people who had had physically experienced twenty-four years of Communist good fortune already knew in 1941 what nobody else in the world knew: that on the entire planet and in all of history there was no more malignant, bloodthirsty and at the same time refined regime than the Bolshevik one, which called itself 'Soviet': and that no other regime equalled it either in eagerness to exterminate nor in inertia, nor in radical objectivity; nor in dyed-in-the-wool 'unified totalitarianism'.

The kind of warfare which developed after the recapture of Kharkov, increasingly disagreeable to us all, went on for a few weeks. Then at the end of March 1943 – the fighting strength of No. 9 Company was twenty-two men – we were relieved by fresh reserves and withdrawn from the front. They allocated us quarters in farmhouses at Olshany, about 30 kilometres west of Kharkov, in order to be 'refreshed' for coming operations.

The replacements which were supposed to bring the unit back up to fighting strength were composed partly of young volunteers, some of whom had been transferred in to us from Göring's shrinking Luftwaffe: understandably they showed no great enthusiasm but then settled in well. In a military unit one quickly learns that for better or worse you rely on each other: a squad, a platoon, a company are communities thrown together by fate, provide a feeling of solidarity and through it a kind of home from home.

147

Naturally the usual chicanery started up promptly again at Olshany in order that the 'new boys' should appreciate to what noble unit they now belonged. As I had now been with the Leibstandarte long enough to be considered a member of the permanent staff I was spared the worst, but a special drudgery had been devised for us drivers: the vehicles had to be brought to a condition of 'fitness for parade'. In practice this meant that not only all visible parts, but also the engine area, the underside and the wheel boxes had to be cleaned to the most pernickety standard. At the beginning of April, still bitter cold, we lay all day in snow and ice under the vehicle cleaning all corners and angles with a tooth-brush. At roll-call the harness master or the Spiess would then investigate the screw threads with a sharpened matchstick: the slightest speck of dirt meant punishment guard duty and show parades until no further excuse for more chicanery could be found.

We agreed the usual arrangement with the owners of the houses forced to accept us as lodgers: they slept around the large oven and we had the floor of compacted earth. If we could get straw we spread our blankets on it at night, during the day it was heaped in a corner. On the whole, this two-month stay at Olshany was a good time for us. The weather gradually warmed up during April and the sun shone, after the conclusion of all roll calls our duties were tolerable, the rations sufficient; if there was lentil soup I used to have two mess tins full, each containing a litre and a half; my other favourites were rice pudding or noodles with dried fruit. My mother sent me some aspirin tablets, which now and again the Russian farmers' wives would accept them for eggs in barter, the going rate was one tablet per egg.

Quite unexpectedly I received three weeks' home leave in June, long overdue: Spiess Nieweck had held it back from all those who showed an aversion to his primitive stables stink. After twenty-one months twice on the Eastern Front and in France, I was a relatively free man for twenty-one days. My leave began with an endlessly long journey through the Ukraine and Poland in a wooden-seat train of the Deutsche Reichsbahn. To sleep I put together a construction with my gas mask and haversack webbing hanging from the luggage rack to support my arms as a rest for my head. At Brest-Litovsk we had to go through a giant delousing establishment and were then given a packet of eats, which all leave-takers had been looking forward to.

After forty or more hours clanking across Eastern Europe the train arrived at Berlin Zoo station where I had to change for Aachen. I felt I was dreaming, and stared at the girls in their summer dresses on the station platforms as though they were beings from another planet.

At home what awaited me was the long-desired luxury of a proper bed, mealtimes by the clock, liquor put by for me and my books, which I spent the greater part of my time reading. I visited friends and relatives and everybody eyed me in my Waffen-SS uniform as if I were an exotic figure of fable, so many adventurous legends being apparently associated with it. The general mood had changed markedly. After the victorious Western campaign in 1940, many from Eupen-Malmedy had been hoping for a peace under the motto 'Home into the Reich' by which the province would finally separate from Belgium and be reincorporated into Germany. My Belgian compatriots – insofar that they had not renounced Belgian nationality in 1920 in favour of starving Germany – had taken this pragmatic route since they could see the advantage that, however things turned out, they would belong to the victors, a very compelling strategy. However, the disaster at Stalingrad several months earlier had now engendered an atmosphere of cautious reserve in the border area, and I felt increasingly isolated.

Amongst the few letters my parents had kept for me was one from the Reichsbahn management at Cologne: they were requesting to have the negatives of my photographs at Hammerbrücke bridge near Hergenrath after it was blown up in 1940. I got through to the sender by telephone and discussed it with him; I went to Cologne in civilian clothes, which was expressly permitted by my leave pass.

It was a cool day and I wore my rust-coloured coat, rather odd to German eyes and which I had bought a few years before in Antwerp. On the return journey to Aachen I had a window seat, and the train was almost empty. When it stopped at Düren, I saw two men dressed in overcoat and hat on the almost empty platform. They got into my coach. Suddenly one sat beside me, the other faced me. I felt something hard pressing against my ribs and one of them said, 'Don't attract attention! Your papers please!'

I took out my identity/paybook and leave pass from my breast pocket and handed them over. The gentlemen stared in surprise, one said questioningly in a loud voice: 'Leibstandarte?'

'Got something against them, have you?' I replied drily.

Then the tension relaxed. Apparently when I boarded the train at Cologne a railway official thought I looked suspicious, after all, didn't British spies in the Ufa films look like that? He had informed the Gestapo and here we all were. The two gentlemen apologised and left, much to my amusement.

My leave passed quickly. I made the journey back in the company of an LAH man from 2nd Regiment who came from Eupen. I fell in with him by chance at the beginning of the journey. He survived the war, but upon his return to his home town he became the subject of persecution there.

When I arrived at Kharkov I noticed that the area around the railway station looked unusually empty, and then I saw that it was cordoned off by a chain of uniformed men in field-grey. Some of those leaving the train were intercepted and led off into a compound. I knew that this was done if they wanted to quickly throw together a unit for some kind of dangerous activity, they called the action 'Heldenklau' – 'stealing heroes'. I crept under the train to the other side and stole across the tracks into the open grounds. Later I heard that they were looking for SS men as permanent staff to set up the new Hitlerjugend Division.

When I rejoined my company and had that 'back home again' feeling I discovered there had been some changes which pleased me and – as it turned out later – were to be of great importance. The loathsome Spiess Nieweck had been relieved and replaced by Danninger, promoted to SS-Staff Sergeant. Chief driver Schubert was in the military hospital with a serious infection and so Danninger, favourably disposed to me, appointed me Schubert's successor. This meant that not only did I get the coveted Horch V 8, on operations I was also leader of the Kfz fighting Tross. In rank I remained SS-Private, therefore a private soldier, but exercised my function as an acting NCO. I had not had to attend an NCO's course or Officers' school but could enjoy some advantages of being an NCO. I was attached to Company HQ and no longer had to do guard duty, and nobody could make me do fifty knee bends or push ups on a whim.

There had been another important change. A new Company commander had arrived: SS-1st Lieutenant Breuer, who proved to be a man of the best type – a model officer who had the men's interests at heart, was educated, easily satisfied and modest: he cleaned his own equipment and clothing himself and therefore had no need of a valet. As his driver I was constantly closer to him than all the others. I soon gained his confidence and he had my boundless respect.

I did not have much time to enjoy my new situation, however. After a few days the alarm and operational orders poured in for the attack on the Kursk Bend known as Operation 'Citadel'. The company was now in for difficult days with the heaviest fighting and losses.

Chapter Six

The Battles of Kursk and Belgorod

W e had all grown to like Olshany. Our company was quartered in about twenty houses in a suburb of the town. As usual we agreed amicably with the owners on the arrangements and slept on the earth floor. As a member of Company HQ I had now more space than in a room with an MG squad which was three or four men larger.

I soon found my feet as the leader of the fighting vehicle Tross for initially few demands were made of me. My real responsibilities did not begin until the advance, when the pool of MTWs had to be as close as possible to the frontline and held ready at all times for the company's operational movements. In the case of rapid movements I was responsible for finding the route in the leading vehicle.

Within the sensitive hierarchy of the Tross the change was bound to cause minor irritations. Grulich and Kiehn had longer service with the company than I and as SS-Lance Corporals had higher rank. Nevertheless, no problems arose with them and they recognised my special status straight away. If I ever had to give them instructions I disguised them as comradely wishes. To my new company commander, Breuer, I was as attentive and conscious of my duties as he could desire, and happily I had practically no further contact with the corporals in the platoons. For all cases I had Spiess Fred Danninger to watch my back, if ever called for he would smooth out more difficult situations with his direct Tyrolean charm.

In the last days of June an unpleasant disquiet blew like a raw steppe wind through the idyllic Russian summer with its constant sunshine. Weapons, equipment and vehicle inspections followed quickly one after another, lorries from the Battalion Tross came rolling in heavily laden with ammunition and fuel, and in general everybody grew tense and nervous. Soon it became unmistakable: our comfortable stay in the tranquil Ukrainian town, where we had almost forgotten that there was a war on, was over.

When the hour came to pull out, the calmness of SS-1st Lieutenant Breuer transformed the usual uproar into smooth routine, and when he gave the signal to move out, I was inwardly very glad to be sitting alongside him in the leading vehicle and not with an MG or mount in one of the MTW's. All the same, we all knew that we were not going to just roll forward joyfully to another victory: we were heading into a bitter struggle, which would cost many of us our lives.

For three years the Wehrmacht had achieved great military successes with the strategy and tactics of mobile warfare. The commanders felt along the enemy front for weak spots, penetrated these with fast panzer groups, which raced into the enemy's rear to cut his lines of supply and then destroyed him within great encirclements. These new methods of strategic warfare had inflicted huge losses on the Soviet Army in the opening months of the campaign. Their casualties were made worse by using the First World War strategy of massed forces defending to the last bullet, or going forward to attack the German guns in massed waves, where they bled to death in front of them.

At Stalingrad the Red Army succeeded for the first time by using the German method. With strong forces attacking from north and south of the city they overran the positions of the inadequately-equipped Italians and Romanians, only weakly motivated for self-sacrifice, and then closed the pocket with a large-scale pincer operation. The Sixth Army, 250,000 strong at the end of December 1942 and prevented by Hitler from breaking out while they still had the chance, soon found itself without supplies of weapons, ammunition, food and medical supplies and was forced to capitulate at the end of January 1943, reduced to 90,000 exhausted and starving survivors. After the war in the Soviet zone of Germany, without any intention of irony, they used to say, 'To the Soviet Union, learning means learning to win!'

The campaign in the East developed into a war with the roles exchanged. Hitler boasted: 'Where the German soldier stands, he stands, and no power on Earth can remove him from there!' which showed that mentally he was speaking from his infantry trench of 1916. Endowed by propaganda with the euphemistic attribute 'Greatest Warlord of all Time'[1], in 1941 this First World War PFC sent the Wehrmacht, totally inadequately equipped, into war against the USSR. After the victories of the first months it soon proved that the leadership was neither capable of guaranteeing supplies nor of controlling more than a fraction of that gigantic region, which stretched to the shores of the Pacific.

At the time of Stalingrad and after, Hitler and his obedient minions at Führer-HQ clung on to every square metre of Russian soil in bloody retreats. By doing so they sacrificed the real assets of the German Army, the men's trust in the leadership, their self-confidence and their belief in getting off lightly when the catastrophic adventure came to its end. In the end, German soldiers were fighting desperately to keep the Red Army, which had shown the most brutal cruelty to the prisoners it took from many units, as far as possible from Germany and their families, and they knew that a miracle was needed to achieve this.

In order to give full measure from the cup of self-destructive madness, the German leadership now did exactly what every experience of this campaign indicated it should not do. It decided to go ahead with Operation 'Citadel', throwing almost all the still-intact divisions and heavy weapons against the strongest defences on the Soviet front, at the salient around the city of Kursk where the Soviets had established a fortress with a radius of fifty kilometres.[2]

Under the protection of the short night I had driven twice to the foremost front line where the platoons were receiving the heaviest fire. The day before, supported by Tigers, SP guns and Stukas, against bitter resistance they had broken through two well-developed trench systems. We brought back eight dead and eleven seriously wounded. Grulich and another driver helped out with their Kfz 69s. Walking wounded had to find their own way to the battalion dressing station.

The fighting Tross had found cover in a broad, flat depression with trees and bushes common in the region around Belgorod and similar to typical Russian gullies. As a safe place to keep the vehicles it was too small: we were exposed to air attack and they were parked too close together. Of the wounded, five with the worst wounds were brought out from the depression by ambulance, the other six had to stay back because Russian fighter bombers appeared at daybreak and attacked any vehicle moving in open country. As we had no anti-aircraft guns, for defence against enemy aircraft Grulich and I set up an MG on a tripod in a field ten metres from the wooded edge of the depression.

Paramedic Rist had treated the remaining wounded as best he could, and we laid them on blankets near my Kfz 15. To give them better protection we started to dig slit trenches; this did not proceed rapidly because the ground was stony and had many tree roots below the surface. After we had been digging out the slit trench for a good two hours, Soviet fighter bombers arrived. Three of the them circled the area in vain in search of prey for some time, and then decided to attack a wooded gulley about 400 metres away. They did some dive bombing on it, cannons chattering, then came a few dull explosions. Two dark clouds of smoke rose up from the woodland.

Suddenly they left what they were doing and headed for us at top speed. We threw ourselves to the ground as the rounds from their cannons swished above us. The first attack lasted only a matter of seconds: an MTW of the third platoon was burning, two of our wounded were hit, one had a shell splinter in the upper thigh, the other took a round in the stomach and bled to death quickly.

In a rage and without any further thought I ran to our MG. Knowing that the fighter bomber had an armoured underbelly and was almost invulnerable to my MG, I waited until one of the machines came within range and showed me his side fuselage as he banked: then I fired. The first burst was good, forcing the pilot to climb rapidly and turn away. I tried to fire a second burst after him but the MG jammed. I removed the hot barrel from the jacket and ran with it to my vehicle at the edge of the gully to fetch a replacement. As I reached my Kfz 15 a few seconds later, I heard the howl of aircraft motors approaching again, bursts were fired through the trees and above the ground. During the night I had obtained a

Russian self-loading rifle from the front line and placed it in the support near my driving seat. I grabbed it, instinctively threw myself on my back and fired in quick succession at one of the fighter bombers, which roared above us in an inferno of explosions and firing. At the moment when I landed I felt a light blow to my right hip, but hardly paid it any heed. Suddenly an Me 109 appeared behind the Russian aircraft, firing at it from all barrels. The Russian reared up, trying to gain height, then tipped over at a steep angle and disappeared beyond the horizon in a giant cloud of dense smoke.

When I gathered my senses I became aware of a deafening silence. Something warm and sticky was running down my right leg, and when I felt it and looked at my hand I saw that it was covered with blood. Rist, who was close by, came over straight away and cut away my trousers. He inspected a hole the size of a bean below my right hip joint and then said, 'Not sufficient for a trip home!' Then he applied a dressing after which I tried a few steps. Rist, watched then told me drily. 'Fit for the front, next!'

In their second attack the fighter bombers, apart from some harmless hits on the bodywork of three MTWs, had not done much damage. My wound was too insignificant to make a song and dance about. Therefore I carried on: the numb feeling in my leg went after a couple of hours. I limped a little for several days, then I forgot it. Four months later, however, I was to be reminded of the incident in a dramatic development, which had a decisive influence on my whole life.

When the German armies attacked the Soviet forces in the Kursk Salient on 5 July 1943, a greatly numerically superior enemy was waiting for them in terrain previously prepared with minefields, anti-tank ditches, trench systems, bunkers, hundreds of dug-in tanks and other obstacles – a gigantic trap.

Probably the best-known chronicler of Operation 'Citadel', the Polish historian Janusz Piekalkiewicz,[3] wrote of the enormous preparations by the Red Army:

Meanwhile, the Red Army had finished work on the defensive line at the Kursk Bend. From April to June 1943 along the central front, for example, they had dug out about 5,000 kilometres of infantry and communications trenches and sown around 400,000 mines and explosive devices. Army General Rokossovski: 'In the sector of 13 and 70. Armies, 112 kilometres of barbed-wire entanglements had been planted and more than 170,000 mines laid. The number of automatic weapons and tanks at the Soviet Army front almost doubled from April to June.' Major-General Fomitshenko: 'In the summer of 1943 when our troops prepared to beat off the enemy attack on Kursk, we disguised our positions in masterly fashion: German reconnaissance aircraft, flying over at less than 20 metres altitude, saw only empty fields. In this apparently barren land however whole regiments with artillery, mortars and tanks were hidden.'

What the Germans were throwing against the very well-prepared Red Army was something like a last offensive in a deadly race against time. The enormously increased deliveries of weapons and vehicles from the United States to the Red Army, the collapse of the German-Italian front in North Africa, the heavy U-boat losses in the Battle of the Atlantic and the destruction of German cities by the Anglo-US air forces were shaping the spectre of defeat even faster for the German Reich.

OKW still believed that it was possible to regain superiority in the field with new weapons developments. There was the 72-tonne Sd.Kfz 184 Jagdpanzer 'Ferdinand', equipped with the 6.4-metre long 8.8cm cannon developed originally as a heavy anti-aircraft gun but proving very effective as a multi-purpose weapon. Its armour was up to 200mm thick. The other 'wonder weapon' hoped to prove decisive operationally was the Sd.Kfz 171 Mk V Panther: 45.5 tonnes with a 7.5cm cannon and two MG 42s, heavily protected forward with armour 80 to 100mm thick and having a road speed of up to 55km/hr.

The Ferdinands and the Panthers had similar problems to the Tigers before them. Many of these steel monsters were soon non-operational. Moreover, in close combat with enemy infantry the Ferdinand was literally defenceless, for it had no MG to ward off

157

Red Army anti-tank squads, and the Soviets soon developed a response to the effective 8.8cm cannon. With their fast, nimble T-34s they ran below these heavily armoured panzers – in the Battle of Kursk additionally favoured by the hilly terrain, difficult to observe – and at short range the armour of the new German panzers was still vulnerable to their 8.5cm cannon.

The Battle of Kursk was also the successful baptism of fire for the Soviet JSU assault gun. Weighing 41.2 tonnes and capable of 37 kms/hr on the flat, they were much more nimble and faster than the Ferdinand and better armed with a 12.2cm cannon and one MG. The Russians also had the robust US standard lorry, 400,000 of these being delivered during the course of the war. The United States played a substantial part in Stalin's victory at Kursk. The Soviet signals also proved superior. The Soviet High Command, 'Stavka', was better informed about the plan and timing of the offensive, and the composition and strengths of the German forces involved, than the HQs of the German front armies. This was due to their secret intelligence service with spies and traitors from Switzerland to Hitler's closest entourage. The Soviets knew all about it. The Commander-in-Chief, Sixth Soviet Guards Army, Lt. General Chistyakov, gave special warning to the commanders of his divisions on the evening of 4 July 1943: 'Hitler's guard is facing you!' he said. 'We must expect the German offensive to be concentrated in this sector.'

On the first day of the attack, the SS-Panzer Corps broke through at several places along the Soviet defence system. The Russians put up a stubborn defence, particularly in the LAH sector where a Guard-Infantry Regiment held its ground. Georg Karck,[4] commander of No. 9 Company, 2nd Regiment LAH, finally achieved the breakthrough. With only a handful of men he blew up five enemy bunkers with hollow charges.

The LAH fought then as before with its usual bravura even though in four years' operations it had become a very diverse unit in origins and standards of training. Many men of the division had been drafted into the Waffen-SS without being asked. There was no talk of enthusiasm for the 'National Socialist cause', not even amongst the volunteers, many of whom had stepped forward encouraged by fanatical parents or teachers or under other compulsions. When a Staff Officer lectured the men of our company on the Nazi 'world view' during the long rest period at Olshany, their boredom with it was clearly evident.

Yet whoever belonged to the Leibstandarte had joined a community sworn to the principle of absolute reliance on mutual support. If the MG gunner needed ammunition, there was no doubt about whether he got it or not: the ammunition runners brought it to him even under the heaviest enemy fire: if a runner became a casualty, the nearest man lying ready would crawl up to haul his box of cartridge belts to the MG. To leave a wounded man to his own devices no matter what the circumstances was unthinkable; whoever failed in this respect, and it was considered 'cowardice in the face of the enemy', would not survive the day.

The rule of unconditional comradeship was not only an unavoidable duty, it exercised a fascination very difficult to describe on everybody subject to it. This binding power surmounted the natural fear of the individual, and where individual decisions were possible, it left no choice. My comrade Hermann Schreiber, whom I met time and again during my nocturnal drives to the front line, was No. 1 gunner at the MG and therefore the most important man in his team. On the third day at Kursk he received a letter from his mother telling him that his brother had fallen, and that by virtue of the enclosed official notification he was entitled to take the fourteen-days special leave provided for such cases. Hermann gave me his letter in reply in which he had written: 'Dear Mother, I am sorry, but I cannot leave my comrades in the lurch!'

At the height of the battle, there began around Prochorovka an open tank battle unique in military history, in which 1,500 tanks and assault guns took part. Soviet armour stormed the German forward sections at top speed and broke through the panzer screen. The T-34s engaged the Tigers at short range, for their thick armour and armament no longer offered them an advantage. Volume 3 of the official *Soviet History of the Great War of the Fatherland* quotes a report submitted to headquarters by the High Command, Voronezh Front, under Generals Krutchov and Vatutin. On 7 July, it records that the decision whether the German divisions would break through to Oboyan hung by a thread. Sixth Guards Army front had been torn open. Behind it were only elements of two Soviet armoured corps. In order to halt the German panzer spearhead, in agreement with General Krutchov, General Vatutin ordered the remnants of First Tank Army to dig in its tanks and set up an anti-tank gun wall.

That night when I returned from my third trip to the forward positions it was almost daybreak and I was dog-tired. In six days our company had taken nine Soviet defensive positions, but had withdrawn 300 metres back from the ninth after dark because it had come under massive fire from Soviet artillery and Stalin-organs. I had brought out five wounded on the first trip, three dead and two wounded on the second.The exhausting night runs had left me hardly any time for sleep over the previous few days: by day Soviet fighter bombers and fighters overflew our green hideout and gave us no peace. Overtired and filthy I was just about to brew coffee on the small but excellent benzene stove, which had become mine with the Horch V-8, when Danninger appeared and bawled: 'Clear the decks, we're going to Olshany! Prepare quarters!'

'Why quarters?' I asked in a daze, 'Is the circus here not going any farther?'

'The war is over,' Danninger said, 'We've had enough of it and are pulling out – to Italy, summer holidays!'

I thought this was a pretty poor joke. Danninger would allow no further discussion on the subject and left with the parting remark: 'We're leaving in ten minutes, Kiehn and Grulich are also coming!'

Surprises did not stick to a mudrat like me for long. I drank my coffee, had a wash, filled up the Horch, checked the oil and wiped over the seat covers with a damp cloth. Scarcely had I finished than Danninger and the other two arrived. We headed for Kharkov. We were not in what you might call 'holiday mood' for we had to drive through open country with no cover in bright sunshine: we were a welcome target for fighter bombers and similar riff raff. We kept the doors open, for if an enemy aircraft appeared there was only one thing for it: bale out as quickly as possible and do hare leaps for some hole in the ground or vegetation in the vague hope of surviving. I had convinced myself that the best chance in such a case would be to feign death after the first attack.

Not much was said. Each man observed the quadrant of blue sky corresponding to his seat in the vehicle. Danninger at my side found it all too much of a bother and nodded off now and again. I kept watch on his sector as well as my own, and also on the terrain to his left: this was not a problem for the unpaved road had numerous tyre tracks, which were easy to follow. Nothing stirred as far as the eye could see, we heard nothing but the reliable droning of our motor. It was as quiet as peacetime, much too quiet for my taste.

All of a sudden we came to a spot where the tyre tracks made a sharp turn right, and only a few carried on ahead. I stopped and said, 'We should go right too.'

'There's nothing there,' Danninger growled, 'Kharkov is straight ahead, and that's where we have to go!'

Following a strong hunch I would not give in and protested: 'But something is not right here. It stinks!'

Danninger sat up in his on-duty posture. 'Enough of the palaver! Drive ahead, that is an order!'

Doubly alert I drove on into the lightly undulating territory with its visibility for miles. In order to reduce our trail of dust to a minimum I kept the speed down, but only gradually so as not to irritate Danninger.

After a couple of hundred metres I saw something very close to me, which raised in me the highest state of alarm. Ducked low in a slit trench an SS private was looking up at me from below the rim of his steel helmet with a bewildered and fearful expression. He raised his arm and pointed insistently to the East. At the same moment I noticed at the side of his trench the side of a packing case with the inscription 'Halt! Here main front line!'

I reacted in a split second without even thinking about it. Just at the moment when Danninger said to me in a threatening voice 'What's going on? Drive on! Or have you got cold feet?', I rammed home the gear lever, stepped full on the gas pedal and raced off to the right.

At that same moment all hell broke loose. There, where seconds before we had been parked, shells began to explode in dark clouds of smoke lit by lightning flashes: 'Ratch-boom', anti-tank guns, at least three: the gunners had watched our approach like hunters, waiting only for us to be as near as possible. I could see next to nothing, shoved the gear into second, then used the overdrive lever to roar off swerving wildly left and right up the slight gradient of farmland. My speed was such that my passengers had to hold on for dear life. I thanked my guardian angel that I had the Horch with its 8-cylinder motor and all-wheel drive to plough across the arable land spraying clods of earth in all directions. The 'ratch-boom' salvoes continued to crash down around us dangerously near, throwing up great plumes of earth: two great holes appeared suddenly through the windscreen but the Horch was master of the situation, bringing us with every second farther from the deadly danger to which we had exposed ourselves. Ivan fired as if possessed, but his salvoes became increasingly more dispersed and then he fired more sparingly. After two seemingly endless minutes we were free of it. The terrain sloped down into a depression hiding us from the Russian gunners. A hundred metres or so farther on I stopped in the shade of a clump of poor trees. We had all got away without a scratch.

We took a few deep breaths and allowed ourselves time to reflect. Then Danninger laid his hand on my shoulder and said in German without a trace of Tyrolean accent and very mannerly: 'You may tell me I am an idiot!' to which I answered at once, 'Jawohl, Stabs-scharführer, with pleasure!'

I got out and inspected the Horch. Apart from the holes in the windscreen and some scratches from shell splinters to the front mudguard and rear box doors, the vehicle was undamaged. I patted the bonnet in gratitude and didn't care if the others saw me or not. When we drove off the motor worked as reliably as ever. Soon we came to a *Rollbahn*, a major highway with many vehicles, followed it south and after an hour we reached the western outskirts of Kharkov and Olshany thirty minutes later.

There we were greeted with great joy by the owners of the houses we had left two weeks previously. I was desperate for sleep and found an empty room containing only a bed frame with webbing. Fully dressed I threw myself down on it and fell at once into leaden unconsciousness. The sun had begun to set when a sharp burning sensation on the right side of my body woke me: it was red and painfully swollen. When I turned the bed over I found on the underside of the webbing thick teams of bloodsucking bedbugs. I carried the webbing out, poured benzene over it and incinerated the bedbugs. Then I felt a little better.

The German pincer attack at the Kursk Salient was one of the Wehrmacht's last strategic offensives, perhaps the last of all. What followed it were at best tactical reactions to the operations of the Red Army, ever greater in scale. Despite the inferiority in materials and numbers, the German armies at 'Citadel' could have won the battle if luck had been on their side, but the luck they had had in the campaigns in Poland and France came from the element of surprise. At Kursk and Belgorod it was not the defenders but the attackers who ran into an opponent excellently prepared in every respect. Nevertheless, judging by what we know today, for some days the German armies had a chance of winning if only temporarily and in a limited area; in the south, where I SS-Panzer Corps broke through the Russian front and headed for Oboyan, for some time it seemed that success was within their grasp.

Yet the decision which destroyed all German chances and successes in the Kursk Salient was made far from Kursk, Prochorovka and Oboyan. On 13 July 1943, Field Marshals von Manstein and von Kluge were summoned to Führer-HQ 'Wolfs-schanze' in East Prussia. 'Citadel' had been relegated to a side-show, for a catastrophe was building in Italy after the Italian Army under General Badoglio had seized power and offered to surrender to the Allies. On 10 July, British, US and Canadian forces from North Africa had landed on the island of Sicily and quickly overwhelmed the Italian defences. Some 300,000 men simply took to their heels, leaving only a few units in position. The Allies rolled forwards over the coastal roads. The only resistance they met came from German paratroops, panzer-grenadiers and anti-aircraft troops fighting as infantry. On 17 July Hitler ordered the immediate withdrawal of the SS-Panzer Corps from the Eastern Front because he needed to use it on the Italian mainland, but during the next few months he left most of it where it was. Only our division, the Leibstandarte, was rushed to Italy.

The allocation of quarters at Olshany was no big deal. The platoons and squads were distributed amongst the same houses as before. It was made easier by the losses the company had sustained over the previous couple of weeks; of the former fighting strength of 120 men, forty-seven had fallen or were wounded. Morale was at rock bottom. We all knew that our successful breakthroughs at Kursk were insignificant pyrrhic victories, which bore no relationship to the effect and enormous losses in men and materials required to achieve them.

We stayed for only three days at Olshany, where twelve 'reinforcements' arrived from Berlin, young volunteers and a couple of 'transferees in' from the Luftwaffe, and then we entrained at Kharkov. As the wheels of the transporter train began to clank, bringing us ever faster towards the West, and ever farther from Kursk and Kharkov, we forgot the horrors of the battle. We were young men, bound to the events of the hour and day, and the certainty that we were leaving the nightmare of Russia if only for an unknown period of time was reason enough for us to be happy.

The author Paul Carell[5] drew the conclusion that the War in the East was not lost at Stalingrad, but by abandoning Operation 'Citadel'. The German armies might have won the battle if the circumstances had smiled more kindly upon them, although the possible *Endsieg* can hardly be more than idle speculation. For my unit, No. 9 Company LSSAH, I can only say that in eight days its fighting strength shrank to fifty-six men. After the gigantic squaring-up neither side was in a position to embark on a great offensive, but the Soviet Union had the greater reserves and resources and therefore the capability to win the war. Furthermore, the Red Army had been fundamentally restructured. The armour had been reorganised and was supported by a tank-building industry with a turnout far higher than the Germans could manage.

164

Deprived of the possibility of launching great offensives, the Germans went over to defence along the entire Eastern Front. The Soviets now had the initiative and the end was only a question of time. According to Marshal Zhukov, at Kursk the Germans lost 500,000 men, 3,000 guns and 1,500 aircraft. So far the Russians have not revealed their own losses. These were certainly not insignificant. For example, Fourth Panzer Army under General Hoth took 32,000 prisoners, destroyed 2,000 tanks and almost as many heavy guns.

On the evening of 5 August Stalin ordered a fireworks display in Moscow and a large number of guns to fire a twelve-round salute as a tribute to the troops of the Central Front.

Chapter Seven

Italian Intermezzo

It always surprised me how often latrine gossip rumours turned out to be true. After a certain subdued confidence about the outcome of the battle following limited breakthroughs along our limited front sector, suddenly we heard it whispered, 'You wouldn't believe it, day after tomorrow we're going to Italy!'

What you dream of you like to believe, and so even the most morose amongst us gave in cautiously to the German soul's dream of southern climes and sun. Nobody who did not experience the Russian campaign can possibly have an idea of how strongly each of us yearned to escape the horrors of this pitiless war without equal, even if only for a while. 'Before I have to die,' I heard young soldiers, no more than overgrown schoolboys, utter on more than one occasion, 'How I would like to know what it is like to sleep with a woman!' A last wish which – if ever – was fulfilled in a Wehrmacht brothel and only brought with it an unmemorable experience.[1]

Two days later we were rolling towards the sun. We men of the fighting-vehicle Tross were loaded on open goods wagons with our vehicles and enjoyed the journey in beaming sunshine, passing first through Kiev, Shitomir and Lvov and then westwards. The train kept up a fast speed, making short stops only for a change of locomotive when its supply of water and coal ran out. Onwards we rolled through Silesia, where blonde German girls waved to us from the level-crossing gates: we stared at them as if they were creatures of fable.

At Breslau the train headed south through Prague, then Bavaria and the valley of the Inn to Schwaz near Innsbruck where we were unloaded. The company now set off at once through the Brenner Pass to Italy. Spiess Danninger, who came from the nearby region,

166

used the opportunity for an unscheduled short break with his family and solicited from our always obliging commander SS-1st Lieutenant Breuer the loan of the Horch with me as driver: thus I spent a day and a half at Landeck in a proper bed and got to know solid Tyrolean fare. Moreover I spent a whole wonderful day lazing about doing nothing.

After the second night we set off back. Up to the Brenner the weather was misty and unpleasant, then the sun of Italy greeted us with all its glory. At the villages we drove through the South-Tyroleans stood at the kerbside and waved to us enthusiastically. Danninger, who had brought a bottle of wine along and meanwhile finished it, surprised me by his reaction. He stood up in front of the co-driver's seat, holding the frame of the windscreen with his left hand and made wild threatening gestures with the other shouting: 'Clear off, you stupid macaroni eaters!' and worse. I increased speed so that the public would not be able to understand what he was shouting, and they reacted thrilled all the more by the temperamental outbursts. After a while I understood what it was all about: Tyroleans from the north were pure Tyroleans, those from the South Tyrol, with many immigrants from Italy, were nothing like those from the North and were therefore objects of his deepest contempt.

I had never had before the chance to drive the Horch along a proper highway and gave the vehicle free rein: on the straight it could do 120km/hr, a phenomenal speed for a cross-country vehicle of the time. Under six hours from leaving we rejoined the company at Reggio, where they had put up tents in a green meadow at the edge of town.

Next day there began a really curious way of conducting warfare. Italy had entered the war on the fall of France in 1940, and in 1943 under the pressure of the Allied landings in Sicily Italy declared that its participation was terminated. The LAH Division was the only unit in the operational area capable of fighting and was accordingly given the task of guaranteeing the security of northern Italy and with it the supply lines to German Tenth Army offering stubborn resistance in the south. That was not so easy to do, for the fighting strength of the division after Kursk was estimated at about 3,000 men. Apparently the bright idea occurred to someone in Divisional HQ that the units with all their vehicles should be constantly juggled while in a state of permanent movement: we were on the move day and night with the endless convoys in order to give the impression of strong units being present in the Modena, Bologna, Florence, Padua, Verona and Milan areas.

This actually did deceive the Italian commanders. We stood for three hours ready to fight on the approach roads to Milan, then five divisions of our former ally capitulated there: presumably they were not keen on taking their skins to market any longer, and furthermore the Fascists, well represented in the police, were doing what they could to seize back power. Within a few days 106,000 Italian soldiers had been disarmed[2] and held in camps; it was said that many of them were then taken for labour in Germany.

We occupied Milan and with the company troop had quarters in an old palazzo with a beautiful, large inner courtyard; the Horch passed through the gateway with centimetres to spare. A Swedish consular official resided there, the house superintendent had a wing of the ground floor with his family; we requisitioned some of the remaining empty rooms.

At the beginning we were left more or less to our own devices, reconnoitred the surrounding area and noticed men and women coming from a large building carrying bags and cartons. We soon established that this was a large warehouse full of good things intended for British prisoners of war, principally chocolate, biscuits, tins of fruit and cigarettes. It had all been cleared out except for some remnants on the floors, amongst these I discovered modest booty in the shape of some tins of Virginia tobacco and Libby's condensed milk, which was very sweet and gave me a never-previously-experienced pleasure.

SS-1st Lieutenant Breuer had a special task for me. 'Take a couple of men and drive east to Brescia. On the edge of town is an airfield with some Italians: scout out the situation and then come straight back, do not start anything!'

The airfield was an extensive installation on which a dozen twin-engined Italian fighter-bombers stood around apparently fully

168

operational. We saw vehicles near some barrack huts at the perimeter of the airfield. Near the entrance where we had halted was a large hangar, which we looked over. It contained some small military aircraft and lorries including a bright red fire engine of which I took immediate charge: I got in and had wonderful fun racing at breakneck speed into town with the siren howling. Grulich took the Horch. As I intended, our spectacular arrival caused quite a stir amongst our Company HQ. This was the type of theatrical entry by which one could impress them.

Breuer smiled indulgently, received my short report and then gave the company orders to mount up. At the airfield the platoons swarmed out and headed for the large built-up area on the western side. Here were two accommodation blocks from which we received fire as we approached. These were searched by two platoons and some men brought out from within and assembled in a small meadow. They were all found to be harmless, the shooters having quickly made themselves scarce.

Meanwhile, together with other members of the company, I went towards the airfield barrack huts, which had aroused my suspicions on the first visit. The first we came to was empty, at the second we found the door shut; I entered and found myself in a darkened room before an illuminated table at which a uniformed man was working furiously at a radio set. When he saw the muzzle of my Russian machine-pistol pointing at him he jumped up as if stung and threw up his arms. I fired into the radio set, waved the trembling Italian outside and led him to SS-1st Lieutenant Breuer who listened to my report and said, 'Tell him he should clear off and get himself some civilian clothing.' This was done, but it left me somewhat bewildered and not altogether in agreement with the decision. The fact was, SS-1st Lieutenant Breuer was a warm-hearted person, not in the least like the brutal SS officers portrayed by the media. He had already let the civilians in the housing block go.

Shortly afterwards I had the opportunity to increase my reputation as the company's 'organiser'. One of our security drives took us to Cremona where SS-1st Lieutenant Breuer told me to check for anybody in the officers' academy there. I went with the Company

Staff in the Horch and one Kfz 69. We soon reached the large complex, sealed off from the road by tall railings, the main gate being locked. With crowbars from our vehicles we quickly overcame this impediment but then an Italian officer ran towards us from inside, shouting excitedly and pointing a pistol at me. Personally, I did not consider the situation threatening but a shot rang out behind me and hit the man in the chest. There was no cause to censure the shooter, but seeing the young, extremely handsome man bleeding to death before me on the ground I felt sympathy and regret at his death, senseless but yet an impressive example of devotion to duty and bravery of which, despite the commonly held poor opinion we had of the Italian soldier's fighting qualities, they were apparently capable.

We stormed the building: my colleagues searched the ground floor; following my proven instincts I went to the upper floor and began to give it a thorough once-over. At first I found nothing of interest, but then in the storage depot I came across a rich trove. It contained clothing of all kinds: the finest shoes and other leathers, a store with bolts of first-class bright grey cloth for walking-out uniforms, but even better a large room full of officers' tropical shirts, baggy assault trousers and khaki short trousers, amongst them LAH large sizes, and even passable caps. I summoned the others and we loaded up to the limit of our vehicles' capacity. In addition from the arsenal I took a number of the coveted Beretta pistols, which I shared out amongst everybody.

When we arrived back at Company with our booty, surprise was complete. Breuer slapped me on the back, called for Spiess Danninger, who was naturally in raptures at the sight of it, and ordered him to have the company parade at once and dress up in the new uniform parts. Swiftly every man had his gear and set to with needle and thread sewing on the collar patches and shoulder straps and fixing the LAH death's head on the caps. All were proud of their new stylish attire and thankful to be rid of the cloth uniforms, unbearable in the summer heat, and the ugly, uncomfortable work dungarees. The whole Regiment admired No. 9 Company and thoroughly envied our men.There was some material left over.

Breuer invited Battalion HQ to come over and receive two bolts of the very elegant uniform cloth, this act dissipating the grave doubts they had about the irregular togs. I sent a few metres of it home, everybody being expressly authorised to do so by Breuer.

In another environment this could not have been achieved, but under the circumstances and in the gentle climate everything was easier and more free, although it did lead to dramatic consequences. No. objection would ever be made to controlled booty from Italian military stocks, but the strict regulations regarding 'manly upbringing' applied: none of us would have dared to relieve an Italian of his watch.

My comrade Hermann Schreiber, No. 1 MG gunner in 2nd Platoon, became innocently involved in an affair, which he related to me very sadly. A year before he had been with the No. 9 Company reserve in France.

We met up for the first time in the wash-barrack hut when I spoke to him with regard to the strange way he was washing his socks.

'Just let me do it,' I told him, 'I'll show you a easier and quicker way!' As we conversed I asked him the usual question, 'Where are you from?'

'From Rheydt, near Düsseldorf.'

'But then we are from the same region! At Rheydt I went regularly to my relations there at holiday times, they had a wholesalers' shop on Bahnhof-Strasse.'

Hermann knew the family and was pleased to meet a Rhinelander, a species spread thin on the ground in the Leibstandarte. Subsequently we met up very frequently and exchanged intimate experiences and discoveries. On 28 February 1943, No. 9 Company's Black Sunday during the Battle of Kharkov, he was amongst the survivors. In Italy Hermann had had the bad luck to be assigned to the firing squad which had to execute three men of 1st Battalion. They had made the basic error of misunderstanding the extent of the looser discipline and in Milan they had robbed a jewellers' store. It became a matter of common knowledge and soon came before a Divisional court-martial, which sentenced the delinquents to death.

Soldiers were nominated for the firing squad from each company, which is how Hermann was chosen. It was an onerous task from which nobody could excuse himself. Hermann did his duty, and it was something of a relief for him to speak about it. He told me, 'It was a good thing that according to regulations one of the carbines handed out had to be loaded with a blank, perhaps it was mine!'

After two weeks of adventurous activities, Lombardy was safely in German hands again. For safety's sake we remained in the countryside, transferred out from the town on the Po to near Pavia. There the company set up tents on a large farm estate. I collected milk, potatoes and the giant, mild-tasting onions of the region and prepared quick dishes on a benzene stove for Breuer, Danninger, myself and often for one or two others, much lauded as a supplement to rations: my roasted potatoes from finely-cut rough tubers with tinned meat were enjoyed immensely.

In general I had it good. While the others had the devil riding their backs in the countryside and had to stand their watches, I had a cushy number, slept on the straw floor at the farmstead often until nine in the morning and spent the day more or less as I pleased. A number of corporals looked down on this with obvious disapproval, but Spiess Danninger would have none of it and gave me special light duty missions such as driving him to and from Battalion and accompanying the despatch-rider Adele on deliveries.

Babucke and Löbel continued to serve up the usual miserable fare, and one day they crowned their dubious culinary gifts in the following way. By misadventure dried peas, rice and dried vegetables became mixed up in the sacks, and they simply shovelled the result into the field kitchen and served it as lunch, which I fetched for SS-1st Lieutenant Breuer as usual.

I was sitting with him and paramedic Sepp Rist at the table before his tent and as he began to eat I broke the silence by remarking, 'Today the kitchen has set a new low, this is the foulest pigswill in the company's history!'

Breuer, always in control of himself, jumped up and went off with fast, stiff strides to the kitchen where he roared at Babucke: 'How dare you offer us such pigswill! If this happens again I shall have you confined for three days!'

Babucke, red as a beetroot, could only stammer horrified, 'Jawohl, SS-1st Lieutenant! Jawohl!' It came as a late revenge for me, which I enjoyed.

A few days later SS-1st Lieutenant Breuer had a conversation with me which was of great importance for my future. I was checking over the Horch, parked under a large tarpaulin near his commander's tent when he came up to me and as if by way of an afterthought said, 'You have now been my driver for a couple of months and have been trusted with other assignments. I know you to be reliable, correct and sensible in critical situations. Furthermore you have a good educational background. I am considering recommending you for Junker school, what do you think of that?'

I knew at once that a great deal hung on my answer. A man like Breuer would not take kindly to any response other than a positive one. Therefore I replied quickly, 'I am a war volunteer, SS-1st Lieutenant, for a career as an officer I would have to sign on for twelve years.[3] I do try to carry out my duties as best I can. I thank you for your recognition and confidence in me, but I have another wish for the future. I believe that I would not be suitable as a fighting officer.'

'So what would you like to be?' Breuer enquired.

'A doctor of medicine!'

'But that is also a possibility,' Breuer countered, 'You could train as an SS doctor: would you agree to that?'

Anything was better than No. 9 Company, which at any time could suddenly have another and far less agreeable commander than this one. So I said simply, 'Yes, I would, SS-1st Lieutenant!'

'Then I shall bear it in mind,' came back his brief answer.

Nothing further was said on the subject until months later when I reaped the pleasurable consequences of this conversation. The first thing that came my way was my promotion to SS-Lance Corporal.[4]

We spent a while making our way to different places in Lombardy. Our tents had stood on the banks of the Po for a good week when the entire company less the supply Tross received the order to swim to the other side of the river. What had not been taken into account and was not immediately obvious was the dangerous eddies in the river. When we reached the other side we were widely dispersed and all exhausted. Two men were missing, we waited for them in vain, then made the long trek back over a bridge. The incident was never spoken of again.

Apart from the two who had drowned, the company had no losses in the entire period of our stay in Upper Italy. We had grown accustomed to the pleasant summery existence when in mid-September 1st Regiment LAH including our unit was ordered to the east. After the military collapse in Italy the partisans in Yugoslavia had become considerably more active and had even spilled over into Istria. It was thought that our presence there might do something to restore the situation.

These irregulars had not yet ventured as far as Trieste and the neighbouring small coastal towns. We spent two days in picturesque Portorose where I could not resist the temptation and with two equally adventurous comrades took a sailing boat from shore for a flying tour of the Adriatic. We kept close to the coast but encountered problems with the variable winds and in order to reach land had to tack, something I had only ever tried out with model boats.

We advanced along the coastal road to Pola at the southern tip of the peninsula to an important German naval base, but only a light occupation force was present. Driving on through the hilly interior of Istria northwards we came to villages, which had apparently been abandoned in haste by their occupants. Then we headed eastwards via Rijeka through the karst and then southwards to the Kapela mountains. After leaving open country we became caught up increasingly in fighting: the partisans fired down on us in ambush from the rugged rock walls. After fighting our way up narrow serpentine roads, we would find nothing at the top. We could only move through the valleys in convoy, going alone in a Kfz or on a motorcycle was a risky business. This cowardly and barbaric way of fighting is outlawed by the Hague Convention, and we found it abominable and even more repulsive than the war in Russia; it was well known that as a rule the partisans massacred their prisoners.

174

We were only successful twice in catching up with a band of them and exchanging fire. At the time I had enough to do guiding the fighting Tross and did not get involved in the firefight myself, but I had a sense of satisfaction seeing the bodies of dead partisans for the first time. One of these actions was a real scrap. We surprised a large number of partisans installed in a village with steep cliffs behind it. Since the longed-for opportunity for an open battle now presented itself, daylight was failing and we did not want the enemy to escape us in the dark, we had no choice but to convey our fighting troops over flat, slightly descending terrain lacking any cover over a distance of about a kilometre. We drove at top speed, our MG gunners fired from the rocking MTWs without regard to the heavy defensive fire. Just short of the village the platoons dismounted and went onto the attack. When they reached the village, the partisans had disappeared into the nearby mountains under cover of dusk. This skirmish cost us some wounded, amongst them my colleague Hermann Schreiber from Rheydt, a through-and-through wound in the upper thigh. I found out later that he was taken to a military hospital in Trieste: afterwards he was assigned to the Junker school in Prague.

There were a few other experiences, which ended less happily. Breuer had another special mission for me and my proven men; we were to reconnoitre an isolated village high up in the mountains which could not be seen from below and take all men under the age of sixty prisoner. We had two light MGs to give protection for all conceivable cases. With colleagues armed with machine pistols ready to fire sitting near and behind me, I set off driving the Horch followed by Grulich with a Kfz 69. It was a long, winding road up the mountain through overhanging vineyards with overripe grapes, which apparently nobody had dared harvest.

The village appeared deserted: when I knocked on a farmyard door with the stock of my machine pistol, nothing happened for a while, then it was opened by a man speaking colourful-sounding but comprehensible German: 'There is nobody else but us here, Herr! We are Croats. The others have fled to the hills. We are not your enemies, come inside and have a look around!'

I signalled to one of my escorts and we followed the farmer across the yard into a low living room. On the wall was a photo of the man showing him as a young NCO in the uniform of the K.u.K Army[5] of the First World War. His plump wife set bread, sausage and wine before us and invited us to tarry, which we did for the sake of courtesy.

The man was obviously no 60 year old. 'Really I have orders to take you with me,' I told him, 'but we will not do that, I shall take responsibility for it.'

When he heard that he was visibly relieved. With effusive utterances of thanks he kissed my hand and concluded with the words, 'I have a pretty daughter, may I fetch her and introduce her to you?'

He went out and returned with a fine-looking, lively girl of about twenty. I greeted her courteously and said, 'She is charming, I wish you good luck in these difficult times. And now we must leave.' In the valley I reported to Breuer what we had discovered and, as he did almost always, he stated his satisfaction in his lordly manner.

In the confused circumstances of ever-present guerrilla warfare, our commanders operated in the manner the situation seemed to call for. We were forced to use the few roads in the valleys bordered by steep walls of rock from where the partisans, at home in this territory, fired down on us from the heights. Luckily for us, apart from mortars they had no heavy weapons and were not adept with their MGs and rifles although they had a clear advantage over us. We were practically served up on a platter while they were difficult to spot in their hideaways amongst the numerous rocks and boulders and it was even more difficult to get to grips with them. Our mortars were of little use against targets situated high up and our small arms with simple jacketed rounds could do very little. We were supplied with explosive munitions, which proved very effective: it must have been terrifying for the partisans in their supposedly safe cover behind rocky uplands to be suddenly surrounded by hundreds of explosive shells all bursting at the same moment. Our use of these munitions clearly infringed the Hague Convention, but the partisans, being non-combatants, also acted illegally with every round they fired at us, and besides there was hardly much difference between the illegal ammunition and our firing at them with, for example, the quadruple Oerlikon anti-aircraft gun. Looking back at the manipulation of the rights and wrongs retrospectively: the Hague Convention originally allowed the shooting of hostages in retaliation for attacks on occupation troops, and it was later made illegal retroactively in order to convict Germans in the dock at Nuremberg, Rome and in France as war criminals.

Increasingly frustrated and embittered by our cowardly leaders we decided that the next time we were ambushed we would seize the opportunity for a spontaneous counter attack. A serpentine road snaked upwards alongside an almost vertical wall of rock; Breuer decided on a *coup de main*, ordered two platoon leaders with their Kfz 69s to follow him and told me, 'We are going up, as fast and as far as we can!'

I pressed ahead like a hound from hell. We arrived unexpectedly quickly at the narrow road with its hairpin bends and were about halfway up the height of the wall when we came under massive fire. Instantly our platoons left their vehicles and returned the attackers' fire with four MGs, the rest of us with our carbines. We were also given support from the company's other eight MGs in the valley: all in all a considerable firework display, which the partisans were not prepared to take for long. After a few minutes we remounted and were soon at the top of the rock wall where we found an isolated house on a plateau occupied by poultry and a pig but no humans. In the house Breuer confiscated maps and other documents. SS-Corporal Hübner was in such a rage that he set fire to the straw roof of the cottage before we departed. Nobody tried to stop him, not even Breuer.

The next day Breuer gave me the job of taking the captured papers with the Horch V-8 to Battalion HQ. This was a drive of some kilometres and I went without an escort. On a long uphill section of a mountain road, to the left of which an abyss yawned, I got into a queue behind some heavy lorries of a bridge-building convoy. There was a long delay, for safety I put the gear into reverse and for some reason decided to leave a largish gap between the Horch and the last, heavily-laden lorry of the convoy immediately in front of me. I had got out to stretch my legs when this lorry began to roll back slowly. Without losing a second I sprinted to my driver's seat, depressed the clutch and attempted to steer my vehicle as far right as possible without power. The lorry had, meanwhile, picked up momentum and striking the forward left mudguard of the Horch hard, drifted off to the left and tumbled into the abyss. More furious than frightened, I found that the damage was reparable. There was an unavoidable palaver between the officer of the bridge-building convoy, a SS-Captain, and the lorry driver, white as a sheet. With razor-sharp logic the officer decided that I had prevented a worse accident and wrote me a couple of lines in evidence. Then with a crowbar from the car's standard equipment I separated the wheel from the crushed metal and was able to drive on.

After my return to company, Breuer was clearly pleased that the valuable Horch had not suffered worse. There were only two vehicles of this type in the battalion, one for the battalion commander, the other for the chief of the heavy company, Breuer, who was very proud of it. In order to bring the repaired Horch up to scratch I had to drive it to a body repair workshop at Cilli. The repair took three full days during which time I had a not especially entertaining but off-duty stay in the small town. Soon enough it would become of fateful significance for me.

The second week of October 1943 brought a highly unwelcome change for me. SS-1st Lieutenant Breuer, my highly thought-of commanding officer, was transferred to Battalion HQ. His successor was SS-1st Lieutenant Rieker, a wheat-blond Holstein giant with a nutcracker face who kept his distance from everybody, never uttered a word and to whom I took an instant dislike. There was nothing for it but to make the best of the new situation and I take care not to leave myself open to anything.

One of the malicious corporals must have said something to Rieker, for on our first meeting he eyed me critically and said, 'You may have had privileges with my predecessor, but you will have to earn them from me. And you will also stand watches!'

On the following night I was patrolling with Kiehn at the edge of

178

KFZ 15/Horch V8; the Wehrmacht's best cross-country vehicle – and almost the only one suitable for war in the East.

Battle of Kursk-Belgorod: troops of an SS panzer division recovering a seriously wounded Red Army soldier (from Janusz Piekalkiewicz, *Unternehmen Zitadelle*). (J. K. Piekalkiewicz Photo Archive)

Kursk-Belgorod, July 1943: Moving into the readiness position to attack.

Kursk-Belgorod: captured Soviet soldiers.

Battle of Kursk-Belgorod: MG group of the '9th' in expectation of a Soviet attack.

(LEFT) SS-Lieutenant General Sepp Dietrich, commander of 1st SS Panzer Division, in a warlord's pose on the special general's model of the Horch V8.

(BELOW LEFT AND RIGHT) On the transport to Italy, July 1943, at the left, the author.

(BELOW) Italy: 'Farmhouse Holidays'.

(ABOVE) Commander's tent with Horch V8.

(LEFT) Proud in Italian summer uniforms: colleagues of the '9th', in 'riot trousers'.

(RIGHT) Bernd Kloska, a recruit in Berlin together with the author.

(LEFT) Others from the company in short trousers.

(RIGHT) Croatia, October 1943: MG replying to partisan fire. The Kfz 69 has recent bullet damage at the rear.

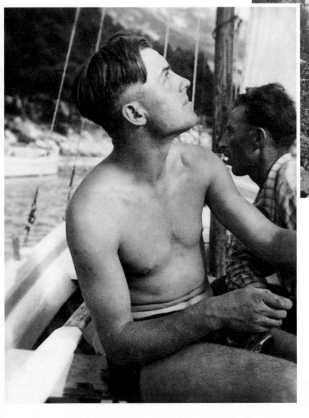

(LEFT) Istria, September 1943: for a change of scene, sailing on the Adriatic at Portorose.

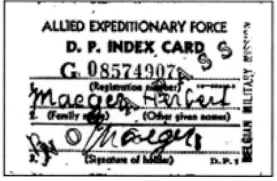

Release document No. 299 issued on 14 August 1945 for 'Obergefreiter' (Senior Private, Army) Herbert Maeger. (Centre) ID document of release from Trebbin PoW Camp requesting passage without let or hindrance for the bearer on his route home. (Bottom) Displaced Person's Index Card issued by the 'Belgian Military Mission', Lüneburg, September 1945.

the village in a clearing where the company was sleeping. It was a bright, moonlit night, which threw the houses into sharp outline. The surrounding woodland was black and threatening, ideal operational terrain for determined partisans who knew the area. We both felt uneasy about the whole thing and avoided speaking as we continued our patrol.

Suddenly about 30 metres away I saw a light like the short flash of a pocket lamp and seconds later a second one between a house and the nearby edge of the woods. As always on patrol I had a rifle grenade to hand, and I threw it as accurately as possible at the target. Seconds later the village came to life. Amongst the first to approach us and to identify himself when challenged was a fairly excited Rieker.

'What's all this hullaballoo?' he snarled; and after I had given him my version: 'You must have seen a ghost! If all this uproar is a false alarm, you're in for it! We shall have a look!'

Where my grenade had exploded was a narrow concrete trough with a small opening. This led into the woods. Somebody must have been in the protected quadrangle and made a run for it because he had left behind his field cap with the red star and a torch.

'Well then . . .' was all Rieker said, 'we can all go back to sleep.' And then to the Duty NCO who came hurrying up: 'But double the patrols! And . . . oh yes, Maeger and Kiehn are relieved!'

Parked on the narrow road which wound its way up the steep slope I was sitting in my driver's seat in the Horch sunning myself and enjoying the overripe sweet grapes from a giant vine, which I had plucked a few metres further up at the edge of the village. The other fighting vehicles of the Tross were lined up behind me. SS-1st Lieutenant Rieker, who apparently liked to wander off alone, had reconnoitred the village without an escort; when he came back he gave me a wave to bring up the vehicle, got in and signalled to the other cars to remain where they were.

'It all looks peaceful enough,' he said as if conversationally, 'we shall drive a little bit farther up the mountain.' This was by no means the invitation for a discussion, and so without speaking I put the vehicle in gear and drove off although I was not happy about it. It was a small, poor village and looked deserted. When we had the last houses behind us the road became steeper and I had to take the hairpin bends with care. Then the road turned to the left, there followed an unexpectedly horizontal stretch and became finally a track hewn into the rock pointing northwards, lying in the deep shadow of a high rock face.

I liked the look of the whole thing even less and I reduced speed. Rieker reacted at once, 'Get on with it, drive on!'

'What happens if we need to turn?' I asked him.

'What's up with you? Scared?'

With caution I drove a little faster. There was good reason for anxiety. A partisan could be crouching behind any jutting boulder and calmly finish us off without any risk to himself. The track was so narrow that I had the rock face no more than a half a metre to my right and little more for the wheels before the abyss to the left. We came to a bend and the road ended. It was simply no longer there, apparently a stretch of about 15 to 20 metres had been blown up.

Rieker appeared unimpressed. 'I shall climb up the mountain alone,' he told me, 'drive back and find another way! I'll wait at the top for you!'

With that he left me inwardly raging but outwardly calm as one had to be with a man like him. The stupid dog was simply a menace, a permanent risk for the entire company, he had as much knowledge about cross-country vehicles as an ox. But this did not help me.

Obviously I could not remain where I was, nor could I leave the vehicle. I could not simply reverse back because the tall rear structure of the vehicle blocked my vision. I had to do something extravagant, and it occurred to me how after some thought. I pushed back the driving seat as far as it would go, selected reverse gear and the low setting for the intermediate gear, pulled the starter button to the right of the steering wheel so far out that the motor increased from neutral revolutions to moderately high, then I let the clutch come up carefully: the vehicle began to roll slowly back. As quickly as possible I stood up and turned to face to the rear.

Upright with my hands on the steering wheel, I steered the Horch back to the departure point of this current adventure. To the right of me the abyss yawned; one false move of the steering wheel would have plunged myself and the car into the depths.

I covered the stretch with intense concentration. It seemed endless but in reality was not much more than 150 metres. When I could finally turn about safely I heaved a sigh of relief.

I did not have much time to recover. Rieker, bent on Valhalla, would be waiting for me alone on the mountain; that had been his crazy but clear order. In driving off I noticed in the village a kind of field path, which led on the sunny south-west side of the mountain into the not especially steep wine slopes. According to the manual the Horch could go up an incline of 45 degrees and I was in the mood to test it out. At great speed I ploughed through stakes and vines on a direct course upwards until it simply petered out. I parked the Horch on a tiny plateau, hung my carbine around my neck and went to the summit. There I found Rieker smoking a cigarette.

He gave me what passed for a friendly look and said, 'I just wanted to find out if I should keep you on as my driver or send you back to the platoons. You can stay!'

The right thing to have said was: 'Thank you, SS-1st Lieutenant' but I made no reply. Rieker looked at me askance but then stood up and said, 'Now we'll go up a bit more and have a look around!'

It was a fine stroll over the extensive crest of the mountain. The panorama was magnificent, insects hummed in bushes and stalks, nobody was to be seen far and wide, the war was light years away.

The idyll was deceptive and came to a sudden end. A few metres to the right of me I saw a quick movement; behind a clump of bushes in front of us a figure literally came up out of the ground, a young man in typical Partisan dress, a field cap on his head with the Soviet red star. He was probably a lone sentry surprised in sleep: with horror in his eyes he raised his arms in surrender. If he had been alert and cold-blooded, he could easily have shot the pair of us in our reverie.

Rieker gave the prisoner a sign to go on ahead of us towards the village, then drew his pistol and shot the man in the neck. I was horrified and could not conceal it. Rieker gave me an unconcerned look and said cynically: 'You probably don't approve. But think about it: it was the most humane thing for him. I could have ordered you to do it. Failing that we would have had to take him back with us, lock him up in the village and set in motion procedures according to the Hague Convention.' It would have had the same result, and I knew that he was right. All the same, my mood was a chaos of protest, sorrow and helpless rebellion. Suddenly my surroundings were strange and hostile. Night was falling and I followed Rieker back to the car without speaking.

Up to mid-October I had preferred to avoid the musty houses if possible and sleep in the rear seat of my Horch. At the higher altitudes, however, the nights were cooler and I shared the double bed in one of the abandoned houses with Grulich and Spethmann. On the second night my right hip and leg began to hurt, within a few hours my upper thigh had swollen up and I had a fever; Rist came straight away and took my temperature: 39 degrees.

After two years and three months that day was to be my last with No. 9 Company LSSAH. Normally I would have been conveyed carefully in a field ambulance to the nearest dressing station or field hospital, but all of a sudden the company broke out in hectic activity, caused by an urgent movement order: the transport train stood ready for immediate loading: as usual everybody knew what the destination was: the Eastern Front around Zhitomir.

I gathered my Seven Things together in great haste and Spiess Danninger had me driven to the battalion dressing station where SS-1st Lieutenant Keppel, who knew me from earlier encounters, told me benevolently, 'Now, first of all we shall spare you another winter in Russia. The main dressing station is loading up already so we'll take you to a hospital nearby and inform the district commandant who will then look after you.'

This was done but turned out rather differently to my optimistic outlook. Within fifteen minutes I was in a small and very modest hospital, its single large ward having about twenty other patients of whom none spoke to me nor wanted to. I never saw a doctor, health care was in the hands of some nuns who brought me my meagre meals sullen and wordlessly. They also brought me some obscure tablets, which worked, enabling me to think despite my high fever. I knew that I was in a town near the southern border of Slovenia: the area, which had previously been part of the Austro-Hungarian Empire, had been annexed into the Greater German Reich under the name 'Südkärnten' – South Carinthia, an arrangement to which the partisans paid little respect, or our military presence there would not have been necessary.

I neither saw not heard anything of the district commandant and decided to act on my own initiative. On the third day of my stay I dragged myself out of bed and dressed, except for my right foot, which would no longer fit into the boot. It was difficult to find my way to the nearest railway station, fortunately it lay nearby. Limping and in pain I broke down, the nuns gave me a crutch to assist my departure, evidently relieved to see the back of me.

I made it to the station in great distress: to survive the endless wait on a station bench I had to clench my teeth as hard as I could. Finally a train pulled in for Cilli, the motorman helped me get in and just over an hour later we arrived at the destination, a small rail junction with a Red Cross office and a military hospital. By now it was evening but I had to wait half an hour before I was given a soft bed and the best treatment in a wonderful hospital situated by a southern slope.

Next morning I was scheduled for the operating table where a very reliable-looking Senior Staff Surgeon was waiting and with a slight Austrian accent calmed me: 'You've arrived a little late, but we'll soon have you up and about.' To my embarrassment, an extremely pretty theatre nurse had to shave my pubic hair; when she blushingly took my penis in her hand and started the procedure with a cut-throat razor, I told her, 'Sister, no cutting away more than is necessary!' to which the Senior Staff Surgeon gave a jovial smile.

When I awoke from the anaesthetic, my swollen and distorted leg was almost normal. The surgeon explained: 'It was a phlegmone, we drew off a litre and a half of pus and took out a large splinter, here it is. Where were you wounded?'

'I got it at Belgorod in the summer,' I told him, 'it made only a small hole in my hip.'

'Have you received the Wound Badge?' he asked. When I said no, he replied, 'Well then, we'll apply for it from your unit.'

Two weeks later the award arrived, and so now I had the Ostmedaile from the first winter in Russia and the Wound Badge, the two decorations which distinguished a true veteran of the front. The scar I have on my upper inner thigh is twelve centimetres long.

After a week I was so much recovered that I could take a daily constitutional, which I did happily. I had a good time in the Cilli military hospital, whose ambience of Austrian charm was much nicer than the usual Prussian coldness. Everybody was pleasant and friendly except for the matron who – falsely – alleged that I behaved as a Casanova in the town. In the event, without any duties I was perfectly satisfied just enjoying the good food.

The time passed quickly. I no longer thought of ever leaving, and then one beautiful day shortly before noon the Senior Staff Surgeon sent for me: 'Actually you have been well again for some time. I kept you here because no doubt you have had bad experiences in the past and your time here has done you good. But now unfortunately I must throw you out, and at once: this evening a hospital train is bringing in seriously wounded men from the Eastern Front. We need every bed. The almoner will provide you with instructions for your provincial military hospital at Aachen, and they will arrange to contact your field unit about your convalescent leave.'

The almoner had already prepared the paperwork and handed it to me with the words: 'You must vacate your bed by 1500 hrs and leave without delay, there are three trains leaving here this afternoon for Vienna.'

In the ward another surprise was waiting for me: there was mail on my bed, a letter from my parents. I had written to them from the hospital and now they announced their visit to me at Cilli. This gave me an enormous headache: the letter had been sent three days before and by now my parents were certainly on their way and would arrive within the next twelve hours. I could not be on the station platform or in the town past midnight or I would come into conflict with the field-gendarmes, something it was better to avoid at all costs.

I discussed the problem with a young tankman from Lüneburg in the neighbouring bed who told me very casually, 'Simple. I shall consult the cards and tell you when your parents will be arriving.'

'I'm in no mood for larking about,' I told him in annoyance.

'This is no lark,' he assured me, 'My grandmother taught me to read the cards and it works! Let me do it for you, what have you to lose?'

'Nothing,' I said sceptically.

He shuffled the pack, laid out some and then said with certainty, 'Your parents will arrive this evening after nine, under no circumstances leave beforehand!'

'If you can predict the future so precisely, perhaps you can tell me how much leave I am going to get.'

'Certainly,' he replied, shuffled the pack again, laid some to the right, some to the left and told me with an absolutely straight face: 'sixty-one days.'

'You know that is crap. Nobody has ever been given sixty-one days leave, and in the fifth year of the war too!'

He shook his head with forbearance. 'We shall see. I shall give you my home address, you can complain there if it is not so. The other thing is, what do I do to get your smart assault pants?'

By this he meant my irregular issue from the officers' school at Cremona, Italian tropical trousers of the best quality in beige. After some negotiating he offered me a Beretta pistol, which unfortunately he did not have with him, it was indoors. He swore to me most faithfully to send it to me at Gemmenich as soon as he got home, but I never heard from him again. After what I was to go through later, I never really felt the loss.

I waited at the railway station as my clairvoyant comrade had insisted. I let the train at 1700 hrs steam off, the last one was due to leave at 2200 hrs. I passed the time in and around the station. Shortly after 2100 hrs a train from Vienna pulled in, I was waiting for it on the platform and was taken aback to some extent when I saw my parents alight. They were surprised and relieved to hear how things had turned out. We made the long journey home on the 2200 hrs train. It was all very pleasant; my father wore his railway official's uniform and for the whole time we had a service compartment at our disposal. The arrival time of the train was not specific and I made use of the circumstances accordingly: slept in late, paid obligatory pleasant visits including one to my relatives at Rheydt, read and, as the metaphor has it, 'swung my legs'.

My instructions required me to attend the military hospital at Aachen-Ronheide where I was received by a Senior Staff Surgeon of similar disposition as his brave counterpart at Cilli.

'We shan't send you off to Russia before Christmas,' he informed me, 'Come to see me on the first Monday after the holidays towards eleven in the morning. Your unit will certainly be patient until then. After that we'll have another look.' This gave me more than another four weeks leave.

On the Monday after New Year 1944 I took the train to Aachen and reported punctually to the office of the Senior Staff Surgeon where a female secretary with apparently little to do told me tersely, 'The boss is not here, come back next Monday!' I thanked her and registered with satisfaction another week gained. I recalled the Cilli prophecy, but it was still a long while until the sixty-first day. That changed in a curious manner. When I reported a week later in Aachen, the Senior Staff Surgeon was present. With a slightly surprised voice he informed me, 'They apparently think a lot of you at your unit! It says here that they are giving you another twenty-one days convalescent leave. Well, very good luck!'

I was quite shocked, thanked him and once in the corridor began to count up. Whichever way I twisted and turned it, it always came out the same: I had left Cilli on 25 November, thirty-one days hath December and I had to be back in Berlin on 26 January – according to Adam Riese exactly sixty-one days! And so it was as the cards had foretold.

Chapter Eight

Six Months Leave from the War

W hen I arrived at the Reserve Company in Berlin I was expecting to be sent back to the Eastern Front. Things developed more favourably, however, than I had thought likely two months before. Spiess Danninger was quite openly determined to fulfil the vague promise made to me by SS-1st Lieutenant Breuer in Italy: I was not given any more details in the company office but told to await a final decision.

I was additionally glad not to have to spend the time waiting in the grim Lichterfelde barracks but was sent off, so to speak, to open country, to a nest with the original name of Markgrafpieske between Berlin and Frankfurt/Oder, where elements of the Reserve Battalion were avoiding the ever heavier air raids. I took the tram to Fürstenwalde, then had to walk ten kilometres.

Scarcely had I got to Markgrafpieske than I received the order to return to Fürstenwalde: I was assigned to a squad at the railway station there, which had the job of unloading open goods wagons bringing coal for the HQ and reserve units at Storkow, Bad Saarow-Pieskow and other locations. I got myself a lorry for the journey back. At the station I found three men in a small barrack hut who made up my squad. Most of the time we had nothing to do but play cards and traipse round the gloomy suburb in which the only attraction was a seedy cinema. Every fourth or fifth day a wagon would arrive with coal and then we had to unload it in record time to release the wagon as quickly as possible for other important war economy work as per the slogan on the banners everywhere reading 'Wheels must roll for victory!' It was no light work, for the coal had to be shovelled out in a wide swing over the wagon's side and far enough to prevent the coal dump reaching the railway track. Highly motivated by the pleasant soft number we had, generally we shifted out the ten tonnes of in a bit less than four and a half hours. Then we would look like coalminers after the shift and had to spend hours making ourselves and our dungarees presentable.

We were hoping to keep this job until summer but were disbanded in March and ordered to Markgrafpieske. There the Spiess of the Reserve Battalion greeted me with a welcome report; he revealed that I was on leave for an unspecified period, after which I would join the Waffen-SS Company of Medical Students at Giessen. Happy at this change in affairs in my life as a soldier, in mid-March I headed off for the town, which was outwardly entirely untouched by the war. No bomb had fallen on Giessen, everything breathed peaceful tranquillity; the citizens showed me and the other students the friendly open-mindedness traditional to the university town.

First I had to complete the formalities, which were unavoidable even in a company of students: report in and receive the special instructions for study and the interior duties. The absolute requirements were to be in the company building, which had been used before the war by a students' association, at 1230 hrs punctually every day for dining and military roll call. At the latter the opportunity would be taken by the unavoidable Spiess to distribute orders and other information, which might appear essential for the maintenance of our morale as soldiers. The company provided the textbooks and lodgings. With a fellow student from Vienna I was given a room in the loft of Frau Wittig's house in Posen-Strasse on the south side of town.

After I had enrolled, there remained a few weeks until the beginning of the semester. We were put to work building barrack huts, which we were to occupy upon their completion. Even after beginning our studies we had to continue this work on Sundays: we made every effort, not without some success, to delay its progress. Apart from that we enjoyed considerable freedom, relatively speaking, which in the circumstances had to be taken advantage of. I had my bicycle sent from home but was not allowed on public transport with it to the outlying institutes.

It was almost inevitable that I should meet a pleasant young female fellow student. Ilse Harmsen lodged in Breslauer-Strasse, was a year younger than I, came from Cuxhaven and wanted to be a veterinary surgeon. She also had a bicycle and we went together to the lectures at the Faculty of Botany. Gradually we grew closer. It was initially a relationship based on sympathy, which developed into young love: corresponding to the times it was limited to romantic intimacy. Amongst our frequent pleasures were evening strolls through the nearby Philosophen Wood.

I enjoyed wonderful months far removed from the horrors of the war. Ilse shared rooms with a student, Gisela, who came from Güstrow, and together with my own roommate the Viennese, the four of us made trips to the Lahn valley and swam in the uninviting brown waters of the river. We also went on the neighbouring mountains Schiffenberg and Gleiberg, both within my sphere of activities ten years later as editor of the *Wetzlarer Neuen Zeitung*.

Our schedule of duties made sure that we were occupied outside lectures, and included barrack-hut construction on Sundays and several hours of sport, mainly light athletics. I also learned fencing and soon received the recognition of the female instructor for my ability with the foil. Later at Junker school I cut a fine figure in this discipline.

At Giessen we also had duty as attendants at a closed institution for mentally ill Waffen-SS men. Behind the barred fences the inmates continued the war in their own manner, the higher ranks playing out all the oppressiveness against common soldiers they were capable of given their condition. It was a depressing job in this dismal building protecting the latter from the worst excesses.

In the short semester holidays we worked ten hours daily on constructing the new barrack huts intended for us. We were just preparing for the second semester when we were unpleasantly surprised by an order which we all found extremely unsettling: the Company of Students at Giessen had been disbanded and converted to officer training at the Junker school, Prague.

Chapter Nine

From Junker School
to the 'Crossbones Division'

robably nobody amongst us was happy about the development, which ended our peaceful interlude at Giessen and
brought us in a train, at least with carriages for passengers and
not cattle trucks, to Prague. Were we to be drilled to become front
officers or would we find ourselves within a framework of what we
had all eagerly crammed for a semester? There was much speculation
on the journey, and all conversations dried up with the threatening
prospect of being slaughtered in Russia like so many others.

Until then I only knew Prague from history books and the film
Die Goldene Stadt with Kristina Söderbaum. The city gave us a frosty
welcome despite the warm season of the year. The Czechs hated the
Germans without regard to the person; there was no trace whatever
of human emotion even towards occupation troops such as I had
known in France, Italy and for that matter Russia. The girls, if we
ever got to see any, never gave us a glance.

On the rare occasions during my stay in Prague when I
ventured into the city centre, I noticed that the citizens were better
fed and clothed than our 'ethnic-compatriots' in the Reich. The
city had been completely spared ground fighting and air raids.
There was no sign of the militant resistance we had encountered
in the Balkans and in Russia: the hate of the Czechs was only
unleashed in the last days of the war when the victory of the
Soviets and their Western allies was certain. The horrific persecution of the Germans in Czechoslovakia, which went on for
months and years across the country, were not individual crimes
but mass actions: besides forcing them out, the overt murders of
hundreds of thousands of victims are even today expressly

approved of by many Czechs as the justified reprisals of one whole people against another.

The Junker school was at Prague-Dewitz in the western suburbs. Here began the fourth chapter of the old story of military basic training I knew three times already from Berlin, Taganrog and Boissy in France, a certain consideration being shown to us in that the sergeant-instructors, mostly of Haupt- or SS-Staff Sergeant rank, saw us as future officers. All the same, everything began with the typical, stupid Army training routine: exercises, cross-country training, weapons training, training manual (HDV) instruction and then the whole thing again from the start. For a change the command function was shared out, for ultimately we had to learn to command.

I was tolerably well versed in all these disciplines and as I had no ambition to be a success at Junker school I couldn't help pointing out the correct version to the instructors when they falsely stated or misquoted something: This unsettled them and certainly was not a plus point in my favour. The school leadership was composed recognisably of officers who stood closer to the Party cadres than the fighting men, they had a tangible 'stable smell', which was not ours.

After two weeks the daily training schedule changed with a greater emphasis on leadership tasks. Into the area of general leadership of troops there now came the tactical and organisational work of the medical units. This latter was basically activity from which I did not want to withdraw although it had little to do with charitable service for the needy. By then my experiences and knowledge had infiltrated my soldierly mentality to such an extent that at heart I found Junker school repugnant.

Although two officers responsible for training assessment attempted to motivate me, due to a strong inner feeling I remained critical and reserved; an attitude which other members of our training course ('Inspektion') clearly shared. One day after early morning sport, weapons cleaning was on the agenda followed by the discipline singular to the Junker school known as 'Instruction in the World View'. In the training programme of our

Inspektion it appeared for the first time and we prepared for a quiet, boring hour.

The lecturer was a bland SS-1st Lieutenant, the village school-teacher type: as an SS officer he obviously belonged to the category 'Home Front'. We suspected immediately that he had never had his baptism of fire, for his tunic was bare except for the Hitler Youth Sport Badge. His discourse began as expected, stale from constant repetition, the diction banal and bombastic. The theme was 'The Law to Protect Against Progeny Afflicted with Hereditary Disease'[1], which had been passed shortly after the National Socialist seizure of power in 1933 and had as its objective the obligatory sterilization of seriously – particularly mentally – handicapped persons, a measure only moderately opposed by the public. Little was known about what was being done, although after implementation of the Law it was no secret in the vicinity of the closed institutions and was accepted without any great emotion. The subject had been discussed at the University of Giessen, where two months earlier I had studied the field of Eugenics, the view there being taken that the circumstances created by the Law were rather positive.

The training hour dragged on. The lecturer continued to reel off his repertoire in a dull and wooden manner: racial hygiene, the need to promote the positive elements in the body of the people, the mission of the state to cull the negative strain, in particular the sterilization of individuals whose progeny might be classified as unwholesome. Up to this point we had sat through the lecture more or less in detachment. Finally the speaker touched upon the measures which had been decided upon about six months previously in a detailed programme. He spoke of the medical operations practised on the afflicted and then uttered a sentence abruptly which – also for me – had unexpectedly dramatic consequences.

'We have decided', he said, 'on a measure to simplify the solution of the problem. Seriously mentally handicapped persons will, after the most thorough medical investigation, be passed on for euthanasia, the procedure will naturally be carried through with scrupulous attention to humanitarian principles.'

There was a rhetorical pause for this to sink in and the air in the room suddenly became icy. Then an SS Junker in the row to the left of me stood up and said in a calm, clear voice: 'I protest formally against this disregard of medical ethics and the Hippocratic oath, to which I feel myself bound as a student of medicine.' Two other young men rose with him. One said, 'I associate myself with the words of my comrade!', the other only, 'I also. What you are propagating is a crime!'

We all sat as if frozen: I felt sudden admiration for these three comrades. They were men of the sister division *Das Reich*, one of them was an SS-Staff Sergeant with the Iron Cross First Class, the other two were SS-Corporals with the Iron Cross Second Class ribbon in the buttonhole, all three were decorated with the Ostmedaille and the Wound Badge. I wanted to jump up and exclaim: 'I too! I too!' but I was as if paralysed, my throat blocked. I remained seated and was filled with bitter shame.

For long seconds there was an almost intolerable, breathless hush. The SS-1st Lieutenant lecturer, his face a pallid mask and struggling to compose himself, clutched the edges of his desk. Finally, after a pause, which seemed to be eternal, he took a deep breath and ordered, 'Follow me at once to the office!' He marched off with stiff strides followed by his three crazy opponents, never to be spoken of again. We waited in consternation, nobody said a word. We knew that these three comrades had put their heads in a noose. After a while an SS-Corporal came from the office to inform us that the lecture was over, the daily schedule was to be followed, this being cross-country duty and a lecture on commanding motorised units.

This incident had deeply disturbed me inwardly and I pondered it until the evening hours. After duty I was in the squad quarters, which I shared with five other Junkers. I was alone with my bed-neighbour SS-Corporal Hans Bender, real name Zdislav Benderis, who came from Lithuania. He and I – as I had determined from cautiously angled conversations – were of one mind in our basic view of what had become of National Socialism, and we had no illusions of what would lead on from it.

193

On the wall was a map on which the front lines had been marked out with pins and coloured cords. In the East the German retreat ran along the East Prussian border, along the Vistula to west of Odessa, and was temporarily stabilized: in the West, Belgium and France, except for Alsace-Lorraine, were fully in the hands of the Allied armies of invasion, in Italy the Gothic Line was being held with difficulty parallel to the Apennine mountains from La Spezia to Rimini. Scandinavia, and the Balkans with their indispensable oilfields, were more or less open flanks with few forces available for their defence.

I stood before this map and said to Bender, 'If we are to get out of this mess, we need more than a miracle: our only reserves exist in our imagination that we are fighting for the ethics of Europe against Bolshevism. What happened today has hurt us all, this development will become a danger to the morale of the fighting troops.' Bender did not reply. He gave me a piercing stare and placed two fingers of his right hand against his lips conspiratorially. I soon saw what this meant. Along the wall from the height of the window to the floor was a large wardrobe, which unknown to me covered a door: behind it was the room housing our squad leader, SS-2nd Lieutenant Lobeck.

Seconds later Lobeck threw open our squad room door and roared at me, 'I heard everything! You know what that means! Remain here in readiness!' He bestowed upon me a look pregnant with malice and left the room. 'My God, you've really trodden in the shit.' Bender said in concern, 'If you want, I'll try to play the whole thing down, a sentence taken out of context or something.'

'Thanks, but just leave it, Hans,' I said in an attempt to calm him. 'Really you had nothing to do with it. Actually, I am quite happy it has come to this. From now on every day here makes me feel sick.'

I knew already: what was coming my way was unavoidable and extremely threatening. I was not allowed much time to reflect on my position. After a few minutes somebody came from the office and reported laconically, 'Maeger is to report to the Chief of Inspektion.'

I buckled up, put on my steel helmet and went. The Spiess waved me through a door into a room in which the Chief of Inspection, SS-

Captain Gerlach was sitting behind a desk, at his side Lobeck with eyes like slits.

I stood to attention and stated as per regulations: 'SS-Junker Maeger reporting as ordered, SS-Captain!' Gerlach looked at me thoughtfully and then said quite nicely, 'If you said what SS-2nd Lieutenant Lobeck says you did, this is a very serious matter. You have questioned Final Victory in a defeatist manner. What have you to say to that?'

I replied, 'I stand by what I said, SS-Captain. The motivation was the incident today in the World View lecture. The three comrades who protested are neither traitors nor defeatists, they have expressed a justified concern.'

'I don't want to draw this whole business out longer than necessary,' Gerlach said. 'Make a believable statement and I will deliver a bearable ruling.'

Lobeck intervened: 'He expressed himself quite unmistakably, SS-Captain! It was subversive to military power and a criticism of the National Socialist ethic. It must not be mitigated in any way!'

I reacted impulsively. To my horror I heard myself say: 'I relinquish wearing the same uniform as SS-2nd Lieutenant Lobeck!'

At that Gerlach lost his carefully controlled cool. 'You cheeky man,' he shouted. 'I sentence you to three days close arrest for insulting a superior officer! You are hereby excluded from further visits to the Junker school and will not take part in any more scheduled duties. You will find out the rest later. Dismiss!'

My squad room comrades received me with distant embarrassment. One of them slapped me on the back without speaking. Insofar as there were any conversations, they were terse and mundane. That night contrary to my expectations I slept well.

At early morning roll call I was ordered to step forward before the Inspektion. The Spiess read out the punishment, which Gerlach had already pronounced upon me, then he cut off my Junker's lace with a pair of scissors. In a strange mixture of emotions I felt despair, depression and yet relief. I spent the day inactive in the squad room, sitting by the window in the autumn sun. Somewhere a radio was playing:

195

Es geht alles vorüber, es geht alles vorbei,
Nach jedem Dezember folgt wieder ein Mai . . .

'Everything is temporary, everything passes away,
After every December, there's always a May.'

and I felt somewhat comforted. Towards midday Lobeck appeared and ordered me drily, 'Clean my room!' I went there and found that there was nothing to clean, everything was painstakingly laid out correctly and spotless. Then I noticed on his desk his pistol holster with a Walther PPK 7.65mm calibre resting on top of it. It was loaded contrary to regulations and I understood at once what Lobeck expected of me. According to his concept of honour, in my situation there was only one way out – to shoot myself. I did not have the slightest intention of giving him the satisfaction and returned immediately to my squad room.

In the late afternoon I was ordered to the office again. I was instructed to report to the arrest building before curfew with one blanket and without rations. Upon doing so, I was shown into an absolutely dark cell inhabited by a co-delinquent guilty of a breach of watchkeeping regulations. Wöhlert was from Lauenburg in Pomerania and belonged to my former Inspektion, but I had had no previous contact with him.

The three days in the arrest cell dragged on and on. The only bright spot was the company of a cellmate. There was nothing consoling to say to each other but our mutual presence shielded against total despair in the absolute loneliness of the black hole. I had smuggled in a Hindenburg lamp[2] and in its dull light we read the shreds of newspaper, which lay around the cell.

Our only contact with the outside world was the rattle of the door bolt morning and evening when the jailor brought us a jug of water. Hunger was initially tolerable but by the evening of the second day so bothersome that all I could think about was food: the revolting millet porridge, which had been our only sustenance for months in the first winter in Russia, would have seemed like a delicacy if only I could have got some. I did not wish to discuss this subject with my

196

cellmate, all conversation between us had dried up, we were two silent figures in the darkness.

In my helpless depression and exhaustion, thinking that I could not tolerate this misery any longer, I heard Wöhlert hammering on the cell door with both fists. He would not desist and finally the bolt was pulled back and someone growled through the crack in the door, 'What's all this racket, anything special?' and I heard Wöhlert reply, 'Hunger, comrade! Hunger! Please bring us a slice of bread, just a little slice!' The door was shut and Wöhlert fell silent. A leaden silence enveloped us. Then the bar rattled again and without a word the jailor handed in two slices of bread. Never, not even later as a PoW, did I ever eat my bread with more devotion and a prayer of thanks.

After the three days arrest were up we both received at the Inspektion office orders to proceed to Berlin, to the Medical Office of SS Headquarters, where we had to hand over a sealed envelope. After a railway journey of twelve hours interrupted by air raid warnings we arrived and were met by the SS-Lieutenant-Colonel charged with our further destiny in his hands.

As we entered his room, his initial dark look changed into one of joyful bewilderment. 'Man, what are you doing here?' he asked Wöhlert, equally surprised. It turned out that both the Lieutenant-Colonel and Wöhlert came from Lauenburg and there was some kind of family relationship between them. After they engaged in a private exchange of news we were invited to sit while with a frown the Lieutenant-Colonel read the report we had brought from Prague. As for me, my defeatism only merited a comment in the margin while the important matter was insulting a senior officer; presumably the Junker school did not wish to have its reputation damaged any further.

'Well, we shouldn't take too tragic a view of the whole thing,' said the man who at that moment had power of life and death over us. 'You both ought to go directly to the Probationary Division, but for me you are primarily paramedics and so far have not yet received a proper training for that, so I shall send you first for six weeks to the medical training school at Bad Aussee. After that we shall decide. Good luck and leave by the central corridor.'

Outside we almost hugged each other at our good luck, we could hardly believe the change in our fortunes. The Probationary Division, for which we were ultimately intended was called *Knochensturm*, the Crossbones Division, because its members did not wear the SS runes on the collar patch, but two crossed stick-grenades, which looked like crossed bones. It was notorious as a squad for suicide missions. We had no idea where Bad Aussee was located in beautiful 'Ostmark' – Austria – but at least it was not Berlin or Prague, and above all not the Eastern Front.

We received new orders and left as soon as we could in good spirits. Bad Aussee received us like a peaceful fable: the medical school was housed in a new, roomy building on the road to Grundlsee, the town itself was a giant military hospital with wards distributed in all available hotels and sanatoriums. For the first time I was happy to be a soldier, my duties gave me pleasure. Four mornings per week we were instructed in all disciplines, in the afternoons we worked shifts alternating across all departments: surgery, internal medicine, infectious diseases, skin and venereal diseases, the X-ray department.

The atmosphere in this renowned spa resort was wonderful. The military hospital side had been markedly affected by the restrictions imposed for the fifth year of war, particularly provisions and dressing materials; there was plenty of Plaster of Paris but flexible metal splints, plaster strips and so forth were in short supply. Used bandages were carefully rolled up for re-use, and washed if dirty. Gauze dressings were being replaced more often by thin crepe-paper rolls.

The situation regarding medication was much better thanks to the highly developed German pharmaceutical industry. Although penicillin had been discovered by Sir Alexander Fleming in 1928 nothing was known of it, presumably as a result of the closing down of German research in the Third Reich. Instead for some diseases, gonorrhoea and gangrene, the more effective sulphonamide developed by Gerhard Domagk was used as Marfanil powder in the treatment of wounds, at Bad Aussee as a combination in cod liver oil: Lebertran-Marpu for short was one of the most used terms in the surgical department. In the other clinical areas the commonest sulphonamides were Cibazol, Eubasin, Euvernyl, Prontosil and Supronal. Everything that I learnt was contrary to what I expected, although in the X-ray department my earlier knowledge of photography came in useful.

I could hardly believe my eyes when in my third week at Bad Aussee I suddenly recognised Hans Bender at morning roll call. He was just as surprised as I, was pleased to see me and he told me that upon passing out from Junker school he had been sent to Aussee because he had no training as a paramedic and had to pass this course with various others. Although Bender had meanwhile been promoted to Junker and was therefore more successful than I, we worked it that we shared the same squadroom and got on the same as we had at Prague.

When it snowed at Aussee in October, Bender, who was an excellent skier, initiated me into the sport in what free time we had: I quickly mastered the thrilling descent down a steep icy track as well as he did. There were any numbers of military skiers available: they were financed by civilian donations for the Russian campaign but were never deployed as the sponsors had intended.

Under instruction I soon won the goodwill of the training officer, an SS doctor in the rank of SS-1st Lieutenant. I was quick to learn how to apply any dressing from the manual with such dexterity that I was chosen to practice this discipline with a few other advanced students. In theoretical work I was the first student who could pronounce fluently the chemical formula 'dimetylamionophenyl-dimetylpyrazolon', the preferred analgesic Pyramidon.

When the course terminated at the end of October 1944 I received my certificate as Sanitäter (paramedic), and the head of the school informed me that with two other qualifiers I had been selected for additional training as theatre nurse and Army surgeon at the Weilmünster military hospital in the Taunus. Before this I was shocked to receive from SS Headquarters in Berlin another week's leave which I spent in Cuxhaven with the student friend of my Giessen days, Ilse, whose parents had invited me: Eupen/Malmedy was already occupied by the Americans.

Ilse's parents still called their only daughter 'Plümchen' because as a child she had been a little on the plump side, and as a grown woman the situation had not changed much. Father Harmsen – big, heavy and blond – was the officer authorised to act and sign on behalf of his firm which made U-boat equipment and was also a Party member: mother Käthe, of slight build and dark, took me to her heart at once. Both read from 'Plümchen's' eyes her every wish, which was at that time myself. Therefore all three had planned a surprise; scarcely had I arrived at Cuxhaven than my engagement was prepared. Father Harmsen, brought up on a farm at Bremerhaven, disappeared for a day and a night, returning with a trunk full of good things, amongst them a large fat goose, which was consigned at once to the baking oven. The following day we celebrated with a hefty North German banquet with nice people from the family and I had a good time – why not? Things had not gone so well for me for a long time.

In the five days of my stay I came closer to the inner family circle and of course was asked a number of questions, which I answered frankly. I was even unmistakably clear about my experience in Prague. Father Harmsen frowned to show his concern, slapped me on the shoulder and said kindly, 'Only thoughts are free, dear boy!' At my departure he presented me with a small pistol to fit into my trouser pocket. The Russians seized it after my capture.

Mother Käthe, with whom I later had a pen friendship, provided me in 1948 with an unsolicited 'Persil certificate',[3] much sought after and honoured for its material benefits, in which she had stated:

Herr Herbert Maeger often visited my abode during his periods of leave. From the conversations I had with him I established that Herr Maeger was clearly opposed to the methods and aims of his sector of the Wehrmacht. Amongst other statements he made the following observation to me: 'If I ever have a son who wanted to join the SS, I would kill him before he did. I was personally neither a member of the NSDAP nor any of its associations.'

I never used Käthe Harmsen's 'Persil certificate' nor similar documents, for I never saw the need to attempt to rehabilitate myself. In 1948 before a Spruchkammer[4] at Weilburg the following dialogue took place between the chairman and myself.

Chairman: 'Were you voluntarily a member of the Waffen-SS or were you conscripted?'

Maeger: 'What would it cost me to have been a volunteer?'

Chairman: 'You could not be an innocent, but a fellow-traveller, which would involve a fine of 50 Reichsmarks.'

Maeger: 'Then I declare myself to have been a volunteer.'

Shortly afterwards the Hesse State Ministry for Political Liberation sent me a bill for the fine which came to 76 marks including tribunal costs, postage and expenses. The written explanation accompanying the invoice stated: 'Because the accused belonged to an organisation declared by the International Court at Nuremberg to be criminal, there was no question of an amnesty', a poorly drafted piece of officialese. Despite what I had to go through it was worth it, I paid the 76 marks and to all intents and purposes I was denazified. Officially, my apocalyptic past lay behind me, but had burned itself indelibly into my soul.

The wonderful days at Cuxhaven passed more quickly than I wanted. My leave pass said that I had to report to the Waffen-SS reserve battalion stationed at Stettin. I arrived in a grey city marked by war and spent a couple of dark days in a miserable barracks before being given my orders to proceed to Weilmünster in the Taunus. The military hospital, located a little away from the valley of the Weil and based around a provincial sanatorium, overspilled into an area larger than the village itself whose inhabitants, as I soon discovered, were proud to be assessed as a 'market town' instead of a village.

My first impression was that Weilmünster did not compare with Bad Aussee. After I had been there a few days, however, I saw its positive aspects. I particularly liked to work in its operating theatre. It was run by Matron Gudrun, a real operating-theatre dragon but very competent. I soon assimilated the knowledge and ability, which the basic training at Bad Aussee repertoire lacked. With three comrades who had long service in the Sanitäter grade at the front, I aimed to be with them as part of an operating theatre team in a front main dressing station (HVP). These HVPs were controlled by the Divisional HQs and received the wounded from battalion dressing stations. They worked as close as possible to the front line; understandably they had no female staff.

The training programme embraced four disciplines: the theatre nursing team assisted the surgeon with his preparations and gave direct assistance at surgical operations; the Asepsis had the job of preventing wound infections in the operation area and keeping the instruments and all materials germ-free; the anaesthesia is self-explanatory and the dressing craft was post-operational measures including splinting and applying plaster casts to limb injuries, for example in the case of bullet wounds to the lower jaw the setting of a head plaster-dressing of two rubber bands, which gave the structure mobility, allowing the patient to eat.

As I proved myself competent in the difficult procedure of administering the anaesthetic as a male 'theatre sister', I was first choice for this task. As it remained the case long after the war, for anaesthesia chloroform was used to induce unconsciousness and to maintain the condition. I also learnt there the generally rare procedure with Evipan for intravenous narcosis, which was only reliable if a precise dose was administered and then maintained by constant injections over the entire period of the operation. By reason of my ability in this regard, after the war at Rheydt Hospital, where I still had hopes of continuing my training in medicine, and from January to April 1946 I passed pre-clinical practical studies there, Senior Surgeon Professor von Tappeiner chose me to handle the Evipan narcosis process in preference to the assistant surgeons.

Soldiers were delivered to the Weilmünster field hospital with wounds or illnesses of so severe a nature that a quick recovery was not to be expected there. The extensive complex of buildings (the town had its own branch line on the Weilburg-Usingen-Bad Homburg-Frankfurt/Main service), could handle 1,200 patients but was not full when I arrived. That changed very swiftly after I had been there a fortnight when a hospital train was announced bringing in 500 cases from a military hospital in East Prussia threatened by the Red Army. All available beds were set up in wards and smaller rooms and the cellars, or better put, basements, because of the structure of the buildings on the slope. These were cleared out as far as possible and renovated.

When the long train arrived, all available assistants were called upon for a major effort. When we entered the converted express-coaches we were met by an intolerable stench. The totally inadequate number of travelling assistants, all exhausted, informed us that the journey had taken six weeks. All other military hospitals along the route were hopelessly overcrowded, and it had taken might and main to arrange for meagre food rations. Treatment of the wounded had been almost impossible for lack of dressings and the manner in which the tiered bunks had been crammed into the coach. It took the hospital staff two days to de-train the pitiable victims of this crazy journey into the prepared quarters. The unloading of the debilitated wounded on stretchers along the narrow corridors of the railway wagons was a punishing task during which many of them died. To get patients uphill into the hospital complex on the slope local farmers helped out voluntarily with horsedrawn wagons.

We of the operating theatre staff brought the worst cases with thigh and upper-arm plaster casts directly into the operating room and experienced there what until them we had considered impossible. In some of the cases the plaster cast detached with contents, the entire leg or arm having rotted. In other cases as we carefully cut away the plaster cast we found beneath it a furry grey layer, which looked like surgical cotton and which we assumed was felt for padding a splint until we found to our horror that it was a thick host of lice. The sight of it made us feel absolutely sick. The suffering of those plagued without being able to get at these vermin must have been unimaginable.

Everybody who survived that transport from East Prussia had gone through unspeakable horror. We worked for a whole week at two operating tables from six in the morning until night in order to alleviate their sufferings. One day remains unforgettable, in which we carried out forty-three amputations. It was amazing that nearly all these cases came through it. As no other volunteer could be found to dispose of the amputated limbs, I took on the job: I wrapped the severed legs and arms in a cloth, carried them to the block where the central heating system was installed a hundred metres away and tossed the body parts into the glowing coals of the giant furnace. The two stokers could not be induced to do it at any price.

The Spiess, without whom no military organisation is possible and who was also to be found in the SS military hospital at Weilmünster, was well informed from my personal file about my obscure path to the locality. If he found anything he objected to in my file, he did not make me suffer for it.

When at evening roll call one day he complained in a loud voice – and with justification – that certain members of the hospital staff had avoided doing their share. I could not help calling out distinctly from within the ranks: 'Those who slipped away, Stabsscharführer, are on the right flank!', which was occupied, as usual, by the office-sergeant and the supply services. My observation which by the SS yardstick a few weeks before would have counted as an impudent provocation had no comeback. Presumably this was an indication that in view of the ever-worsening situation, a major reconsideration had set in regarding the sense of uncritical subordination in the ranks.

The Weilmünster operating theatre team of nursing sisters and male trainees proved their worth with that great call upon their services. Relying on the routine we had set for ourselves, we came through the following few quieter weeks with no major problems. Amongst ourselves and with the assistant surgeons there was a good understanding. The Senior Surgeon, SS-Lieutenant-Colonel Dr Klemm on the other hand was a different case, to put it mildly. A vain career type, who apparently fitted his own mental image of the elite, was always spotlessly dressed. He treated the patients and ourselves as the extras to his starring role, but he was excellent with the scalpel, which we had to respect. He already had some concerns about the war's end for himself and this may explain why he gave preferential lodging and treatment to some wounded US troops delivered to Weilmünster.

On the theatre plan at six one morning the first operation was an appendectomy, a relatively harmless procedure. Everything was ready; the patient, an army sergeant aged about thirty, was already under narcosis on the table, the assistant surgeon SS-1st Lieutenant Dr Siebel and we others stood ready waiting for the Senior Surgeon who had not turned up for the case scheduled by himself. After about a quarter of an hour, Sister Gudrun told me to ring his quarters. I did this and he answered tersely, 'I am on my way!'

After another ten minutes I rang again at the request of Dr Siebel and received the same reply. Meanwhile, we were having concerns about the patient, whose circulation was not good. After another five minutes Dr Siebel decided to scrub up to avoid any further loss of time. He had hardly begun when the Senior Surgeon stormed in, looked at the situation, saw that Dr Siebel had begun scrubbing up, and said merely: 'Well, I see that everything is proceeding here without me!' Then he turned on his heel and left the scene.

Dr Siebel had no surgical training and now the patient had lain under narcosis for half an hour with an inflamed appendix. Since we were all looking at him expectantly, and an appendectomy amongst insiders was considered one of the simplest procedures, which sea captains in emergencies on the high seas had carried out successfully, he bravely took up the scalpel and got on with it. After ten minutes he had still been unable to locate the appendix despite a thorough search in the open abdomen. At his request I rang the Senior Surgeon for the third time in order to inform him: he replied laconically, 'I have no more time for it today.' And hung up. We all stood around speechless and at a loss. Then the patient was sown up again, and died three days later.

Insofar as I had anything to do with them, the population of Weilmünster were friendly people, considerably more forthcoming than the inhabitants of my previous military hospital localities. When I had free time in the evenings or on Sundays, I would walk the couple of kilometres to the 'market' and go into the 'Posthaus', a roomy restaurant with its own butchery business where the plump female proprietress would serve the soldiers of her 'garrison town' with a big stew or a plate of baked potatoes with jellied meat.

On the way to this welcome addition to the sparse and monotonous hospital fare I regularly passed by a mixed goods store.

Both its display windows had been shattered by the only bomb dropped on the nearby railway line. Two replacement panes about the size of a hand towel had been fitted into the wooden boarding. One day I went in because I needed some shoe polish, which a very pleasant middle-aged woman readily sold me. I was alone in the shop and we entered into conversation as a result of which the shop owner, Lisette Rippel, invited me for dinner the following Saturday evening. I was then introduced to her daughter, Ilse. Father Rippel had been killed in a motorcycle accident on 13 March 1933, as Lisette, inclined to occult beliefs, emphasised; since then the two of them had run the shop and with great industry had won a faithful clientele for themselves. After a second visit I asked the Rippels if they would look after my valuable medical books, which I wanted to bring up from bomb-threatened Giessen, and they agreed readily.

The upshot was that I wrote to Weilmünster in March 1946 enquiring if the books would be available for collection. I received in reply a very warmly worded letter informing me that I was welcome to call at any time. That was in the days when in the British zone of occupation, in which Rheydt fell, former Waffen-SS men were required to report in. I did not like the sound of this; the adventurous railway journey to Weilmünster took two days. At Weilmünster I was received like a family member believed lost. Naturally I stayed awhile, taking walks with Ilse through the almost undamaged town, along the idyllic Weil river and over the slopes of the Taunus, sprouting the first green of spring. It was inevitable that we would grow closer. I found a new home, a good wife and faithful life partner; when she died of a serious illness ten years later I felt her loss very deeply.

Apart from my work in the operating theatres at the military hospital I was given other functions, such as visits to change bandages and supervise blood transfusions. The latter were still being made then with a primitive three-way transmission equipment. Regular blood donors were the soldiers at the Weilburg NCO's school. All that mattered was the blood group, refinements such as the Rhesus factor were not included in the standard. On two occasions I experienced how patients died within a few minutes of the transfusion as a result of errors.

Now and again I was Duty NCO for night duty in the central office, once the Senior Surgeon's room at the Hesse provincial sanatorium. I was very happy to do this for I was alone in the large room with great shelves of books up to the tall ceiling with which I could pass a few recreational hours. As Duty NCO I had access to all the service forms and rubber stamps. One night I toyed with the idea of writing myself orders to proceed to the military hospital at Koblenz, where I knew that US forces had arrived. Had I given in to temptation I might had got far enough and then had to think up some story for the remaining part of the journey. In the end I realised that even if this adventure succeeded I would be in dereliction of my duties, and this might have been harder to bear than the risk of staying where I was and soon being ordered to the collapsing Eastern Front.

My transfer was imminent, and so Christmas 1944 marked the sad transition into an extremely disquieting new stage of my career as an SS soldier. I had no illusions as to what awaited: the penal division of the notorious General Dirlewanger – the Crossbones Division.

Chapter Ten

By Tram to the Front

'I am now going to Berlin, and from there by tram to the front,' I had told them at Weilmünster upon receiving my orders to report to SS Headquarters. The past, the debacle of my departure from Junker school at Prague had caught up with me. I knew that I was facing a difficult future.

At the conclusion of the operating theatre course at Weilmünster we received a proper certificate, mine being endorsed 'Very good'. My three colleagues were sent to join the reserve battalion for paramedics at Stettin, my orders were to report in Berlin. Upon taking my leave of the Spiess at the Weilmünster military hospital, he gave me a very meaningful look and remarked: 'Up until now you have got away with the business very lightly. I wish you continuing good luck. You will be getting a good assessment from here. But whether this will be of any help to you . . .', and left the sentence unfinished.

It was a long journey that took several days because the railway tracks were continually severed by the incessant air attacks. I arrived at Kassel on the evening of the second day. The city was an empty, cold, stone desert upon which the moon shone down: it was almost half an hour until I came across a patrol who pointed the way to a soldiers' home in the cellar of a public building. There I at least got a hot drink and a bed on which to stretch out.

In Berlin a different wind was blowing. My patron at the Medical Main Office, SS-Major Gerlach, was still competent in my case but told me with a shrug of the shoulders: 'Now I am not able to do much more. Your next posting is to 36th Waffengrenadier-Division whose commander is SS-Brigadier Dirlewanger, if that name means anything to you. I will try to do what I can to get you into the divisional main dressing station corresponding to your qualifications. You will have a better chance there.' I had heard of Dirlewanger, the commander of the penal division: the chances of surviving under his command were close to zero.

As it happened, however, I was put on ice for three weeks at a barracks at Lichterfelde, which had no windows as a result of the incessant Allied bombing raids: the rooms were, therefore, unheated. I was assigned to a repair squad fitting window panes from morning to night. Soon I could do it as well as an apprenticed craftsman. What surprised me was that despite the obvious general industrial collapse, there were always new panes of glass available.

Berlin was anything but pleasant. The rations were miserable, because of the concentrated air attacks I spent the nights crouching in the air raid shelter. Therefore I was rather relieved towards mid-February when I was given orders for Trebbin. I had been appointed a member of the operating theatre staff of the permanent staff of the new 36th Waffengrenadier-Division, formed from the remnants of its predecessor, the Bewährungs-Brigade[1] Dirlewanger. The new division was the last stop for men condemned at court martial, transferred into it as a punishment and released concentration camp inmates: the Divisional HQ were officers 'guilty of less serious offences' who had been transferred in as 'probationers' and were therefore, to some extent, privileged to wear insignia of rank. They retained the SS runes and, as I was, spared the 'crossbones' collar patch.

For almost three weeks we were engaged in senseless drills in the country, sixty men in a gymnasium with two-tier bunks nailed together from rough planks. One night I had a dream in which I was crossing swampy land alongside a ditch, panzers firing at me from my left, Russian soldiers approaching me from my right. I awoke bathed in sweat, the nightmare still intensive. A few weeks later the same dream played out in reality at my capture.

In the course of the next few weeks I got to know a few more miserable Brandenburg villages with the same nonchalant, disapproving attitude towards soldiers; it was quite impossible to get a plate of soup or anything fit to eat in a restaurant in order to supplement the poor rations, quite different to the 'Ostmark', or in

Weilmünster, where one could always count on a small additional mealtime at the 'Posthaus'. The quality of regular rations for Wehrmacht other ranks generally left much to be desired. For breakfast we received dreadful ersatz-coffee, heavy damp Army bread, two tablespoonfuls of marmalade made mainly of red beet and colouring and a blob of margarine. For supper instead of the marmalade there was a triangle of cream cheese wrapped in tin foil or a couple of centimetres of grey sausage made out of ground sinew and bones mixed with so-called 'Bratling-powder', the constitution of which was unknown.

From the day of my enrolment in September 1941 I had never had enough to eat. All the boastful words such as: 'Everything for our brave soldiers, for the best soldiers in the world the best equipment in the world and first-class food' proved to be just empty talk. There was really only enough when we had the opportunity to feed ourselves as we had done for example in France, when I bought potatoes, milk and butter from farmers to make my bucket of potato purée, some of which I would share out to my squad room colleagues.

In the four-man operating theatre staff to which I was appointed I kept the rank of SS-Lance Corporal, which was two grades below that of SS-Staff Sergeant, as befitted my duties. For some time we loafed around, at the end of March 1945 we set up the divisional main dressing station in the school at a village west of Guben. We had a good supply of equipment and medication. At first there was relatively little to do because the front was quiet. Army Group Centre had dug in on the left bank of the Oder with around 700,000 men from all the rearward services everywhere: we had hardly any fighting reserves. On the right bank of the Oder the Soviet Army prepared for the last decisive battle. They had enormous material superiority and were confident of victory.

After limited incursions on 14 and 15 April 1945, in the early hours of the 16th the Soviets opened their Berlin offensive with an enormous mass of tanks and artillery, 2.5 million men in eighteen armies and an unprecedented concentration of artillery of almost 43,000 guns, howitzers and mortars, one gun to each five metres of frontline, and 6,287 tanks and assault guns.[2] The German advanced front line was literally crushed but despite the destruction caused by the enormous artillery bombardment, in the sector of 36th Waffengrenadier-Division the retrieval of the wounded went on: field ambulances arrived in a steady stream at our main dressing station. The rows of stretchers in front of the operating theatre lengthened, men suffering from shock, loss of blood, privation: those still conscious showed in their faces their despair at having been delivered to an almost inescapable fate. Each of us knew that this battle was the last act of the twilight of the gods for the Thousand-Year Reich and that the Soviets up to this phase of the battle habitually murdered our wounded, paying no regard to the Red Cross flag. Taking prisoners was not provided for in the Soviet logistics.

The offensive stretched our resources from the moment of its inception. We simply could not handle the numbers of wounded even though our operating theatre staff worked alternately eighteen to twenty hours daily at two tables, myself almost exclusively as anaesthetist: the constant breathing-in of chloroform and ether affected my liver and it took years for me to recover from it. The two surgeons at the main dressing station, also transferred into our unit, did their work worse rather than better, overcoming the problems with cognac, apparently available to them in unlimited quantities. The main burden was undertaken by a Jewish surgeon from Jülich who like many of his fellow sufferers had been recruited from Mauthausen concentration camp and wore the SS uniform with the 'crossbones squad' insignia in place of the SS runes. As the anaesthetist I was nearly always at his side at the operating table: I would put the wounded under, which in their condition of total exhaustion as a rule required only a small dose of anaesthetic, then he would do the emergency operation, limited to the absolute minimum so as to get the table free for the next case. The extraction of bullets and shell splinters, the sealing of blood vessels and injections of analgesic medication was obviously a priority.

While dressings were being applied to wounds I would have short periods of rest, which included preparing a label to be attached to

211

the breast of the uniform jacket of the patient. At each end of these labels were detachable red and green strips. If both strips were detached it meant 'after care back to unit'. If the green strip was left attached this meant 'walking wounded military hospital', if the red strip was left attached this meant 'transport to military hospital'.

Our pair of staff surgeons, insofar as they did their duty at all, leaned towards the desires of the command structure: a wounded man with only a through-and-through of the arm, a light splinter wound to the head, buttocks or a leg was labelled 'back to unit' after treatment. I would ask the poor devils as often as I found the opportunity: 'Do you really want to go back to your unit?' and nearly always received a silent shake of the head. There were men there, 'Frontschwein', who had been on the Russian front from the beginning: they wore the proof on their breast, from the Ostmedaille to the Infantry Assault Badge, the Iron Cross, the Wound Badge in Silver. They lay on their stretchers with pale faces, exhausted, all hope gone. To have sent them back to the collapsing front so close to the end of the war after years of unspeakable sufferings on the Eastern Front would have meant certain death. In many cases I left the red strip attached to the label, which meant transport to a military hospital by the next ambulance, and so I was certainly able to save the lives of many. I had no way of knowing that their chances had greatly increased. At the beginning of the Berlin offensive, Soviet fighting forces had been ordered to use less brutality against German prisoners and wounded. Ilya Ehrenburg's rousing call for ruthless revenge had come in for official criticism: in Moscow the plan was now to ease the way for a Communist post-war Germany. At least some sections of the Red Army accepted the change in attitude and even behaved in a more humane manner in many cases.[3]

I knew what I was risking with my unauthorised relabelling. It was a time in which words such as 'sabotage' and 'sedition' were not just bandied about. If I had been detected, I could easily have finished up hanging by the neck from the nearest tree.

The last weeks on the Oder front live in my memory as a chaos of blood, defeat and despair. All the brutality of an absolutely ruthless Nazi leadership was now turned against its own troops in the total collapse. Our division was part of the Army Group of the notorious Field Marshal Schörner, whose inspection routes were lined with hanged soldiers. Most were stragglers, separated from their units in the confusion and unable to show field gendarmes a movement order. Schörner, who used to be accompanied by a 'flying court' gave these stragglers short shrift before having them strung up.

At the beginning of May, when his army was bleeding to death between Oder and Elbe, Schörner got into a Fieseler Storch, which he kept constantly on hand for his own use, and had himself flown to the Americans, where he was invited for breakfast. Certain of today's publishers celebrate the deserter Army Commander-in-Chief with splendidly bound books and hail him as one of the great heroes of the Second World War.[4]

Looming Armageddon came upon us with abstruse conditions and orders. Twice we had to abandon the operating theatre, and the wounded on its tables, in order to dig foxholes at the edge of the village to stop expected attacks by Russian armour. We had no weapons, not even a hand grenade or a sidearm. Now and again we did at least have a couple of hours sleep. The wildest rumours were circulating; one evening during a roll call an army order with the following contents was read out to us: the German Government had concluded an armistice with the British and Americans; we were now fighting as allies against the Soviet Union and had only to hold out for a few days until help came from the West. This proved again that there was no lie to which a demoralised leadership would not stoop in order to cling to power for one day longer.

Everybody could see that the end was near. Ever present was the fear of falling into the hands of the Russians. We knew that the front units had been wiped out and that their remnants were in wild flight to the West. All organisation had broken down. Of our two surgeons one had made off, the other was constantly drunk and babbling. We did what we could and actually managed to get all but two wounded, both in a coma, away to the military hospital. The ambulance drivers did their duty to the last.

Suddenly no more ambulances arrived, the sounds of fighting became louder and clearer, a sure sign that we were cut off from all front activity behind the lines. Everybody took off in the space of a minute: I was caught on the hop and found myself alone in the operating theatre where so shortly before there had been such bustle.

Through a window I saw a line of Russian riflemen approaching from the edge of a wood and within rifle range. My field pack stood ready: into it I crammed my most important belongings, a glass of morphine substance I happened to see on a table, slung my paramedic's satchel with dressings and medicaments over my shoulder and headed out for the last stage of my career as a soldier. It must have been 24 April 1945.

Without giving thought to what might be awaiting me, I strode towards the West to catch up with the survivors of Ninth Army, who also had no idea in mind but to get away from the Russians as quickly as possible and from the threat of damnation in Siberia. They had only one goal: the Elbe, the Americans and the vague hope of a life in freedom.

Chapter Eleven

The Death March to the West

Making my way westwards I was left to my own devices. I never saw any member of my medical company again on the route. I lost no time in joining up with stragglers of the mass of German soldiers flowing back. The military units had almost all disbanded: the many stragglers, in small groups or alone like myself, met up by chance. There was also a blend of units still able to fight, mostly SS with armoured vehicles. Between them were officers of the rearward services and Army administration officials with heavily-laden lorries and cars hoping to get their booty to safety. Many of these vehicles failed on the woodland paths, offering the starving masses of exhausted soldiers the welcome opportunity of a free feed. It was the common will to keep on to the West, never making camp, in the flight to the Elbe, the demarcation line between the Americans and the Russians. It is estimated that about 4,000 men actually reached this destination.[1] They got through west of Potsdam behind General Wenck's Twelfth Army blockade line and at Tangermünde, where US General William Simpson permitted them to cross. If this questionable success of the Final Battle was bought at a price, thanks were due to the 100,000 men of Twelfth Army who enabled 300,000 civilians to be saved from the Soviet troops.

The history of those days is the chronicle of the great death march of the remnants of the beaten German Army, fighting for pure survival. The Russians had meanwhile taken almost the entire region between the Oder and the Elbe and were attempting to encircle the last remnants in a small pocket, but even now a large portion of the German forces proved in these last dramatic days what they were still capable of. Lacking heavy weapons, which they had long since been obliged to leave behind, they broke

215

through Russian interception positions repeatedly, destroying Soviet tanks in close combat. These were not operations resulting from tactical or strategic orders, but developed from a plan-like movement of troops westwards. The losses were enormous; the Russians maintained incessant artillery fire on the German lines of retreat through the woods, explosions against trees having devastating effects.

With the materials from my paramedic's satchel, I rendered what first aid I could in the hope that the victims had at least a chance of survival. This forced me to fall back. I found an abandoned bicycle, which enabled me several times to return to the head of the group to which I had attached myself until I was halted by two field-gendarmes aiming machine pistols at me. They ordered me, 'Get rid of the bike and satchel, pick up a rifle and get forward. Towards the Elbe!'

I was thinking of asking them where 'forward' was, but then produced my Red Cross identification and said, 'I am a paramedic. I am tending the wounding so far as I can and that is why I need the bicycle.'

The answer from the senior man was terse and precise, 'Do what you are told or you will be shot!' I was strongly tempted to kill them both, but lacking a weapon had no chance and was forced to knuckle under. So I became once more an infantryman.

I continued ever westwards, determined to reach the Elbe at any price. I discovered bread, a couple of tins of food and a loaded pistol in an abandoned lorry. I also found another bicycle in a usable state, which I rode down a narrow lane leading into the small town of Halbe. Here I had another fearsome experience. North and south of Halbe the Russians had occupied strong positions. The line of retreat through the town was being kept open by the remnants of the German divisions; the defence was so fierce that it had forced the Russians back and now they were firing on it from both sides with mortars and artillery. Everybody aiming to get to the West had to pass through the Halbe bottleneck, and Halbe was an inferno.

I ran alongside others, pushing my bicycle for dear life between armoured vehicles and through the streets lined with ruined houses.

Over several sections the road was strewn with corpses; for hundreds of metres one could not set foot down on the ground for the dead. Soldiers fell around me under the artillery barrage. Whoever was hit or tripped died crushed by panzer tracks literally dripping with blood. It was a scenario of hell beyond the powers of imagining of those who never experienced it. Breathlessly I found steps leading down into a cellar where I was safe and spent some time. After a while the firing fell off a little and so I set off again for my life. Then I reached the edge of the town and the worst of the fire storm was behind me. I pedalled away as furiously as my lungs and aching lungs allowed, and then threw myself into the grass alongside a road in order to rest awhile. I had got away with it again.

At the end of 1996 my wife and I followed my route over its 130 kilometres from the Oder to Beelitz and on the way visited the woodland cemetery at Halbe in which more than 22,000 victims of the battle are interred. The cemetery is growing constantly as more and more remains are discovered: it is thought there are still 30,000 who were hurriedly buried in the woods around the town.

After the end of the murderous battle at Halbe, according to the official figures of the Red Army it had claimed the lives of 60,000 German servicemen; 120,000 prisoners had been taken, more than 300 tanks and assault guns, and 1,500 artillery pieces captured.[2]

About four kilometres west of Halbe, the Berlin-Dresden autobahn crosses the road from Halbe to Teupitz. It was there that the Russians set up a blockade with tanks and infantry in order to liquidate the remains of Ninth Army, which had escaped the hell of Halbe and were making for the Elbe. A colourful crowd of soldiers from all branches of service gathered at this intersection, most of them unarmed. In the ensuing chaos, Soviet tanks and artillery fired into them. As I cautiously approached this witches' cauldron a few rounds exploded so near that I dropped my bicycle, which had my field pack bound to the rack at the rear, in the centre of the carriageway and dived behind a slope for cover. After about thirty seconds I thought the coast was clear and went back to my bicycle.

Suddenly I found myself at the centre of a fresh salvo: three shells exploded on the highway, none more than three metres away as I could see seconds later by the craters they left. I had had no time to react: I stood with my hands on the handlebars, still on the road. Confused and disbelieving I looked myself over, but found that as if by some miracle I had escaped injury. Then I hurried off, pushing the bicycle at the double. I found a sand pit and checked myself and the bicycle over more closely. I was safe and sound, the bicycle frame had two holes from shell splinters but was still usable. My field pack had been penetrated by a splinter.

A crowd of about thirty men gathered around me. They had been forced off the autobahn by the Russian blockade. After a brief discussion we were in agreement about our situation: we found ourselves within a large encirclement and in a mini-encirclement, which was becoming more threatening by the minute, for the Russians were bringing up reinforcements to tighten the pocket.

In this situation the assembled, pitiful remnants of the German Army gave an example of the kind of wood from which they had been cut. Practically without leadership – nearly all the officers everywhere had been the first to decamp for the West – and without having taken part as a body in a battle previously, they organised themselves into a fighting force from nothing. With what modest stock of anti-tank limpet mines, hand grenades and machine pistols was available they launched an attack, the like of which could not have been better taught in any war academy. In less than twenty minutes the blockade had been broken. Four Soviet tanks lay smoking and wrecked. The Russian infantry had not been keen on standing its ground and had withdrawn. To give them their due, there was no reason for any of them to prove their bravery, the war was practically over and all that remained was to get out the vodka.

Because of the constant artillery fire falling on the routes of retreat, littered with wrecked vehicles, I decided to advance parallel to the highway but some distance off. I came across many corpses, both German and Russian, and then I arrived in a kind of no man's land.

In a wood at Märkisch-Buchholz I had the most horrific and gruesome experience of my entire life. Because of the bombing raids on Berlin, Wehrmacht Staffs had been evacuated to tents and Nissen huts with many female signals auxiliaries. Apparently they had been surprised by Soviet troops. So far as the eye could see, the wood was strewn with the naked corpses of hundreds of young women, each gutted from breasts to pubis and left to die. I shall never be able to rid myself of the image for as long as I live. If I correctly interpret statements by Red Army veterans to the television cameras after the collapse of the Soviet Union, even for them the memory of what they themselves or their comrades did in uncontrolled bloodlust – or often when under the influence of alcohol – or from simple psychopathic vindictiveness, is a heavy burden on their consciences.

In 1945 the writer Ilya Ehrenburg had incited it all at the urging of Stalin with an appeal published in many Soviet newspapers and fliers distributed to the Red Army:

Kill, you brave Red Army soldiers, kill! There is nothing of which the Germans are not guilty. Follow the instructions of Comrade Stalin and crush underfoot the Fascist animal in its lair. Break with violence the racial pride of German womanhood, take them as your rightful reward. Kill, you brave Red Army soldiers, kill.[3]

The walls of the ruined Reichstag in Berlin bore for years the painted slogan:

The Russian sword is up the German vagina!

I cannot estimate how much time I spent alone and deeply troubled amongst those hundreds of dead young women in the silence of the wood. Then I heard voices and hid behind a tent. Three German soldiers appeared with a Russian prisoner. When they saw the field of corpses, they raised their rifles and without a word shot the Russian. I found this unjustifiable for I had got to know enough Soviet soldiers – prisoners and defectors who had served us usefully at the front as so-called 'Hiwis' (auxiliary volunteers) – that they were people as we all were, many of them good, others sadistic and brutal, just as many Germans had been brutalized by a system, which even treated themselves as if they were subhumans.

Before I began to write my war memoirs, I decided that I should report every atrocity I had seen. Over the decades I have been asked more or less tactfully what I knew about Nazi war crimes, especially when the questioner knew that I had been in the Waffen-SS. Again and again I have seen how difficult it is to separate information and opinion in this connection. As regards the Russian campaign, it is to be doubted that the Soviet Army was conducting 'total war' from the very outset as Goebbels loud-mouthed in 1943, they simply dealt with their prisoners without mercy.

All armies in every war commit excesses. They are committed by individuals mostly as a result of stress during battle, also often as subjective reaction to fear. As I have already described, I have seen Russian prisoners shot to death even with their arms raised in the gesture of surrender: possibly this was not done from cold brutality, but in the panic of battle. These were exceptions, however. Of crimes against the civilian population, with whom we often enough in winter, and as a general rule, slept in the same room and shared bread with them, or of mass shootings, I personally saw nothing.

As I stood in that wood at Märkisch-Buchholz amongst those countless butchered young women, I thought my own fate was sealed. This was the bestiality of which German propaganda had so often warned and was the motivation for hundreds of thousands of German soldiers, and I, to fight on against the Soviets long after everything was lost.

If the Soviet Union, before embarking upon the conquest of Germany, had declared itself opposed to the brutality of National Socialist policies in Russia, and announced that it would proceed on the basis of humanitarian conduct, without any doubt the war would have ended months earlier and probably set the post-war history of the Soviet Union and the world along a different course.[4] As it turned out, the chain of inhuman cruelties was pre-programmed for military conflicts up to the present time.

In May 1996 my wife and I laid a wreath on a tree stump in the wood of the murdered signals girls. My heart was almost as heavy as it had been fifty-one years before. In 1945, however, it would soon become clear to me from my own experiences that there are both decent and mercilessly cruel people in all nations and in all armies.

It was close to nightfall, and the narrow track led through an endless wood into the setting sun. To the right and left of us, forced aside by panzers, were abandoned and burnt-out vehicles of every kind. Where two paths met I halted; there lay about twenty wounded men, apparently the victims of an artillery attack, calling out to me. A senior-grade officer cadet and an NCO joined me, and while we were discussing the situation two vehicles came towards us from the east. We pointed our weapons at them and forced them to stop. They were two War Economy Ministry officials or paymasters with their drivers, the loading surfaces of the trucks full of cases and sacks. We forced them to unload it all and watch as we distributed the food and drink. Then we got them to help us to load the wounded and then drive on.

Our small group continued on foot. We came to a young soldier leaning against a tree amongst many bodies. He had a stomach wound, but was fully conscious and quite calm. I stayed a while with him in conversation and seeing that his condition was hopeless gave in to his wish to let him have something to drink. He knew that he was dying and asked me to pray with him. The end came quickly.

After that I went on alone, and suddenly an armoured scout car and two armoured personnel carriers came up. The occupants were Waffen-SS who stopped me and wanted to know who I was. Extremely suspicious, they told me to my face that they considered me to be a member of the ominous 'Seydlitz-troop'. This unit was named after General Walther von Seydlitz – offspring from a well-known family of the Prussian nobility – who had been a Staff Officer with Sixth Army at Stalingrad and after its surrender had founded the 'Anti-Fascist Association of German Officers' in Soviet captivity. It is kept quiet that Seydlitz, in combination with the 'National Committee for a Free Germany', recruited an armed force from German prisoners and defectors to hunt down their former comrades south of Berlin in the last days of the war.

I found it difficult to overcome the doubts of the men in the armoured vehicles since I was neither wearing German uniform nor could I produce my identity/pay book. I had got rid of them two days previously because I thought it dangerous to exhibit the SS runes on the collar patch. The same went for my photograph in the paybook, which contained the entry that my last unit was 36th Waffengrenadier-Division, and therefore the penal division; but what Russian would have taken the time to read it or ask me to clarify what that meant. I was wearing a fur-lined bomber jacket, which I had found in the stowage compartment of an abandoned Mercedes, apparently a trophy taken from a Soviet pilot.

Finally, I managed to convince the SS men, who now invited me to join their group, but this seemed too risky, and I decided to remain independent. Thus I made slow progress forwards for the next two or three days, staying in the woods if at all possible and avoiding open spaces. The farther I advanced west, the signs and remains of the fighting became less: only relatively rarely did I come across vehicles and corpses.

On our tour of remembrance in May 1996, I rediscovered many places from those fateful days at the end of April 1945, which remain indelibly in my memory. At each spot, besides sadness for the many dead, I felt the same depression as I had then in the desolation and despair of the bare pinewoods of Mark Brandenburg, seemingly extending without limit.

It was in the early evening of a sunny spring day when at the edge of the forest I came across a small group of a dozen soldiers including a woman in men's clothing. We conversed and decided to carry on together. For that purpose we had to cross a swampy terrain with several isolated bushes. When we left the forest at dusk, we adopted automatically the formation of a scouting party: I led, the others followed me dispersed with about twenty paces between them. Suddenly a shot rang out, and from a trench in front of me a Russian soldier rose up, probably from a listening post. I shouted: '*Ruki wjersh!*' and he raised his hands. He was probably one of the last Soviet prisoners to be taken in the war on this Halbe front. I let him precede me by a couple of hundred metres, then I gave him a signal to disappear into the bushes, which he did gratefully.

A little farther on we came to a tall field barn; as we approached it several figures emerged with their hands raised. It transpired that they were Germans who had been hiding there. 'Keep down low, you idiots!' I called to them and headed for some bushes to my right, which seemed within easy reach.

Then – I found out later that it was 1 May and south of Beelitz – I re-lived the dream I had had two months previously: I was standing in a swampy meadow up to the knees in a muddy ditch. In front of me in a tall hedgerow, in which I had intended to seek cover as it grew dark, I suddenly made out well-camouflaged Russian soldiers behind an MG, left and right of it rifles pointed at me, faces below steel helmets looking at me expectantly.

For a short eternity I held my breath. Then a voice said, '*Chände choch, Kameratt, Krieg kaputt, Chitler kaputt, skoro domoi* (soon you go home)'. I dropped my pistol into the mud and raised my hands. A figure came out of the hedgerow and approached me. A smartly dressed junior lieutenant addressed me from the edge of the ditch: 'What time?'

I glanced automatically at the watch on my left wrist: 'Half past eight'.

The lieutenant, a young man in his early twenties like myself, stretched out his hand. 'Give me watch!'

I took it off and was just in the act of handing it over when there was a deafening impact and all I could see was black. I wiped my hand over my face and there stood the Russian officer in the same spot but now coated with black mud. A Russian tank about 300 metres away had fired from the far side of the swamp and the shell had landed in the quagmire exactly between us. By a miracle the mud of Mark Brandenburg had saved us from something far more serious.

The lieutenant shook both his fists at the tank using a half-dozen of those filthy swearwords in which the Russian language is so rich. Exhausted and hungry, helpless and stuck in the mud quite literally, I saw the funny side of all this and laughed out loud. The Russian, still in a rage, gave me a threatening look, but then he also started laughing, ever more wildly, hammering his fists on his knees. My comrades had sized up the situation and hid themselves in the nearby bushes. Finally the Russian lieutenant offered me his hand, pulled me up out of the ditch and led me to a nearby village. With a short order he drove away a number of soldiers who had come up apparently with the intention of searching me, then brought me into a schoolroom where other Germans lay around apathetically. He went off for a short while before returning with a bowl of hot soup and bread, a blanket and pillow, and wished me goodnight. I slept like a log. Next morning I learned that I had been captured by a Ukrainian company. And I saw how their soldiers were bringing out German wounded from the nearby woods and treating them well.

Not until I was researching for this book did I discover that by mere hours I lost the chance of crossing the Elbe and reaching the West. Until the early hours of 1 May 1945, Twelfth Army held the line west of Beelitz enabling the remnants of Ninth Army to make their escape.

Chapter Twelve

In Trebbin PoW Camp

My first night in Russian captivity was also the best during my time as a 'Plenny'– Russian for prisoner of war. After breakfast with tea next morning the first stage of an uncertain future began, which did not bode well for any of us. Behind all hopes and fears stood the giant, threatening spectre of a danger, which I like the others dare not express in one word which filled us all with crippling fear: Siberia. In addition we were all mentally and physically exhausted. Nearly everybody had behind him weeks of heavy fighting, long marches, severe deprivation and the tensions of the desperate attempt to break through to the Americans.

What set off on the morning of 2 May was a lost crowd of about twenty men. An SS officer reported us present to the Soviet district commandant with *Stillgestanden*! and *Augen rechts*! It was just like the barracks parade ground, and from the reaction of the Russian soldiers standing around we could see the respect they had for the discipline of this sad remnant of the defeated army.

Then we were led off to the first assembly point for large and small groups from all directions. The guards had their hands full bringing some order to this mob of desperados. A young Soviet senior lieutenant, by whom we all had to pass, said to me: 'Are you an officer?'

'No.'

'Student?'

'Yes, a student of medicine, paramedic grade.'

'Stay with me.'

He gave his men an order and after a short time dressing material was supplied with which I provided some medical care to wounded

225

comrades as well as I was able without instruments and medication.

After a couple of hours we had to fall in again, and what was then set in motion with slow, dragging steps was a column, constantly growing, of some thousand men. By late afternoon it was a grey stream of prisoners stretching farther than the eye could see, making its way northwards to Berlin. I spent the first night freezing in the open, the second perched together with many others on the terrace roof of a house, the third in a ditch alongside the highway.

For four long days we marched, too apathetic to notice the time of day and the route, too bereft of hope to think about what lay ahead of us. Whoever was unable to go any farther and knelt down or fell received a solid blow from a rifle butt from one of the guards standing to the right or left of us: if he failed to stand at once, he would be shot in the back of the neck. It so happened that the same Russian who cold-bloodedly executed a German one minute would hand to another a slice of bread the next. Only seldom did civilians at the roadside attempt to give us a drink of water or ersatz-coffee. It was clear that the population was afraid and kept themselves hidden away.

Within our ranks were some distraught women in male clothing. Red Army soldiers inspected everybody in the column thoroughly, in the case of doubt with the hands. The women were sifted out and led away; often we heard their despairing cries from somewhere nearby. For us men, our absolute helplessness was a new, deeply depressing and bitter experience.

Once – we had camped in a large meadow during a pause in the march – there was wild screaming from the vicinity. Soviet soldiers came out of nearby houses dragging out a captured comrade and drove him with curses and blows behind some vegetation. A few shots rang out; the Russians came back alone. The poor soul had on a Russian uniform greatcoat, which he had found somewhere and wore to protect himself against the cold of the night. Possibly a Russian had given it to him as a present. I realised that I was wearing a Russian pilot's jacket and the sweat ran cold down my back.

The long march of the German 'plennys' with nothing to eat and only occasionally some water, led in a wide arc to the north, then along the Berlin city boundary eastwards, and finally south until we reached Trebbin, on whose troop training grounds three and a half years earlier during my recruit training at Berlin-Lichterfelde I had been forced through the mill for a week. The destination of the column of prisoners was a former camp for forced labourers consisting of about twenty barrack huts. There we were thoroughly searched again. I was relieved of my camera and a Philips pocket lamp, which was driven by a tiny dynamo with hand movements. Hours later I found them on a rubbish heap, dismantled to their constituent parts. I kept my field pack by hiding it in the barrack hut in the interval after it had been searched and before the personal search.

In the late afternoon we occupied the huts, 100 men to each 5 x 5-metre squad room with only five double-tier bunks for us all. For the most part we slept diagonally across one another like corpses: there would be a grim struggle if somebody found he could no longer breathe underneath it all.

Next morning the old army routine began to function once more. Soon there were senior squad-room and barrack-hut men, who could still command and roar as though army discipline still prevailed. The first day at the camp we spent on body counts, repeated over and over. When the number present came to more than 20,000, the Russians were finally satisfied. Then as a reward we received the first hot meal, one peeled potato per man. Mine was fairly small, I ate it with great devotion. Over the next few days the rations were much the same: barely half a litre of water soup daily, a slice of damp bread, a level tablespoon of raw brown sugar. Whoever had a marriage or engagement ring could exchange it with the kitchen bulls for a special ration of soup: one of them, with whom I traded my engagement ring for a ladle of pea soup, showed me a half-metre long cord full of rings.

Two or three days later wooden posts and boards were unloaded in the camp, rusty nails and hammers were distributed. These were for putting together tiered bunks to stand about two metres high along three walls. Once erected they looked like shelves. We lay in the tiers like sardines in a tin. There was so little space between the bedboard and the bunk above that turning in bed was difficult. In the centre of the room hardly enough space was available for a rough table and a couple of benches. Only the windows and doors were kept clear. I was unable to sleep in the narrow bunk space and had the idea of fitting an old door with one end resting on the upper edge of the door frame, the other attached to the ceiling by hooks and rope. This was a comparatively luxurious eyrie: I had hardly any peace of course for the door was being opened and closed frequently making the thin barrack hut walls tremble. It was comparatively tolerable, however, considering the fact that we got nothing to eat all day and were almost starving.

Everything in the camp revolved around food, or should one say hunger. Food of any kind was as precious as life, for it guaranteed our continued existence. Strong discipline was in force. To steal from a comrade had been a serious enough offence in one's unit, in the camp the punishment was so harsh as to amount to a death sentence. If not killed immediately, the delinquent would be put in the pillory without food and water for the day.

There was a real camp market where a man could obtain anything if he had something to offer. Legal currency was an 'active' cigarette made of real tobacco. Three cigarettes bought you the Russian substitute tobacco machorka, a ladle of thin soup or a slice of bread. Amongst tradable objects was anything of use in the camp: cooking utensils, cutlery, shoes, clothing or equipment of all kinds, for upon capture many camp inmates had lost everything.

There was trade in empty food tins, it was amazing what a skilled craftsman could make from them and sell off to the Russians. They were especially interested in the brown jackets and greatcoats of the Organisation Todt, similar to Red Army officers' clothing in quality and colour. Any prisoner who could do without the same went to the camp fence: as a rule in the late afternoon Soviet soldiers would arrive and pass a shovel under the barbed wire on which, after agreement by means of the usual shouts and signals, the objects for trade would be exchanged. An OT greatcoat was worth a whole loaf. It was unknown for a prisoner to be cheated.

The Soviet camp commandant, a Jewish colonel, apparently thought a lot of the Waffen-SS, and recruited all his camp police from their ranks. His motto was: 'Wehrmacht shoot, SS shoot, all shoot, for me no difference!' Whenever possible every prisoner avoided the Polish guards at the camp gates who were armed with wooden cudgels and used them indiscriminately at every opportunity. Not only the Poles lashed out. Between the barrack huts and the perimeter fence the earlier occupants of the camp, the foreign workers, had laid down a small garden. Many 'plennys', as a result of the disorganisation of being months without a proper diet, were now hardly able to stand. Although all that remained of the garden was more or less sand and soil. Some prisoners dug it over in the hope of finding something to appease their hunger. They gathered a couple of pitiful roots and some grass and were trying to heat it up into something edible in a tin. For this purpose they had to light a small fire, which was strictly prohibited. The Russian guards in the watchtowers looked away but then along came a German lieutenant with much shouting and a large cudgel and set about the half-starved cooks with it. He overturned the tin with its contents and trampled out the fire, crying: 'You worthless swine, I shall teach you to obey orders!' Some of his fellow officers, still in good physical form due to their better nourishment, stood by nodding approvingly. At that it became too much for one of the Russian guards who fired a couple of rounds from his machine pistol near the raging officer's feet. The officer took the hint and made off rapidly.

The adaptability of captured German officers was amazing. In the first couple of days they were never seen. Nobody wore shoulder straps or other rank insignia or decorations. When it suddenly became known that officers would receive special rations and better accommodation, lo and behold! they appeared fully uniformed. Without doubt there were many excellent and brave officers in the Wehrmacht who had the wellbeing of the men at heart and did not spare themselves; without them the military successes of the first great campaigns would not have been possible – one may take a view on their ethics as one will. It is also equally certain that not many of them survived to the last year of the war.

The officers at Trebbin inhabited their own barrack hut in relatively comfortable numbers and laid great stress on the barrier between officers and men. It was not long before a Colonel von Bismarck led a deputation to see the Soviet camp commandant with a special request: they wanted the hospital barrack hut, full of wounded and sick, cleared out and placed at their disposal since it was the best hut in the camp. The camp commandant made a note but regretted with coolness that he was not able to accede to their request.

Besides the hunger, camp life was dominated by boredom. Apart from the morning count, which could take hours, there was scarcely anything else to fill the day. Fortunately it was May and the weather was dry so that the prisoners were able to spend almost all day in the open. They made their slow rounds through the camp alleyways. Many had been captured alone and were forced to find a community to join.

The daily bread and sugar ration was distributed in portions for twelve men, and this dictated the size of communities. The daily handing down of the meagre rations was a festive event every time, with everybody looking on watchfully. So that justice prevailed, we had devised an excellent system: every person in the group took his turn at dividing up the portions, his own turn to choose on that day coming last: next day he would have first choice.

The camp authorities did better arranging the hygiene than the food; the former foreign-workers camp had a large barrack hut for ablutions. Thorough delousing with large quantities of DDT powder, creating a fog so thick that we could hardly see each other in it, kept us free from the plague of these vermin.

The enforced idleness was an ideal breeding ground for endless discussions about God and the world, but more than anything for rumours. The most persistent of the rumours stated that we were all going to be sent to Siberia for forced labour, giving rise to a dull, apathetic despair. Despite that, some of the 'plennys' showed an extraordinary zest for life. Apart from the able commercial types, already preparing for the later black market, others took bets on cards or numbers games. These attracted more uninvolved onlookers than clients, for not many had the cigarettes, tobacco or money to buy in. Nevertheless, it was astonishing what personal belongings some prisoners managed to have retained despite the Russians' 'filching'.

Personally, I had saved my field pack with some underclothes, socks, soap, shaving gear and the precious glass with about a litre of morphine, which I was able to smuggle out on my release. In the camp morphine was not something one could trade. Together with my field pack it was stolen in Duisburg some months later, but that is another story. I gave up shaving after I was shaved bald in common with everybody else and grew a full beard, which gradually looked quite stately.

One was constantly more aware of hunger from being idle. Involuntarily we would find ourselves drawn towards the kitchen barrack hut in the centre of the camp; the cooking was also done here for the camp guards, naturally incomparably better and more plentiful meals than for us. Near the kitchen was a fenced-in area for the waste bins in which, as I discovered, the bones were disposed of from the Russian meat dishes. Plagued by constant hunger, I decided to pay these bins a visit during one night. This was strictly forbidden and the guards had orders to shoot at any anybody seen at night moving between the barrack huts. I crept cautiously along the walls of the huts to the little square where the scraps of food and offal were dumped, tied up the lower wire of the fence with a shoe lace and wriggled through. The disgusting smell of rotting vegetable matter was matched by the delicious aroma of cooked meat remnants. With extreme caution I took possession of the bones, gnawed at them and sucked out the marrow. For the first time in weeks if not months I had a pleasant feeling of a full stomach. After that I risked the trip almost every night.

Selections began in the camp around the end of our third week there. What this portended was only too clear to everybody. During the daylight hours the occupants of one barrack hut after another had to go to the parade ground with bared upper torso. A drunkard of a Soviet doctor with the rank of captain, the violet NKVD political police ribbon around his cap, inspected the ranks, stopping before each man, looking him over and then deciding his fate with either the word 'Healthy', which meant a camp in Siberia, or 'Sick'. The latter won at least a temporary stay in the camp with the vague prospect of release into Germany at some time in the future.

The selections went on all day. When I stood with my roommates on the square the sun was shining but I was understandably very worried. Would I have to show the inner side of my left upper arm with the tattooed blood group, the 'mark of the SS'?

The best I could do had been to beg a caustic pencil from a camp paramedic to cauterize it out, the fresh scar looked like it could have been an injury, but who gets wounded under the arm?

In any case I decided to see how it played out: I had already ignored the camp order to all SS men to report themselves: there was a considerable risk in doing that but the game I now had to play was a gamble – all or nothing.

With a thousand others I stood in the sun with a heavy heart. The Russian doctor made his way closer with his three assistants. Finally he stood before my neighbour and roommate. I remember that he came from Jägerndorf in West Prussia, had been in a concentration camp as a Communist and then transferred to the Dirlewanger penal division. He was rather on the small size but despite all his sufferings and privations he made a stocky impression. The doctor gave him a quick once-over and confirmed, apparently with satisfaction, 'You healthy.'

'Please,' my neighbour said to the interpreter, who stood at the doctor's side, 'tell the captain that I am a Communist, was in a concentration camp and then from there I was sent to the penal division. Here is my paybook in proof.' He had taken the precious document form his trouser pocket and offered it to the doctor.

The interpreter translated. The Russian doctor squeezed his eyes together, took the paybook, threw it on the ground and trod on it with his boot. Then he took three paces forward to my neighbour, spun him round by the shoulder, gave him a firm kick in the buttocks and shouted: 'You Communist? *Otshin karasho*! You Sibirr, Sibirr got many Communist!' At this instant, despite their own miseries, probably everybody who witnessed this scene felt pity for this poor wretch.

Then it was my turn. Gaunt as I was from my long sufferings in the last weeks at the front, the long march to the West and into captivity, my shoulders stooped, my nose projecting long from my bald shaved head, I did not need to put too much effort into making myself a pitiable spectacle. Something diverted my attention for a moment from the tension of the situation: I felt an insect crawling over my naked left shoulder: a small May beetle had decided to rest there. The Russian doctor drew himself leisurely to his full height before me and said, 'You sick, you go home.'

A millstone fell from my neck. The May beetle decided it liked sitting on my shoulder. Ever since they have been my lucky beetle. Whenever I see one in a position of danger for itself, I take it gingerly to safety. This may sound like some fabulous adornment to my story, but that is exactly how it happened.

At the beginning of June I suddenly went down with a fever and severe headaches. I reported sick, stood in a long queue of fellow sufferers and was finally examined by a German surgeon-major, who sent me to sick bay. When he visited me the following day he asked if I were a student. I replied: 'Yes, medical student, I am of paramedic grade and an operating theatre assistant.'

'Well, that's first class,' he said, 'You are urgently needed here. In sick bay we have almost no trained personnel. I shall try to have you transferred into the camp permanent staff. In any case, you must be prepared to care for TB and pneumonia patients. What do you say to that?'

I reflected briefly. I knew that in the camp there were not only soldiers. The Russians had rounded up small children, people with serious lung diseases and old men and simply imprisoned them. The risk of infection with such undernourishment was not inconsiderable; on the other hand it gave me the chance to escape the problem of being SS. Finally I said: 'Yes, I am prepared to do it!'

Some days later he spoke with me again on another visit: 'Unfortunately, I can't transfer you to the permanent staff, the Russians won't allow it. But there is a way round it. When you are discharged from here, report sick again. Say you have heart trouble. Then we can admit you as chronic sick. But we shall have to let the Soviet female camp doctor in on it, because otherwise there could be difficulties.'

233

That was how it went through. I was assigned to a ward in which only the most serious cases with advanced tuberculosis, dystrophy, and acute pneumonia were detained. The triumph of my new position was to be officially a patient with a proper field bed and blue-white chequered sheets. On the door was a plaque with the word 'Pneumonia' in capital letters in Cyrillic script. That kept the Russians away, for they had a morbid fear of infectious diseases. The exception was the female military doctor of captain's rank, a friendly, rather plump but really pretty and sympathetic young woman who ran the infirmary hut. She asked me a couple of questions in tolerable German, then seemed satisfied with my motivation and qualifications and left me with an *Otshin karasho!* After that she came regularly to make her inspections but never found any cause for complaint.

Suddenly I was of paramedic grade again, practically an assistant to Dr Schreckenbach, mainly occupied all day giving regular injections, keeping patients' medical records updated and caring especially for the most ill persons in the room in which I had my own 'sick bed'. I had several helpers for the simple work.

There was no shortage of medication of all kinds. Very close to the camp was an abandoned Wehrmacht medical supplies depot, which for reasons best known to themselves the Russians had not bothered to plunder. We were therefore in a position to offer better care to our patients than had been possible at our main dressing stations and to a certain extent field hospitals too. That may have contributed to the fact that in the two months of my activity in the camp infirmary we did not have a single fatality. In critical situations we did what was humanly possible. I remember an evangelical parson from Thuringia by whose bed I spent a whole night and day giving regular injections for heart and circulation, alternately Cardiazol, Symphatol and Strophantin. After sixteen hours he was out of danger. After that we had many good conversations.

That we had no deaths on the seriously-ill ward to which I was appointed as nurse was a matter of pure luck but added to my standing with the infirmary doctors as also with the responsible

German physicians of the camp. The death of a 'plenny' was always considered a serious matter by the Russians because of the bureaucratic pedantic investigation it unleashed. That may appear strange to all who knew and know about Russian camps, but it was so. In the few cases in which death seemed imminent, the patient would be loaded into an ambulance and taken to the nearby military hospital camp so as to avoid having the death appear on our camp's statistics. I accompanied such a transport two or three times and experienced the depressing feelings of a prisoner passing into East Germany through the camp gates only to return to the bleak existence behind barbed wire. I did toy with the idea of attempting to escape on these excursions, and had the opportunity to do so, but without papers it would have been a very difficult undertaking to get far.

As I have said, there were medicaments aplenty, but there was a shortage of syringes and especially cannula, of which I only ever had three and the syringes plus needle and cannula had to be sterilized with a spirit stove. Finally I came up with a method, which would have been unthinkable in a proper field hospital. For intramuscular and subcutaneous injections I boiled only the needles and cannula and used the syringes for the same medication over and over again.

Anybody engaged in doing something will sooner or later make a mistake. If the activity is a medical one, the error can be deadly. Amongst the pneumonia cases, which I tended in the infirmary hut where I was always on call was a large, blond SS man, one of several I injected daily in the buttock with Transpulmin. For this he had to lie on his stomach and that particular day he refused to do so outright: I could not coax him to do it or get him to obey my order. Unnerved by the resistance and unaware of the possible consequences of my next action, I injected the Transpulmin into the front side of his upper thigh.

At first all went well, but after an hour he complained of pain in the toes of the left foot, which felt cold. I reported the matter immediately to Dr Schreckenbach who merely said: 'Well, there you've hit an artery. Transpulmin is an oily preparation, which can damage the extremities of the foot. Let's cross our fingers and hope it doesn't get worse. There's only one thing to do; keep him as warm as possible. Don't take it to heart, something like that happens to everybody in our line of work once.'

I filled field flasks with hot water from the camp kitchen, it and wrapped these around the patient's foot with strips of fabric. The tips of the toes went yellow and then blackish. After two days to my relief the process stopped. For the victim of my early healing artistry the whole episode had a happy outcome. It delayed his recovery from the pneumonia for so long that when the 'healthy' group was shipped off to Siberia he was still unfit to travel and had to remain behind with the 'sick' in the military hospital camp. From there he was presumably discharged.

Hunger also ravaged the infirmary. At the medical depot pure bean coffee in compressed tablet form had been stored long term but remained usable, for me a welcome and long absent refreshment. I injected the members of my ward including myself regularly with Hepatrat, a highly concentrated mixture of liver extract and vitamins: the preparation, of which great quantities were available, gave the body not only valuable substances, it also took away the sensation of hunger in the bodily tissues, which differs from primary visceral hunger.

At the end of June rumours began to circulate in the camp that the chronically sick would soon be sent home. This prompted the 'kitchen bulls' to ask me what could be done to make them eligible for release. Using my previously exploited talent for 'organisation' I gave them Atebrint tablets – actually a prophylactic against malaria – which gave the skin a yellowish colour simulating jaundice. I advised them to report to me daily for 'monitoring', bringing a full mess tin from the officers' kitchen. In this way I obtained for my seriously ill cases a nourishing dietary supplement, which I shared out fairly. For some weeks we seriously ill of the ward lived in a manner of which normal 'plennys' could only dream.

Meanwhile transports were leaving ever more frequently for Russia with prisoners classified fit for work. Gradually the camp emptied. At the end of July 1945 the infirmary was emptied into a military hospital camp about a kilometre away. I discovered what an enormous stroke of luck had prevented me from being accepted into the permanent staff, for these people, together with all medical staff including the doctors, were sent off to Russia. Dr Schreckenbach, to whom I owed so much, spent almost five years there in camps. He told me, 'Man, you're a lucky dog! Now you'll be going with the sick into the military hospital and will be released.' He had already begun to start learning Russian.

It happened as Dr Schreckenbach had prophesied. To be on the safe side, for several days I ate pure coffee-powder tablets and made myself ill with gastritis in case a Russian doctor should want to examine me. The decision lay in the hands of the young female camp doctor who knew my special status. Possibly it had impressed her that I had taken over the cases with tuberculosis. Meanwhile, I had been officially diagnosed as having a 'stomach ulcer'.

In the military hospital camp I spent another two weeks on a very stringent diet, but still had a proper field bed, though on the 'second floor'. Then I was ordered to attend for medical examination anticipating release. In the room of a barrack hut we had to line up in pairs with naked upper torso. There was a table at which several NKVD officers were sitting. Those in the right-hand file were looked at by a Soviet doctor, those on the left by the female doctor from the infirmary. I arranged to be in the left-hand file.

The procedure for everybody was 'Left arm up!' I raised my arm with the fresh scar in the armpit and the faint, but still visible remains of the 'O' of my SS blood-group tattoo. I held my breath. The doctor gave me a long stare, then she nodded to the table with the NKVD people, told me nonchalantly, '*Karasho!*' and turned to the next man. The fateful second had passed. I approached the table, a paper was rubber-stamped, I took my release permit No. 299, written in Russian and made out for 'Obergefreiter Herbert Maeger' – the army rank of senior private corresponding to SS-SS-Lance Corporal. It was 15 hrs on 14 August 1945.

My release permit proved to be of great significance in two respects: it not only gave me freedom, but now I was in possession of a personal ID after having got rid of my identity/paybook and tunic as a precaution in the last days of the war. I still had my pre-war Belgian ID from 1939 but I kept this in reserve until such time as I could best judge what reaction it was likely to provoke.

Chapter Thirteen

The 'Homecoming'

One day later the camp gates opened for the first batch of released prisoners. We were free. We were also aware from the reports of unfortunates who had finished up back in the camp how quickly this freedom could be lost: a Russian who found a released prisoner unable to account for his whereabouts, or who was simply in a bad mood, could tear up the permit and make a man a prisoner again.

We had orders to report to the Trebbin town hall, which I did immediately. There I received a certificate in German which read:

Obergefreiter Maeger Herbert, born 10.11.1922 has been released today from the Trebbin prisoner of war camp for Walhorn by virtue of paperwork presented. The above mentioned person has been given provisions by me to last him until 17.8.45. It is requested that he be allowed to travel without hindrance and where possible to be given as much help as possible on his route home. The Mayor (rubber stamped Trebbin/Teltow District).

The formula 'by virtue of paperwork presented' – apparently what it should have stated was 'according to paperwork presented' – would prove very useful later. As it was well known that the Russians rarely released prisoners, I could interpret my certificate credibly as follows: My paybook 'presented' had been retained by the NKVD; in it was entered that I had been attached to the Probationary Division, therefore I had been one of the first to be released from the camp by the Russians as an unscheduled measure.

I was still in Trebbin and my primary aim was to find the shortest way to the railway station to take a train to Berlin. After a while a westbound goods train came in, but it was so overcrowded that I had to climb up on the roof of a wagon. Another released prisoner joined me, his hurry was as great as mine. In Berlin we spent the night in a corner of the station, next morning we got on the first train going west, travelling on the roof again, for it was still warm and we could stretch out up there.

With a small watery sausage and a hunk of bread in my stomach, which we had received as our first civilian fare at Trebbin, we decided to go as far as we could on the train. Finally at nightfall we were so hungry and thirsty that we could hold out no longer. When the train stopped in open country, we got off and walked randomly into a wood.

After covering a long stretch we saw the light of a dairy farm. We must have looked a pitiful sight, for a man we met on the ramp filled our mess tins with cream, which we drank greedily. This was not a wise move, stomach and intestines rebelled at once at the un-accustomed fatty liquid and we spent the next half hour at the edge of the wood with diahorrea. Hungrier, thirstier and weaker than before we quenched out thirst with water at a farmhouse and accepted a piece of bread. Here we were shown the way to the nearest railway station.

The journey continued in stages towards Hamburg. As I had no other contacts in this region I decided to go to Cuxhaven to visit my war-fiancée, Ilse Harmsen. That was some way off. We came at first to Boizenburg, the last station for trains coming from the East. I had linked up meanwhile with a comrade from Hamburg and we decided to steal across the demarcation line clandestinely. First we had to find a spot which we could cross from the open terrain. As a result of cautious enquiries we determined that this would only be possible over a short stretch between the Elbe and Lübeck-Elbe Canal, the only natural obstacle there being the small river Stecknitz.

We took a train to Schwanheide, the last railway station before the zonal frontier which, as we were informed there, was heavily guarded by the Russians. We were given nourishing food at a small farm – I shall never forget that huge portion of goulash made with prunes – then we found a barn in which to sleep. The night was pitch black as we crept off towards the frontier – and were stopped at once by a Soviet patrol. They brought us back to Schwanheide and locked us up with other soldiers and civilians who had also had bad luck.

After a while – it was still dark – we were led out apparently for interrogation. When the attention of our guards was distracted for a moment, I nudged my colleague and we disappeared behind the corner of a house into the night. A couple of rounds were fired at us, but apparently the Russians were not interested in giving chase. Fortunately they had not deprived us of our release documents.

It seemed too risky to make another attempt to cross the demarcation line secretly, and so we had to think of something else. First we returned to Boizenburg where more and more released prisoners were gathering, and like us could go no farther westwards. Many of them were wounded with dressings, amputees or sick. I went to the town administration to enquire for food coupons and, when asked, told them what I had been doing at Trebbin camp. They wanted to know if I would be prepared to help set up a hospital to receive released prisoners of war. I agreed and once more had something to keep me busy; the military hospital, which soon filled with patients, was located in an old school. As lodgings I was given a loft in the house of an old master joiner and his family. My hosts were not delighted to have me forced upon them.

So passed three weeks. I received no pay for my services, the rations were very meagre again, my loft was draughty and at the beginning of September rather cool, and autumn was coming, so obviously something had to happen. Enquiries revealed that it was relatively easy for foreigners to cross the frontier. For that I needed a civilian appearance. The contacts I had made at Boizenburg included the stationmaster and his young wife.

I got from them a well-preserved renovated jacket, the wife sewed a black-yellow-red cockade, the Belgian colours, for me to wear in the buttonhole and so equipped I presented myself to the Russian district commandant, producing for the first time my old Belgian border pass from 1939, which I had looked after carefully. My story, which I also kept to later, was that as a Eupen-Malmedyer unfit for the forces I had been studying medicine at the University of Breslau during the war, I had got caught up in the big refugee-trek and now just wanted to go home.

I had practised putting on a guileless facial expression and this must have worked convincingly. My hair had grown a bit and was now the length the Russians wore it, I had shaved off my beard, and I spoke a few sentences of French, which a Soviet officer standing nearby seemed to understand.

The Russians noted everything down and told me to report to the kommandantur every morning with regard to my repatriation. It was only a few days before a lorry arrived from the Belgian military mission to bring out five or six other 'Belgians' cut adrift by the war. One of them might have been a Belgian, but on the journey the others admitted to being Germans who had also tumbled to the 'repatriation' fraud.

We were taken 30 kilometres to Lüneburg on the far side of the Elbe to a displaced persons' camp made up of Third Reich railway coaches. The building in which we were housed looked like a high school: it had proper beds and first-class food. A Belgian lieutenant seemed to find my story plausible, being so impressed by my Belgian ID card that after only a few questions he handed me an Allied Expeditionary Force/D.P. Index Card, which kept me well fed and got me free travel on the former Reichsbahn for weeks. He mentioned by-the-by that upon my arrival in Belgium I would be subjected to a stiff investigation: this was important information for me. A roommate at the DP camp, a former concentration camp inmate, was more dubious and asked me some trick questions. I was able to convince him to a certain extent with chatter and detailed descriptions of Belgian fine cooking for which – as I told him – I could hardly wait.

The DP camp was guarded, but we were at liberty to leave when we wanted. I made use of this and asked around daily when the transport could be expected. Meanwhile the good food helped my recovery. After about ten days in the camp we were told that within the next few days we would set out on the journey to Belgium. Things were now getting too hot for me, and so I went to the railway station and took the first train to Hamburg, from there thanks to my new ID document I was given a special compartment for Cuxhaven, where I arrived in the early morning.

I can describe what happened in one sentence. I found my fiancée and her parents in depressed mood, two days later they made the tearful confession that she had grown to love another: she accompanied me to the railway station. I felt that I had lost something, but did not take it much to heart. It was a time in which scarcely anything had durability, often enough not love either. I concluded that I should make for my relatives at Rheydt. At Duisburg station I found an air raid shelter, which had been set up as a temporary refuge: for a pillow I used my field pack with the few belongings I had managed to keep during the months of captivity.

That morning on the platform waiting for the train to Rheydt I had my last horrific experience of this dreadful war; on the next set of tracks a train arrived made up of open trucks. Former German soldiers sat or lay inside crammed together. In one of them which stopped opposite where I stood I saw pining infantrymen in torn uniforms, a number of seriously wounded men bleeding and some unmistakeable corpses.

I asked an amputee on the transport where they had come from, he said from France; the train was full of men unfit for work and who had been released by the French.

'What is the reason for the fresh wounds and corpses?' I asked.

'When we came through Belgium, men and women on the bridges threw down railway sleepers into the open goods trucks,' he replied.

During the short conversation on the platform I had set down my field pack for a moment out of my sight, when I turned to pick it up it had gone. Perhaps it was a good thing, for my possession of the liquid morphine might have led to some awkward questions if I had been searched.

After my experience at Duisburg it was clear to me that nothing good awaited me in Belgium. I also believe that whatever the circumstances I would have decided for Germany, if only to spare my future children those experiences I had known as a child and adolescent in a disputed border region. Germany had become the country of my destiny. I had gone through difficult times in the uniform I had worn for four years, and in it I had seen many good comrades die. I felt bound to them in a loyalty, which had nothing to do with the flag or a questionable ideology. Moreover, I had learnt that it is not so important where one stands; what is decisive is what one does. This alone is the maxim which makes all decent people, irrespective of their language and country, companions in what is good.

I gained one more experience for my future life, which I owe to fortunate circumstances in a thousand dangers: once a man knows that life can be worse than death, that therefore dying can be easier than what one has to bear, he loses his fear of failure and develops a tranquillity in all dangerous situations and in all tasks with which fate challenges him.

After several decades my past caught up with me. In 1971 a bureaucrat discovered that I did not have German nationality, and since I had repudiated my Belgian citizenship, in law I was stateless: this had to be entered in my personal ID and passport. It was advised to submit an application for German nationality. I objected that this would be an official admission of never having been a German to date, a *de facto* recognition of the basis of the judgement of the Belgian war court in its indictment of me in 1947. I was told this was insignificant. With some inner resistance I saw that there was nothing for it but to sign the application. On 21 June 1971 I received my certificate of citizenship, broadmindedly awarded free of any charge. With it at last I had a Fatherland again.

The Belgian war tribunal at Verviers had condemned me in my absence on 19 February 1947 with this formula:

Maeger Hubert, Herbert, Joseph, found guilty as a Belgian of having borne arms against Belgium or against the allies of Belgium, this particularly in his status as a member of the Waffen-SS [. . .] is hereby sentenced to life imprisonment.

The Eupen daily newspaper *Grenz Echo* had also come up with an accusation against me in that on 10 May 1940 I had burnt a Belgian flag 'with cynical pleasure' at Hauset. It was false: the village mayor took out an affidavit afterwards that I had not been in Hauset on the day in question.

The fact that I had not appeared before the court prevented me from entering Belgium subsequently. When I travelled to France I had to avoid going through Belgium. In the autumn of 1973 I asked the German Foreign Office to try to clear up the situation but ran into a wall of incomprehension and after months of empty phrases received a letter abundant with explanations why nothing could be done.

After some reflection I turned to the West German ambassador in Brussels, Peter Limbourg, who assured me by return that he would take up the matter forthwith. I have to thank his personal intervention and also that of the President of the German Cultural Chamber and coordinator to the Head of Cabinet at the Belgian Interior Ministry, Johann Weynand, for obtaining from the Belgian Justice Minister H. Vanderpoorten on 10 October 1974 a decision raising the last restrictions still in force against me.

After decades, I could finally bring myself to justify my motives and actions in this connection in writing, for which I saw only my own conscience, and not a court, as competent. I wrote:

> It is true that by my origins and language I had and have strong ties to Germany; I felt and feel also an inner relationship with Belgium, to which I owe much for my education and upbringing. From this the knowledge arises that one's personal suffering must be a constructive experience for a better Europe.

In the autumn of 1974 I returned to the land of my birth for the first time in thirty-one years. I found it had become foreign to me.

Epilogue

I wrote this book, whose contents to some extent go beyond the portrayal of my personal experience, for two reasons. First, I believe I am duty bound to correct false representations, which have been spread aboard in important areas, and secondly, I consider it necessary to provide a picture of the milieu, which I was blackmailed into joining as an eighteen-year-old.

The Leibstandarte was not a unit in which a person trained in the Humanities could feel at ease, but neither was it composed of the brutal criminals, which many publications have made it out to be in words and pictures. In particular, the allegation regarding the treatment of Russian prisoners of war does not correspond to the facts. That Soviet soldiers who surrendered – some situations excepted – were simply 'put down' must be refuted by the fact that three million of them were held in German PoW camps and about a million decided to continue fighting on the German side under General Vlassov.

The SS was in many respects a contradiction in terms: in formation and development it was not an homogenous organisation. In its original role as 'Schutz Staffel' or 'Allgemeine-SS' in the typical black uniforms worn until the outbreak of war it was a Party association: within the Waffen-SS political functions were exercised only by the so-called cadres – especially in the SS-Führungshauptamt in Berlin. Alongside these the SS-Verfügungstruppen, from which the concentration camp guards were recruited, the SD as political police and the Death's Head brigades[1] were all answerable personally to Himmler.

Because of its special status the SS was not popular even in the National Socialist Party. Heinz Höhne said of it in his book:

246

The secret circle of the SS allowed no unauthorised persons to peer into the interior of their organisation; the Schutz Staffel of the Führer-dictatorship had to remain a mystery, to the citizen sinisterly and incomprehensibly similar to the Jesuits, which the SS copied down to the smallest detail though officially radically opposed to them.[2]

The German-American publisher Karl O. Spaetel expressed his doubts in a study that the SS could be assessed collectively and thought that it did not consist of just one type of man but 'criminals and idealists, idiots and intellectuals'.

The Viennese-born US citizen Professor George H. Stein drew the following conclusion in his book:

Without diminishing the scale of the appalling crimes of Himmler's followers, the latest investigations have shown that the SS was actually more varied, refined and complex than that monolithic organisation of criminals who sat in the dock at Nuremberg.[3]

Everybody who dons a military uniform in wartime, whether conscripted or voluntarily, faces a challenge to all those features in his education and upbringing which went into the making of his personality. A conflict of loyalty between his individuality and the demands of the group whose member he becomes is unavoidable and can only be overcome in that kind of totally manipulated community if he has the chance to act according to his conscience in decisive situations. On whichever side we stood as soldier-actors of an infernal regime – and also if a benevolent fate shielded us from having to commit abominable acts – we all carry in our hearts until the day we die, invisible and ineradicable, the mark of Cain alongside our memory of desperation, hunger, depression, bitter cold, dying comrades and fear of death.

Not denied and undeniable are the extraordinary military achievements of the Waffen-SS, especially in the East, where the most enormous soldierly demands were made of them. Heinz Höhne described it thus:

A new world surrounded SS soldiers: cruel, ruthless and light years away from the world view of the Black Order [. . .] The hammer blows of Soviet Stalin organs, tanks and massed infantry hardened the reputation of SS soldiers as the fire brigade of the German Army of the Eastern Front. [. . .] Soviet Major-General Artemenko stated upon his capture in the autumn of 1941 that the tactical efficiency of SS 'Wiking' Division exceeded anything he had ever seen.[4]

Bravery and fearless courage were only facets of this bloodiest of all wars, however. Nobody who survived its horror came away from it undamaged. The pain of bodily wounds was much less for many than the agony of remembering unspeakable cruelties committed by people against other people forced to participate in an inhuman event.

This applied in a special way to the war in Russia. It cannot be denied that terrible crimes were committed under the sign of the SS runes in the concentration camps. That such was the case must in the first instance be laid at the door of those who prepared this fearsome war and unleashed an inferno attributed indelibly to Germany. Moreover they bear responsibility that hundreds of thousands of young people were made responsible collectively for the crime, young people who believed they were fighting for the defence of the West and therefore serving a good cause. In the end, whether survivors or fallen, they lost their honour: their loyalty had been shamelessly betrayed years earlier by a leadership without a conscience.

Notes

Introduction: Between Two Fatherlands
1. Source: *Meyers Lexikon* (1925), Vol 2, Belgium/History, p.75.

Chapter One: Recruit in the Leibstandarte
1. *Beute-Germaner* = Booty-Germanic, a person of German race integrated into Greater Germany by virtue of the reconquest of former German lands of which he was an inhabitant. (Transl.)

Chapter Three: First Half of 1942: Six Months on the Russian Front
1. The 'Gefechtstross' included the transport vehicles for the fighting troops, the 'Versorgungstross' the vehicles for the catering, ammunition and fuel supply together with workshop vehicles and the company office.
2. Slang for SS-Stabsscharführer, equivalent to the British CSM.
3. Carl Dirks and Karl-Heinz Janssen, *Der Krieg der Generäle* (Berlin, 1999), pp. 130–43.
4. Franz Halder, *Hitler als Feldherr* (H. A. Jacobsen, 1949).
5. Dirks and Janssen, *Der Krieg der Generäle*, p. 79.
6. In contrast to the Wehrmacht, SS doctors had military ranks.

Chapter Four: Second Half of 1942: France – Dieppe
1. The religion of Nazism was pantheism. The flailing arms of the swastika represent the Sun in revolution and the arms themselves the four 'turns' on the Sun's circuit as seen from Earth, i.e. the longest and shortest days of the year, and the equinoxes of spring and autumn. In all National Socialist communities worldwide each of the four phases was celebrated by a huge festival of fire, hence '*Sonnenwendfeir*'. The Sun was not held to be God, but as the most visible symbol of God, for in his table talk of 24 October 1941, Hitler stated: 'Whoever sees God only in an oak tree or

tabernacle *but not in everything there is* cannot really be religious, he is on the outside of religion.' For SS neo-paganism see *Die Gestaltung der Feste im Jahres- und Lebenslauf in der SS-Familie* by SS-Obergruppenführer Fritz Weitzel, published with Himmler's approval in 1939. (Trs).

2. Kfz = Kraftfahrzeug, motor vehicle. The Kfz 69 was a 6x4 personnel carrier.

Chapter Five: My Second Winter in Russia

1. SPW = Schützenpanzerwagen, armoured personnel carrier, also known as 'Coffin', a half-track with normal wheels forward.
2. 1a = chief operations officer.
3. Sonderführer = Specialists from all walks of life given military rank for the duration.
4. Source: Paul Carell: *Schlacht zwischen Wolga und Weichsel* (Augsburg, 1999), p. 81.
5. MTW = Mannschaftstransportwagen, personnel transport vehicle.
6. *'Wenn der Landser nicht mehr mosert, ist die Lage äusserst beschissen.'*
7. Rifle grenades were fired from a small mortar fitted inside the rifle barrel. They could also be thrown by hand.
8. Probably refers to the red heart symbol worn by 320th Infantry Division.'
9. Oberwachtmeister (Army rank) = Warrant Officer Class I in Cavalry and Artillery.
10. PSW = Panzer-Späh-Wagen, armoured reconnaissance vehicle.
11. Peter Young, *Der Grosse Atlas zum II. Weltkrieg* (Augsburg, 1998). Retranslation into English.
12. The Wehrmacht had at least twenty different types of *Jagdpanzer* (= tank-hunter) The design was a panzer chassis carrying a heavy gun, often a 7.5cm Anti-tank or an 88, in a fixed armoured turret open at the top. Unfortunately the author does not specify the type which surprised these two T-34s. See Alex Lüdeke, *Panzer der Wehrmacht 1933-1945*, section *Panzerjäger/Jagdpanzer* (Stuttgart, 2010), pp. 70–96. (NB: Pen & Sword is publishing my translation of this book. Transl)
13. A nickname for the higher NSDAP functionaries on account of their uniforms with rich gold lace.
14. Paul Carell, *Verbrannte Erde – Die Schlacht zwischen Wolga und Weichsel* (Augsburg, 1999).

15. Source: *Der Spiegel*, 35/1999.
16. Bernd Wegner, *Hitlers Politische Soldaten – Die Waffen-SS 1933-1945* (5th edition, Paderborn, 1997).

Chapter Six: The Battles of Kursk and Belgorod

1. *Grösster Feldherr aller Zeiten*, shortened sarcastically by German troops to 'Gröfaz': at the 1918 Armistice, Hitler had the rank of Obergefreiter = senior private, non-NCO. Contrary to popular belief he was never a corporal, which in the German scheme of military ranks is the lowest NCO grade.
2. Kursk lies about 120 kilometres north of Kharkov.
3 Janusz Piekalkiewicz, *Unternehmen 'Citadel' – Kursk und Orel: Die grösste Panzerschlacht des Zweiten Weltkrieges* (Augsburg, 1998).
4. Source: Paul Carell, *Verbrannte Erde-Schlacht zwischen Wolga und Weichsel* (Augsburg, 1999). Karck, then an SS-2nd Lieutenant, was the author's company commander during his training with No. 4 Replacement Company LSSAH in Berlin.
5. Carell, *Verbrannte Erde*.

Chapter Seven: Italian Intermezzo

1. By this he probably refers to the battery of prophylactic measures to which a soldier in a Wehrmacht brothel was subjected before and after the session. Tr.
2. Source: Werner Haupt, *Deutsche Spezialdivisionen 1938-1945* (Wölfersheim, 1995).
3. The Leibstandarte had no volunteer reserve of officers, only career officers.
4. A rank equivalent to senior private with the authority equal to a lance-corporal in the British Army, but was not in itself an NCO rank.
5. Kaiserliche-und-Königliche Armee in the Austro-Hungarian monarchy.

Chapter Nine: From Junker School to the 'Crossbones Division'

1. *'Gesetz zur Verhütung erbkranken Nachwuchses'*.
2. A small flat shell made of tin and filled with Stearin.
3. A character reference linked by association with the need 'to wash one's Brown Shirt white'.

4. A German civilian tribunal set up after the war under the control of the occupying powers for the 'denazification' process. The ruling it handed down in each case was one of either: *Hauptschuldiger* – Major offender: *Belasteter* – person burdened with guilt; *Minderbelasteter* – person burdened with a minor degree of guilt: *Mitläufer* – fellow traveller and *Entlasteter* – persons against whom no finding of guilt could be made. The above terms in the masculine case include the feminine case. Six million Germans in the western zone of occupation were judged.

Chapter Ten: By Tram to the Front
1. Probationary brigade.
2. Janusz Piekalkiewicz, *Der Zweite Weltkrieg* (Augsburg, 1993); Peter Young, *Der grosse Atlas zum II.Weltkrieg* (Munich, 1974).
3. Tony Le Tissier, *Durchbruch an der Oder* (Augsburg, 1997).
4. Field Marshal Schörner was the last Commander-in-Chief of the German Army by Hitler's Testament. On 5 May 1945 commanding Army Group Centre during the Prague Offensive, he devised a plan to attempt a fighting withdrawal to the west so as to surrender to the Americans and not the Russians. On 8 May 1945, the day when the general surrender came into force, he was with the Americans negotiating. He then 'deserted his command', if that was possible after the capitulation, and flew to Bavaria not due to cowardice in the face of the enemy but to avoid capture and trial as a war criminal. Subsequently he spent a large part of his last twenty-eight years in prisons in Russia and West Germany for war crimes. His 'abandoned command', mainly SS, fought on until 11 May. (Tr.)

Chapter Eleven: The Death March to the West
1. This is the Soviet estimate made around the time. The German literature disputes this as a low figure, some sources putting those who escaped the Halbe Pocket as high as 30,000, not counting civilians. (Tr.)
2. Tony Le Tissier, *Durchbruch an der Oder – der Vormarsch der Roten Armee 1945* (Augsburg, 1997).
3. *Frankfurter Allgemeine Zeitung*, 28 February 1995.
4. The Soviet Union could never have kept such a promise, as all belligerents were well aware. In the 14 April 1945 edition of the newspaper *Pravda*, Alexandrov, chief ideologist of the Communist Party of the Soviet Union,

dismissing a fresh appeal by Ilya Ehrenburg to exterminate all Germans, explained that 'the Red Army never did have, nor ever will have, the goal of wiping out the German people'. He admitted that this change in political thinking *could only be forced through by the leadership using the most draconian measures*. The atrocity at Märkisch-Buchholz occurred two weeks later. Not only would it have been difficult in the extreme to convince the German Government, Wehrmacht and people that the Red Army was actually capable of acting on humanitarian principles, but even the Soviet Government doubted that it could. (Tr).

Epilogue

1. All SS men wore the aluminium Death's Head emblem on their caps, and the Totenkopf units additionally on the right collar patch instead of the SS runes. The Panzer Arm of the Wehrmacht wore a similar Death's Head on the jacket lapels but only to denote its line of succession from the Totenkopf hussars of the Kaiser's Army.
2. Heinz Höhne, *Der Orden unter dem Totenkopf: Die Geschichte der SS* (Essen, 1990).
3. George H. Stein, *Geschichte der Waffen-SS* (Düsseldorf, 1966): extract is a retranslation into English.
4. Höhne, *Der Orden unter dem Totenkopf.*

Index